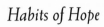

Habits of Hope

ɔʌ

THE VANDERBILT LIBRARY OF AMERICAN PHILOSOPHY

offers interpretive perspectives on the historical roots of
American philosophy and on present innovative developments
in American thought, including studies of values, naturalism, social
philosophy, cultural criticism, and applied ethics.

Series Editor

Herman J. Saatkamp, Jr.
Indiana University & Purdue University at Indianapolis

Editorial Advisory Board

Kwame Anthony Appiah (Harvard University)
Larry A. Hickman (Southern Illinois University)
John Lachs (Vanderbilt University)
John J. McDermott (Texas A&M University)
Joel Porte (Cornell University)
Hilary Putnam (Harvard University)
Ruth Anna Putnam (Wellesley College)
Andrew J. Reck (Tulane University)
Beth J. Singer (Brooklyn College)
John J. Stuhr (Pennsylvania State University)

Other titles in the series include

Dewey's Empirical Theory of Knowledge and Reality
John R. Shook

Thinking in the Ruins
Wittgenstein and Santayana on Contingency
Michael P. Hodges and John Lachs

Pragmatic Bioethics
Edited by Glenn McGee

Transforming Experience
John Dewey's Cultural Instrumentalism
Michael Eldridge

Habits of Hope

A Pragmatic Theory

PATRICK SHADE

VANDERBILT UNIVERSITY PRESS

Nashville

© Vanderbilt University Press
All rights reserved

First Edition 2001

05 04 03 02 01 5 4 3 2 1

Library of Congress Cataloging-in-Publication Data

Shade, Patrick, 1965–
Habits of hope : a pragmatic theory / Patrick Shade.— 1st ed.
p. cm. — (The Vanderbilt library of American philosophy)
Includes bibliographical references and index.
ISBN 0-8265-1361-1 (alk. paper)
1. Hope. 2. Pragmatism. 3. Philosophy,
American—20th century I. Title. II. Series.
BD216 .S43 2000
128—dc21   00-010465

Extended quotations from *Different Seasons* by Stephen King © 1982 by
Stephen King. Used by permission of Viking Penguin, a division of
Penguin Putnam Inc. Extended quotations from *The Grapes of Wrath—
Text and Criticism* by Peter Lisca, editor. Copyright © 1972 by The
Viking Press, Inc. © 1939, © renewed 1967 by John Steinbeck. Used by
permission of Viking Penguin, a division of Penguin Putnam Inc.
Extended quotations from *John Dewey: The Middle Works*, volume 6 ©
1978, volume 7 © 1979, volume 9 © 1980, volume 14 © 1983, and *John
Dewey: The Later Works*, volume 1 © 1981, volume 6 © 1985, volume 9 ©
1986, volume 17 © 1991, ed. Jo Ann Boydston, by permission of
Southern Illinois University Press and the Center for Dewey Studies.

Published by Vanderbilt University Press
Printed in the United States of America

For my parents and Bryan—my teachers in hope

Contents

Preface

The following discussion presents a pragmatic theory of hope based on the insights of classical American philosophy, especially as represented by the works of C. S. Peirce, William James, and John Dewey. Though none of these thinkers developed such a theory, their works are ripe with implications about the life of hope. Perhaps unsurprisingly, the resulting vision of hope is naturalistic and so rooted in our interactions with environments, both social and natural. Since habits are the fundamental structures of such interaction, they function significantly both in the formulation and realization of hopes; consequently, I have chosen as my title *Habits of Hope*. Though this phrase refers to a specific dimension of the life of hope, it also appropriately describes what is central to and also unique about a pragmatic theory.

The central aim of this work is to develop a theory of hope that successfully explains the two senses in which hoping is, or should be, practical. The first concerns the need to make hopes realizable, while the second captures hope's ability to sustain us and foster growth. Succinctly stated, hope needs to be practical (realizable), because it is practical (productive) to hope. My general argument is that a pragmatic theory of hope provides a compelling explanation of hope's practicality. In particular, such a theory emphasizes three dimensions of the life of hope—particular hopes, habits of hope, and hopefulness—the interweaving of which accounts for hope's practicality.

In the introduction, I discuss the need for a practical theory of hope and then sketch key pragmatic ideas used throughout the book. These include pragmatism's commitment to contextualism as well as the means-end continuum. In chapters 1 and 2, I discuss the first sense of hope's practicality—that is, its realizability. I situate hope in the context of the human being understood as an interactive biological

organism, highlighting the roles of habits, intelligence, and the imagination; also relevant is the role of the self, understood as the reconstructive dynamic of the organism. I then discuss particular hopes by
focusing on their ends, understood as future goods that are arduous but
nevertheless possible to realize. Chapter 2 examines those habits of
hope that are the primary means in realizing particular hopes. The central three such habits are persistence, resourcefulness, and courage,
though each of these consists of a complex of other habits.

Habits of hope also play an important role in developing hopefulness. In chapter 3, I discuss the nature of hopefulness, contrasting it
with despair and examining how it contributes to the second sense of
hope's practicality. I argue that we can develop hopefulness as the regnant habit of the self, such that our hopefulness nurtures and sustains us
as we grow and meet life's trials. In chapter 4, I argue that the interweaving of the three dimensions of the life of hope accounts for hope's
nature as *conditioned transcendence*. Hope is *conditioned* because it is rooted
in our habits (and the environment which they implicate), yet it is also
a form of *transcendence* because the very activity of hoping both requires
and enables us to transcend antecedent limitations of agency. I also
consider alternate theories which focus on unconditioned hopes but
argue that these theories undermine hope's practicality. They transform
its conditioned transcendence into an unconditioned transcendence,
thereby impeding hope's realizability.

The conclusion highlights a main point interwoven through all the
other chapters: the active role we play in developing, sustaining, and
enriching the life of hope. There is much we can do to promote practical hoping, whether by developing the basic habits of hope or by expanding them into communities of hope. Our success depends on our
willingness to embrace hope's practicality and to actively resist the debilitating effects of fear and despair. When we do, we become active
participants in the life of hope, buoyed by it even as we support its
basic structures.

Throughout the discussion, I glean insights from a variety of examples, four of which play dominant roles. Two of these involve fictional
characters drawn from John Steinbeck's *The Grapes of Wrath* and Stephen
King's novella *Rita Hayworth and Shawshank Redemption*. The other two

examples are drawn from real life; they focus on the trials of Cedric Jennings (whose tale is recounted in Ron Suskind's *A Hope in the Unseen*) and Martha Manning (from her autobiographical work, *Undercurrents*). These examples demonstrate hope's power in the lives of men and women, children and adults, professionals and convicts. Combined with pragmatism's emphasis on growth and progress, the examples help bring to life not simply the dimensions of hope, but also different possibilities for *developing* and *living* a hopeful life. The result is, I hope, a rich, concrete account that highlights how we can make hoping practical without sacrificing its unique capacity to sustain us and to help us grow.

Acknowledgments

While the genesis of this work was personal, its development and completion have been thoroughly social. Though some hopes may live within the shelter of private thoughts and efforts, few do. I find it one of life's surprises (and joys) that something as typically personal and intimate as hope is best nurtured in social contexts.

Special thanks go to John Lachs, whose patience, encouragement, and direction accompanied me every step of the way. His numerous comments and consistent support have been invaluable. During the early stages of the book's development, Ed Ellis and Lisa Bellantoni were most gracious with their time and input, providing productive sounding boards and friendly criticism. Tom Alexander reviewed the manuscript and made helpful suggestions, many of which found their way into the final version and made it a stronger book. Micah Luce kindly gave computer assistance when it was much needed. Marshall Boswell, Clayton Littlejohn, and Anita Davis graciously read the final manuscript. I extend a heartfelt thanks to all for their contributions.

Finally, I bear a debt of gratitude to family and friends who continue to teach me how powerfully hope nurtures enriching growth and provides a guiding light in the bleakest of times.

Abbreviations

References to John Dewey's works are to the thirty-seven-volume critical edition edited by Jo Ann Boydston and published by the Southern Illinois University Press. The volumes fall into three series, The Early Works (1882–1898), The Middle Works (1899–1924), and The Later Works (1925–1953). Quotations are cited in the text using the following abbreviations: EW, MW, LW. Consequently, LW 6:3 refers to volume 6, page 3 of The Later Works.

Quotations from William James's works are taken from *The Works of William James*, edited by Frederick H. Burkhardt, Fredson Bowers, and Ignas K. Skrupskelis, published by Harvard University Press. Quotations are cited in the text using the following abbreviations:

ERE: *Essays in Radical Empiricism* (1976).
  P: *Pragmatism* (1975).
 PP: *The Principles of Psychology*, 3 vols. (1981).
 PU: *A Pluralistic Universe* (1977).
SPP: *Some Problems of Philosophy* (1979).
WB: *The Will to Believe and Other Essays in Popular Philosophy* (1979).

Also cited

MS: *Memories and Studies*, ed. Henry James (New York: Longman's Green, 1920).

Habits of Hope

Introduction

Hope and Practicality

Hope's Prevalence and Importance

Few people are unfamiliar with hope's prevalence in human life. Indeed, most of us can readily generate long lists of things for which we hope, for ourselves and for others, in the near and far future. I may hope, for instance, the extra effort I put into my job will lead to a promotion or that a sick friend soon finds relief from her pain. Similarly, most of us hope that our loved ones always remain close. We also tend to invest ourselves in the hope that we can more effectively address our deep-rooted prejudices in order to promote greater justice. And the list goes on.

Every stage of life, from childhood to old age, reveals the pervasiveness of hope. Children usually hope to find like-minded playmates. Stories such as Roald Dahl's *James and the Giant Peach* illustrate that, though they might not be able to articulate it, children frequently hope to overcome fears and achieve greater confidence in meeting life's trials (whether coping with unsympathetic family members or dealing with the playground bully). Teen-oriented movies (for example, *Rebel without a Cause*) testify that young adults hope to gain greater independence from their parents in defining their own lives. Adults invest in hopes for personal and professional growth and stability, sometimes even seeking to realize their hopes through their children. Finally, the elderly tend to foster hopes for the continued good health and reliable physical coordination which allow them to engage in necessary and enjoyable activities.

1

These examples reveal that hope's object is conditioned by our current activities and the likely trials that accompany them. In turn, these trials are conditioned by the dynamics of the broader social and natural contexts in which we act. Our economic standing, for instance, often directly influences the things for which we hope. While adults typically hope for growth and stability, the particular form these hopes take depends on specific material needs and resources; an affluent adult may hope for a tax break, while one who is poverty stricken will more likely hope for adequate employment to secure basic needs. Similarly, our moral and religious values condition the specific form of our hopes. Consider a lonely elderly person, most of whose close family and friends have died. If she has a strong faith in the afterlife, she may hope for release from this life, especially in anticipation of reunion with the deceased. By contrast, if she lacks such a faith and thinks this life is the only one we have, she will quite likely hope to make new friends. Finally, our natural environment can also influence the kinds of hopes we have. Those living in climates with extreme temperature shifts may focus their hopes on weathering the harsher seasons, while those living in temperate climates often form hopes without regard for nature's cycles. Hope, then, tends to be conditioned by the multifarious dimensions of the contexts in which we live.

The scope of hope varies as widely as does its content. For instance, our hopes may concern objects or events that affect us as individuals (getting a promotion, for instance), our families (finding and maintaining a safe neighborhood in which to live), or most of society (establishing economic stability and political peace). Moreover, hope's compass can include the earthly goods of this life or extend to those of an afterlife (eternal salvation). Indeed, hope can even have itself as its own object, as when we hope to remain hopeful throughout the course of life. As with hope's content, context also conditions its scope, though perhaps in less obvious ways. Differences in temperament (selfish or magnanimous), maturity (young or old), and social status (active leader or invisible worker) likely influence the reach of our hopes. For instance, while the young tend to be preoccupied with hopes concerning themselves, adults and the elderly frequently harbor hopes that include others. Moreover, as I will argue in the following chapters, hope's scope frequently depends on the reach of one's agency at a particular time of life.

While we readily recognize the prevalence of hope, a genuine wariness of investing our energies in it nevertheless abounds. Such skepticism is usually rooted in the simple fact that, though it promises much, hoping can be very dangerous. Many who have eagerly poured energy into realizing its ends have also tasted the bitterness of pursuing futile hopes. Indeed, for every book chronicling the successful realization of one hope, there are tomes filled with the stories of those which failed. Why is hope so fraught with danger? Generally speaking, hope has as its object an end (whether a thing or an event) whose realization lies beyond our present agency; that end may be remote or directly obstructed, yet insofar as we hope for it, we nevertheless remain committed to pursuing its realization. Whether it be the hope that extra efforts at work will lead to a promotion or that trying experimental treatments will rid one's body of cancer, hope's ends lie beyond the boundary of what can be easily or readily secured. To invest (or continue investing) energies in hope carries the danger that we will waste our precious resources, whether material or personal. We then will not only have suffered the loss of a desired end; we will also be less able to secure *other* ends. Since resources are limited, expending them on hopes can be risky and perhaps unwise.

Unsurprisingly, then, many voices warn that we tread the waters of hope at our own peril. Greek tragedies frequently emphasize hope's darker side. For example, the chorus in Sophocles' *Antigone* warns Creon that

> [f]or the future near and far, and the past, this law holds good: nothing very great comes to the life of mortal man without ruin to accompany it. For Hope, widely wandering, comes to many of mankind as a blessing, but to many as the deceiver, using light-minded lusts; she comes to him that knows nothing till he burns his foot in the glowing fire.[1]

Hoping may be a natural and attractive human activity, especially when we are at a loss to readily secure desired ends on our own. Yet those who pursue hopes play a dangerous game, for hope is unpredictable and typically prodigal in nature.

Other warnings about hope can also be heard. Stoics and Buddhists recommend that we curtail if not extinguish our hopes rather than run the risk of discouragement and disappointment. To hope is to cling to what we cannot and perhaps should not attempt to control. Critics who are cynically minded show outright contempt for those who hope. They argue that hoping indicates we are either naive enough to believe the world can deliver what we desire or so desperate that we have nothing else with which to save ourselves. If we could secure a hoped-for end by our own means, cynics mockingly remind us, we would already be engaged in the process of doing so. Hoping is really only a concession that we have reached the limits of our agency. Unable to secure what we desire, we place our confidence in, and so give ourselves over to, the caprice of forces beyond our control.

The growth of agency and control witnessed over the past century, forged largely through scientific and industrial forces, has not silenced these voices of skepticism. Indeed, it has inspired some to protest even more loudly. The Industrial Revolution seemed to signal the beginning of the fruition of our deepest hopes for material and social progress. Technological advances have in fact enabled us to realize goals for which we once only dimly hoped: quickened transportation and communication have all but obliterated spatial differences; development of cures and preventative vaccines for sickness has enabled us to increase the average life span; and techniques for wresting nature's energy sources have given us greater control over her. These advances, however, have not been without concomitant curses. Technology has grown to the point that, rather than being a means to the improvement of human life, it creates greater demands on our already taxed energies. As computer technology grows increasingly more sophisticated, it rapidly becomes obsolete, forcing its users to learn new systems every few years. Additionally, while the Internet allows us to communicate with virtually every part of the globe, many people feel more, rather than less, distant from each other. The growth of technology has thus left many humans alienated from their technological tools and from each other. Similarly, having tasted the growth of their powers in

solving pernicious riddles of human sickness, some doctors have become so obsessed with solving "The Riddle" that they push patients
into treatments that forestall death but increase suffering.[2] And finally,
by unleashing nuclear power, we have created the almost paralyzing
threat that we will be annihilated by our own hands. Though we have
accomplished more than we once dreamed possible, realization of ancient hopes and dreams has created means that have taken on a life of
their own. Be careful what you wish for, as an old adage says; you may
get it.

In the midst of such skepticism and wariness, however, we can also
discern another voice, gently yet persistently speaking on hope's behalf. Certainly hoping has its perils. Rather than a wholesale dismissal
of hope, however, we can and should differentiate good hopes from
bad. Consider the Greek historian Thucydides' account of the Melians'
debate with Athens during the Peloponnesian War. According to
Thucydides, the Melians justified their continued refusal to submit to
the Athenians by explaining that they still hoped they could defeat the
superior forces of their enemy. The Athenians responded by noting
that hope

> *is* a comfort in danger, and though it may be harmful to people
> who have many other advantages, it will not destroy them. But
> people who put everything they have at risk will learn what
> hope is when it fails them, for hope is prodigal by nature; and
> once they have learned this, it is too late to take precautions
> for the future.[3]

From history, we know that the Athenians were right; the Melians'
hope was a bad one. Yet we should not therefore concede that *all* hopes
are like the Melians'; neither should we swear off hoping because of its
prodigal nature. Implicit in the Athenians' response itself is a vital distinction between sensible and blind hopes to which we must attend.
Blind hopes belong to those who have few or no resources with which
to realize their hoped-for ends and so who lack any grounds for thinking these ends are genuinely realizable. Pursuing such hopes is akin to
acting on blind faith and carries an extremely high risk of failure and

loss of energy. By contrast, those with sensible or practical hopes *do* have grounds for maintaining their hopes; these grounds include their own resources or "advantages." Practical hopes are more sensible in being more plausibly realizable. Those who pursue them thus avoid or minimize the dangers of hope's prodigal nature. They have a faith that is not blind, but supported by conditions which contribute to the realization of the end. Of course, differentiating the sensible from the blind, knowing when an end is "realizable," is no small feat. A central task of this book is to articulate the generic conditions of good, sensible hopes. The practicality of such hopes depends, as the Athenians knew, in no small measure on having "many other advantages."

Even while acknowledging that hopes need to be practical, we must not overlook the fact that part of hope's attraction and power lies in its ability to sustain and get us through dark times. The prophet Isaiah captures hope's productive side in declaring that those who hope in the Lord "shall renew their strength, they shall mount up with wings like eagles, they shall run and not be weary, they shall walk and not faint" (Isa. 40:31).[4] Hoping can be sustaining, nurturing—indeed, *advantageous.* Hope can sneak into and warm even the hardest of hearts, invigorating them to beat with the promise of greater fulfillment and a better future. So while hopes entice us, we must recognize that they also nurture us. Empirical evidence shows that patients who maintain their hope for recovery have a greater chance of actually getting better than those who do not.[5] Without hope, many give up and succumb to their disease; with hope, others are able to break through barriers and discover strengths they did not know they had. Hope can push us beyond practical limits to what does not lie readily within our means. Indeed, we should recognize that, as another adage reminds us, we mustn't limit our hopes, for if we do, we shall never find what lies beyond them. Hope is expansive in nature, and so we must not limit it unnecessarily.

An adequate theory of hope, then, needs to capture two features of hope. On the one hand, hopes need to be practical—that is, they need to be related to actual conditions and powers through which they *can* be realized. Otherwise, pursuing them leads to the dangerous waste of vital but limited resources, such as time and energy. If hoping exhausts

our resources, it is better not to hope. On the other hand, hopes are
productive in drawing us beyond present practical limits, showing us
new horizons and leading us to discover (or generate) new means of
exploring them. *Hope needs to be practical* by having grounds; yet it should
not be restricted to present activities and conditions, *for it is practical*, in
the sense of productive and expansive, *to hope*. Hope thus has two
modes of practicality: being grounded in real conditions and being
productive of new and better ones. Together, I shall argue, these two
modes constitute hope's essential nature as *conditioned transcendence*.

My goal in this book is to develop a theory of hope that adequately captures and relates these two modes or senses of hope's practicality.
I propose a *pragmatic* theory, drawn from the vision of human life developed by classical American philosophers such as C. S. Peirce, William
James, and John Dewey. My basic argument is that a pragmatic theory
of hope articulates the two senses of hope's practicality without sacrificing one to the other. Many traditional accounts, for instance, rightly
emphasize hope's power to sustain us. When they ground this sustaining power in something unconditioned or absolute (and so beyond
human agency), however, they undermine our active engagement in
the life of hope. Theological accounts often (though not always) err in
this way, rooting hope in God's absolute power so that we become
mere bystanders or observers to this vital activity of human life. For instance, a colleague once told me that unless hope is grounded in the
unconditioned, it is susceptible to the vagaries of finite conditioned existence that plague every other human activity. Hope, my colleague argued, needs to be able to live and survive in the darkest corners, at the
darkest times. It needs to be that one indestructible resource which remains when all others are gone. Unless this is so, hope cannot sustain
us. (Such a view shows the influence of the story of Pandora, who,
upon removing the lid the jar of gifts given by the gods, found that
only hope remained.) Hope *does* need to sustain us, but insisting that it
be able to do so in *every* possible situation is to drain it of actual connections with actual states of affairs. A hope whose realization can only
or primarily be affected through an unconditioned supernatural agency
leaves us with nothing to do but await its arrival. The first sense of
hope's practicality is thereby undermined, and all the dangers of hope

addressed above sully its power. By contrast, a pragmatic theory emphasizes the active role we need to play in hoping, underscoring our human responsibility for realizing hopes, whether our own or those of others. We must use intelligence in forming and pursuing hopes, drawing on our various resources (especially our habits) while also recognizing that hoping is itself, when properly developed, a productive resource in meeting trials and enriching our lives. By emphasizing hope's rich practicality, we can thus avoid the charges that hope is empty, necessarily dangerous, or too mundane to sustain us.

The core of my argument is that hope's twin senses of practicality, pragmatically understood, flow from the interrelation of three aspects of the life of hope: particular hopes, habits of hope, and hopefulness. Exploring these aspects constitutes the primary task of the following chapters. In the remainder of this introduction, I will further explain my reasons for developing a *pragmatic* theory of hope and then sketch its main contours.

The Pragmatic Context of the Discussion

Hope has long been a frequent theme in literature and religion. We have already noted its appearance in Greek tragedy and history. Additionally, the book of Isaiah has as its central theme Israel's hope for deliverance and restoration. St. Paul furthermore emphasizes hope by pairing it with faith and love (1 Cor. 13:13; see also Rom. 8:24–25). Moreover, philosophers have also frequently treated hope. Drawing on St. Paul as well as St. Augustine and Aristotle, St. Thomas Aquinas develops hope as one of three theological virtues.[6] Immanuel Kant gives prominence to hope in his system by identifying the question, "What can I hope?" as one of the three interests of reason.[7] Other philosophical treatments include Søren Kierkegaard's compelling account of hope and despair in the context of the self and its ultimate ground,[8] Ernst Bloch's monumental phenomenology of hope in a Marxist context,[9] and Gabriel Marcel's discussion of the centrality of the I-thou relationship to hope.[10] More recently, Joseph J. Godfrey has examined the constitutive elements of hope and interwoven themes from Kant, Bloch, and Marcel to distinguish ultimate hope (or hope with an aim) from fundamental hope (or hope that lacks an aim but that is a basic disposition).[11] I will say more about these theories later. Here I address more fully my choice of developing a pragmatic theory of hope.

My first reason is that the issue of hope is implicit in most pragmatic philosophies, though it is seldom thematized. Consequently, a careful discussion of it will clarify an important but not fully developed theme of pragmatism. Pragmatists frequently talk about matters closely related to hope, such as meliorism and faith, as well as particular hopes for social progress. Indeed, in celebrating inquiry as a central means to promoting technical and moral progress, pragmatists continue the tradition begun in the Renaissance which identifies experimental empirical methods as the ground of hope. Discussions of wedding thought with action and of making practice more intelligent abound in pragmatic discourse, so much so that we should expect the *practicality* of hope to be an explicit theme. But the language of hope is largely absent from these discussions, perhaps due to its traditional connections with religion and theology. One notable exception is the work of Cornel West, a writer with sympathies for the pragmatic tradition. His recent book, *Restoring Hope*,[12] is a series of interviews with prominent speakers on the theme of hope in African American communities. Though a rich and fruitful series of dialogues, this unique book does not articulate a *theory* of hope, pragmatic or otherwise. (I will nevertheless draw from it where appropriate.) My goal is to develop a pragmatic language of hope that acknowledges hope's significance in human life and articulates its various and complex dynamics. As we will see below, the life of hope includes, in addition to the particular ends for which we hope, habits of hope and hopefulness, both of which are fundamental dimensions of hope that pragmatists typically do not articulate but are in a prime position to develop. All three dimensions are needed to account for the twin senses of hope's practicality.

A second closely related reason for developing a pragmatic theory is that it will provide a fully conditioned and naturalist, as opposed to supernaturalist, account of hope. In a pragmatic context, hope is situated in a worldview that embraces the finitude, the ultimate contingency, and yet also the creative dimension of human existence. Humans are complex biological organisms in constant interaction with environments, whether natural or social. *Hope functions as a means to improving interaction,* especially by enabling humans to transform their environments under the guidance of practically defined ends. Consequently, hopes are among the chief tools that we have for making the environment more suitable to our needs and purposes. Unlike theological and standard philosophical theories of hope, a pragmatic theory does not appeal to what is unconditioned, either as the ground of hope (usually God) or as the proper aim and meaning of hope. Rather, it roots hope in the finite, temporal, and communal conditions of human existence. Though capable of transforming human existence, hope does not allow us to escape conditionality and finitude. A pragmatic account celebrates this point without sacrificing hope's expansive power.

A pragmatic theory consequently gives special attention to the role of concrete grounds and agencies such as habits, intelligence, and community, all of which are central to formulating and realizing hopes. In particular, if hope is to be practical, it must take into account habits developed through previous interactions with the environment; otherwise, hope lacks roots in reality and becomes indistinguishable from fantasy. Indeed, insofar as hope is a focal activity that can energize us, pulling us on to active exploration of alternative possibilities, an adequate theory of hope requires understanding its interplay with habits. Moreover, hoping contributes to the creative transformation or reconstruction of habits, some of which are vital to the self. We can develop hope into the habit of hopefulness, a habit which structures how we orient ourselves to possibilities; hope can therefore become an integral dynamic of our creativity. Pragmatism's special emphasis on developing and reconstructing habits makes it an ideal context in which to examine the conditions which limit—but also make possible—the realizations of our hopes. Since hope is tied with habits, the seat of human agency, we bear great responsibility for the success of the life of hope.

The third reason for developing a pragmatic theory of hope is its ability to successfully explain and show the close relation between the twin senses of hope's practicality. This makes it an obvious candidate for being an adequate theory of hope. Demonstrating this is, of course, the heart of the following discussion. But here two important points can be made. First, in providing an account of hope as fully conditioned, emphasizing its practicality in the first sense, pragmatism enables us to see how hope is closely related to, and capable of reinforcement by, other human activities. Hope has its distinctive qualities, but it is in large measure continuous with other familiar and significant human activities such as wishing, dreaming, planning, and experimenting. Second, hope's second mode of practicality is largely an outgrowth of the first. The successful realization of hopes, aided by making hopes practical and continuous with other activities, can be, if properly developed in light of habits, *productive of* a disposition to act in a hopeful way. Consequently, I will argue that nurturing the life of hope, especially its dimension of hopefulness (the development of which requires the other two dimensions), helps us reconstruct ourselves and our societies as productive, intelligently growth-oriented agents. A pragmatic view of human nature thus highlights hope's power as a tool for human self-construction and reconstruction.

In the process of developing this account, I will explore how hope contributes to the formation of the self. Few will contest that it plays some role, but of course we must ask what that role is and how central it is. Skeptics, of course, consider that role to be rather incidental, providing the self with a reprieve, a momentary and perhaps refreshing escape from the drudgery of real life. By contrast, we could argue that hope functions as the necessary basis for the formation of the self, such that apart from it one is not truly a self. Another option, though, and the one developed here, is to contend that hope functions to energize and sustain the self as it reconstructs itself in the teeth of trying circumstances. As such, it marks a *particular* form of integrating the self which focuses on *growth* and the *expansion* of abilities. We must nevertheless consider whether hopes always or even primarily affect the self positively; some may damage rather than transform or reconstruct the self. My goal is to show how we can foster hoping so that it nurtures and enriches our lives.

The Pragmatic Scaffolding

In this section I present general features of pragmatism that provide the scaffolding for the discussion which follows.[13] Issues directly pertaining

to hope's practicality—habits, action, faith, intelligence—will be dealt
with in detail in the following chapters. Here I wish to situate the discussion by highlighting pragmatism's commitment to contextualism;
this commitment, together with an emphasis on empirical method, differentiates pragmatism from much of the philosophical tradition.

Contextualism is the view that everything, whether an object or activity, is embedded in a context. The context of a thing is that network
of relations and conditions relative to which it has the identity, meaning, and value that it possesses. Stated negatively, contextualism is the
thesis that nothing is without relations or conditions. Nothing is isolated from *all* other things, although neither is anything significantly related to all other things. Nothing has an identity, meaning, or value which
is completely fixed with respect to every context. Positively, the contextualist thesis is that everything has limiting conditions and is what it is,
at least in part, because of its relations to those conditions.

Pragmatism acknowledges that we frequently take context for granted, as when I assume that I share the same language with my conversation partners; this poses no special problem so long as the context is in
fact shared. We usually attend to context only when something in our
interaction indicates that we do not share the same context, be it of
language or of values, as when we come to disagree about the meaning
of a word or the value of a particular act. In such cases, the "same" thing
is being used differently. To understand its use, we must appeal to how
the thing functions in its broader context, for use is a function of context. Contextualism, then, invites a functionalist understanding of
things, since it contends that things are what they are as they function
in context—that is, as they are in relation to one another.[14]

Though context is normally taken for granted, ignoring it can lead
to the denial of context per se. Especially in philosophical inquiries,
where we already operate at an abstract level, such a denial generates
many problems. Consider philosophical treatments of the nature of
thought, for instance. When abstracted from the problematic contexts
in which it both arises and functions, thought tends to be viewed as a
special power belonging to an immaterial mind that exists outside of
nature. By contrast, the pragmatist understands thought as a natural operation that arises in complex biological organisms when their

interaction with the environment is interrupted. Thought (or better, *thinking*) is then understood as a form of problem solving and so as a dynamic of the reconstruction of natural energies and materials. Indeed, its success depends on how well it directs reconstructing such resources so as to restore interaction. Viewed from this pragmatic perspective, ideas and ideals are not mental entities that belong to an immaterial mind, but rather plans for action which arise in response to, and are tested by their success at resolving, problems of interaction.

When they deny context, philosophers treat what would otherwise be functionally different operations of natural interaction as fixed and separate agencies or realities. Once this move is made, the dominant philosophical problem becomes showing how what is obviously related in our experience can in fact (or, more accurately, in theory) be united. John Dewey spent most of his philosophic career arguing that philosophical dichotomies—such as those between thought and action (in *The Quest for Certainty*), mind and body, experience and nature (in *Experience and Nature*), or ends and means (in nearly all of his works)—are the pernicious result of philosophers' denial of context. Such a denial, he nevertheless argued, is not surprising, given the abstract nature of most philosophical considerations, for

> [t]hinking takes place in a scale of degrees of distance from the urgencies of an immediate situation in which something has to be done. The greater the degree of remoteness, the greater is the danger that a temporary and legitimate failure to express reference to context will be converted into a virtual denial of its place and import. Thinking is always extended, but philosophic thinking is, upon the whole, at the extreme end of the scale of distance from the active urgency of concrete situations. (LW 6:17)

Abstracting from original contexts—to the point that context is altogether dropped out—philosophic thinking creates artificial distinctions ("mind and matter," "ends and means"), which in turn create stubborn intractable philosophical problems. What would otherwise be functional differences, dependent on conditions of context, are

transformed into ultimate (or "metaphysical") separations. While understandable, the philosopher's denial is nevertheless deeply problematic, creating difficulties where there need be none, leading Dewey to
contend that "neglect of context is the besetting fallacy of philosophical thought" (LW 6:17).

If we are to understand hope from a pragmatic point of view, we
must begin by situating it in its generative contexts and noting how it
operates there. First, hope functions in the life of *human* beings—that is,
of complex biological organisms engaged in constant interaction with
equally complex environments, be they natural or social. In the next
chapter, I thus will begin developing this theory of hope by situating
the discussion in the context of the human being so conceived.
Second, hope functions as a complex mode of interaction, involving
creative integration of desires, habits, and intelligence, whereby humans pursue remote ends not promoted by their current environments.
This pursuit can itself transform the environment, making it more conducive to a rich human life. Consequently, hope is pragmatically conceived not as a private mental state, but as an activity belonging to an
organism in dynamic relation with its environment.

Hope, then, should be treated as an activity, as hop*ing*. To better understand hope as an activity, we should examine carefully the pragmatist's contextual treatment of means and ends. An activity is distinct from
mere action. The word *action* can have a number of meanings. It can indicate the mere change from one state to another, or mere sequentiality. It
can also signify an organic connection of various episodes (some of
which are means and others ends), in which case we have activity.
Activity, in pragmatic thought, refers to a specific union of means and
ends that is lacking in mere action. According to Dewey, an activity is "a
series of changes definitely adapted to accomplishing an end" (MW
6:361). In such a case, no part of the series merely precedes the one that
follows it; rather, each part is chosen as a means to that following
change, which then becomes an end. More specifically, as Dewey notes,

> [t]he connection of means-consequences is never one of bare
> succession in time, such that the element that is means is past
> and gone when the end is instituted. An active process is

strung out temporarily, but there is a deposit at each stage and point entering cumulatively and constitutively into the outcome. A genuine instrumentality *for* is always an organ *of* an end. It confers continued efficacy upon the object in which it is embodied. (LW 1:276)

An end does not simply follow its antecedents in the series; it completes or fulfills what precedes it. Insofar as what has preceded is constitutive of or contributes to the realization of that end, it functions as a means to that end. As such, the end is not the termination of a process, but its culmination.

Means are chosen relative to ends, which can be variously called "aims," "purposes," or "ends-in-view." The last designation is especially appropriate, since it captures the sense in which means are chosen with the end *in view* as a guide or principle of selection in the activity. An object (for example, a tool) or way of acting is chosen not because it is a means per se, but because it is a means *to that end*. Ends-in-view thus function as principles of selection relative to which things become means; what does not promote realization of the end is not a means and so is not selected. Unsurprisingly, an end-in-view is itself an integral part of the process. Dewey explains that

[t]he end-in-view is a plan which is *contemporaneously* operative in selecting and arranging materials. The latter . . . are means only as the end-in-view is actually incarnate in them, in forming them. Literally, they are the end in its present stage of realization. The end-in-view is present at each stage of the process; it is present as the *meaning* of the materials used and the acts done; without its informing presence, the latter are in no sense "means"; they are merely extrinsic causal conditions. (LW 1:280)

Ends-in-view do not function in activity simply as ends; they also function as means to the end that is in fact realized. Materials only become means to the realization of an end when they are chosen in light of and organized by ends-in-view. Consequently, ends-in-view are functionally means as well as ends.

Choice in the selection of means indicates the operation of *intelligence* in the activity. Dewey argues that conscious deliberate choice of means signifies "foresight of the alternative consequences attendant upon acting in a given situation in different ways, and the use of what is anticipated to direct observation and experiment" (MW 9:117). The aim or end-in-view guides the selection of appropriate means by providing a focus or goal relative to which proposed means can be evaluated as efficacious and consequences assessed as desirable. Intelligence, then, indicates the ability to identify, connect, and assess means and ends in light of one another. Means that have undesirable concomitants are then either modified or discarded. Similarly, ends too can be revised; if we find that unwanted consequences would follow were an end realized, or that no means can be found to it, the end can and should be either modified or discarded. The process of realizing an end requires experimentation and subsequent adjustment of means and ends as guided by intelligence.

Consequently, means are means only in relation to ends, and ends are themselves also means. Pragmatism thus offers a contextualist treatment of means and ends whereby each is in continuity with, rather than in separation from, the other. The continuity of means and ends allows us to emphasize three points.[15] First, means are means *for* ends. Apart from some end (be it simple or complex), there are no means, only causes. Second, ends themselves function as means in directing the process of their realization. Strictly speaking, an end-in-view may not coincide with the specific end actually realized; the end-in-view may overshoot or fall short of what is actually possible or needed. But this is where the role of intelligence comes into play. Ideally, the greater the degree of intelligence used in formulating the end-in-view, the closer its relation will be to the actual end. Overlooked conditions carry unforeseen consequences that may interrupt or further frustrate activity; we must survey existing conditions carefully and, on that basis, predict necessary means and likely consequences. Third, actualized ends themselves serve as means *in further processes*. This is most apparent in cases where one practices to acquire a skill (for example, a steady vibrato in playing the violin), which in turn is itself a means to further ends (for example, playing a poignant passage of music with deep emotion).

In light of this means-end continuum, the separation of ends from means—as happens when an end is thought to be final, an end-in-itself and so never a means—is an abstraction which typically results from the denial of context. No end is final in the sense of being either devoid of instrumentality or an absolute standard formed external to experience. To say an end is *only* an end, never a means, indicates *not* that it has *special* value, but rather that it has *limited* value in the wider context of life. Though no end is final, some ends are more comprehensive than others. Such ends command our attention in virtue of their expansiveness and are valued more than proximate, limited ends. Nevertheless, not even comprehensive ends are ends-in-themselves. Rather, they are products or outgrowths of the means-end continuum, indications that means and ends have been sufficiently integrated to produce complex ends that require the coordination of many activities and so of many ends. Consequently, the growth of comprehensive ends is an end implicit in, and not externally imposed upon, the means-end continuum.

Indeed, such growth lies at the heart of the pragmatist's commitment to progress and meliorism. Progress in better adapting natural materials to ends conducive to human fulfillment occurs when means and ends are integrated intelligently. Events or conditions are, then, not mere *effects* of antecedent causes, but *consequences* imbued with value resulting from intelligent, directed choice. Humans, of course, have limited abilities, and the environment demonstrates its own resistance to our ends. Yet, gradual adjustment of both human activity and environmental conditions secures human values. Progress is no accident but results from employing better methods of control in realizing human ends. This view of progress is *meliorism*, described by Dewey as "the idea that at least there is a sufficient basis of goodness in life and its conditions so that by thought and earnest effort we may constantly make better things" (MW 7:294). Optimism differs from meliorism in that it is a spectator's sport. The optimist knows or has assurance that things *will* work out for the best. By contrast, the meliorist is fueled by hope to *make* or *contribute to the development of* a better world. Hope has no real meaning amid the assurances of the optimist, but it finds a natural home in the meliorist's world.

Hope, as an activity, needs to be understood in light of the means-end continuum, particularly as enriched by intelligence. In this regard, it shares much with other common human activities. Hopes are notorious for directing the acquisition or, in many cases, development of the means necessary to realize them. In addition, hoping can be an intermediary step between dreaming and planning. Consider, for instance, someone who wants to mount an expedition to Mars. To the degree that he lacks the means—either because he is not sufficiently talented and resourceful or because no means whatsoever are available to anyone—his desire is a dream. Thus it is commonplace to say that older people *dream* of being younger again, that clumsy people *only* dream of becoming ballet dancers, or that the slave dreams of his freedom when there is no chance of such. The moment realization of the slave's desire becomes a possibility, either for himself or for others (for instance, he hears of other slave owners who have freed their slaves), it then becomes more plausible to say he *hopes* for his freedom. As the necessary means come within his grasp, pursuit of such a hope becomes increasingly a matter of formulating plans. Thus there can be a continuum of dreaming, hoping, and planning.

Not every desire, of course, begins as a dream and develops into a plan. We readily have the means for some ends, and so we plan outright for their realization. And similarly, some ends remain dreams, never to be realized. Some hopes also remain hopes, incapable of being transformed into plans that can be realized. In such cases, we may persist in our dreams or hopes, though usually at our own peril. But as ends, unless they really serve as mere distractions or amusements amidst life's trials, their function is to motivate and direct our efforts at their realization—that is, to be ends-in-view which are themselves means. Central to a pragmatic theory of hope, then, is recognition of hope's continuity with dreaming, wishing, and planning.

Dimensions of the Life of Hope

Thus far in the discussion, I have treated hope quite generically. As I mentioned above, though, the life of hope can and should be more carefully articulated as consisting of three dominant dimensions: particular hopes, hopefulness, and what I call habits of hope. These three can only be distinguished abstractly; as we shall see, they each interrelate with one another to constitute that rich and complex activity of hoping. The preceding discussion of the means-end continuum provides the basis for explaining their integration. While interrelated, each dimension provides special insight into the life of hope, and so it is appropriate to emphasize each singly. Consequently, I treat each separately in the following three chapters. The fourth chapter draws together these strands, showing how they interweave in the rich tapestry of the life of hope.

For now, a brief sketch of each dimension is appropriate. Particular hopes, such as those discussed at the beginning of this chapter, comprise the dimension with which we are most familiar. These have at their core some specific end, whether an object or an activity, which we seek to realize. For example, my particular hope may be to get the job for which I am currently interviewing, or it may be to be cured of cancer. Many activities, such as dreaming and planning, also involve ends; ends hoped for are usually more remote than those for which we plan, yet more accessible or real than those about which we dream. Consequently, understanding particular hopes requires more than simple reference to an end; what is distinctive about them is that they involve *a commitment to the desirability and realizability of an end in the face of some obstacle which marks the limits of our agency.* I *hope*, rather than plan, to be cured from cancer, for not only are there no guaranteed cures, but even therapies and experimental drugs work for some people and not for others. Nevertheless, there are (or should be) grounds in virtue of which I commit myself to this end, even though there are obstacles to its realization. The end should at least be possible, not just generally, but *possible for me.* In this context, we can see the first mode of hope's practicality: the demand that hopes be practical in being realizable so they do not drain our resources.

Habits of hope significantly contribute to this commitment to the hoped-for end. Pragmatically understood, habits are powers or ways of acting we develop through interaction with the environment which structure how we deal with external forces and internal energies. By their means, we are capable of performing increasingly complex modes of activity; habits provide the basic building blocks on which we develop new responses and new behavior. Habits can be individual or social, but in either case they are our primary tools or means of acting. While we can draw upon a vast array of habits in realizing any end, *habits of hope* are those vital abilities which directly and indirectly nurture our commitment to and realization of remote, obstructed ends. Chief among them are persistence, general resourcefulness, and courage. Although our hopes are partly contingent upon conditions beyond our control, it is by means of these habits that we play a substantial role in realizing them.

Habits of hope provide a hinge between the other two dimensions of hope. Insofar as they maintain commitment and also foster progress toward the realization of an end, habits of hope are means to particular hopes. Perhaps less obvious is the manner in which they are also means to hopefulness. Hopefulness differs from particular hopes in that it lacks a specifiable end; rather, it is an *orientation* of open, attentive readiness to possibilities that promise satisfaction. To be hopeful is to be not only attentive to fulfillments that are pregnant in current existential conditions but also ready to act in pursuit of them. As such, we live within a rich horizon of meaning, defined not only by past accomplishments but also by future achievements. By contrast, to despair is to be closed off, not from possibilities per se, but from possibilities which would bring growth, satisfaction, or fulfillment. Despair, or hopelessness, is an orientation of being paralyzed and so entrapped by the obstacles that define the problematic situation out of which hope arises. Its hallmark is disconnection from the meanings and values that move us. While we can be hopeful on occasion, hopefulness can also be a fundamental characteristic that endures over time. We develop hopefulness as a sustaining habit by coordinating habits of hope, especially those productive of openness with those concerning our readiness to act; these habits reinforce the fundamental features of hopefulness, deepening their functioning in our general activity. Since such habits both nurture *and are nurtured by* our connection with others' agencies, the social nature of hope becomes especially clear in the development of hopefulness. While hopefulness is fostered through and indicative of the growth of agency, both individual and social, despair signifies the paralysis or limitation of agency. Once developed as an enduring habit, hopefulness proves an important resource in combating despair in ourselves and in others.

The significance of hopefulness consists in its capacity to energize and sustain us, even when particular hopes fail. Though related to them, hopefulness can enjoy various degrees of freedom from the success or demise of particular hopes. The realization of particular hopes usually energizes us, expanding our powers and giving us confidence to explore further possibilities. Success with particular hopes (and their means, habits of hope) thus fosters hopefulness and thereby promotes the pursuit of additional hopes. Continued failure to realize hopes, by contrast, can have a deleterious effect on hopefulness, pushing us toward the paralysis of despair, but this is not necessarily the case. Though repeated failure of hopes sometimes drains our energy, at other times such adversity makes us all the more determined to pursue other hopes. For example, if my hope to gain a promotion at work is continually frustrated, I may despair, or I may focus my energy on generating hopes in other areas of my life—for example, the hope for success with my personal relationships. In such a case, hopefulness remains alive and active. There is thus no necessary link between the success and failure of particular hopes and the growth of hopefulness; much depends on the degree to which hopefulness defines one's character. While there is a complicated *interrelation* between the realization of hopes and hopefulness, the two also enjoy a certain *independence* or a looseness of play. This independence is vital, since without it hopefulness would crumble with the demise of particular hopes. The chief value of hopefulness is its capacity to sustain us and keep hope alive when our particular hopes fail. It thus helps us avoid despair. Consequently, hopefulness embodies the second mode of hope's practicality in that it can both energize us and help us avoid the pitfalls of despair.

We can sketch the relations between the different dimensions of hope by noting that each functions as both an end and a means. Particular hopes, as distinct from habits of hope, provide the ends for which we hope. Such ends are ends-in-view and so also means in guiding the selection and organization of materials which will serve as means to their realization. Included among such means are habits of hope; without them our commitment to an end (or end-in-view) falters. Habits of hope that we do not possess, and yet need, can become ends developed through the process of hoping. The ability to persist, for example, can be acquired or expanded when commitment to a hoped-for end requires it; hoping provides the opportunity for the development (or, more often, the further development) of each of its dimensions. Hopefulness, in turn, is an end generally (though not always[16]) realized through the development of habits of hope. Moreover, hopefulness, especially in the degree to which it is developed through the *coordination* of habits of hope, can itself become a habit of hope. As such a habit it sustains us in pursuing particular hopes. Moreover, hopefulness can become the dominant habit of the self, in which case it functions as a further means to the life of hope; it then provides the basis for a hopeful person and, in turn, for a hopeful community.

My goal in the following chapters is to clarify and further develop the foregoing analysis. If I am successful, I will show that a pragmatic theory of hope both captures and integrates the twin senses of hope's practicality. The result will be a theory that shows hope's essential meaning to be a *conditioned transcendence* and, as such, a vital part of human creativity. If it is to be realizable, hope must be practical in being continuous with current conditions. And yet, hope is itself practical in that its pursuit changes us and our environment, thereby transforming and taking us beyond current conditions. *Hope signifies the growth of agency.* Moreover, in pursuing hope we can become not only more hopeful people, but also more productive and more creative people. And finally, we can become a people unified in hope, not only in some abstract ideal but also in the concrete habits which make a community.

To summarize the main points of this introduction, particular hopes are remote blocked ends that we consider both desirable and realizable enough to be worthy of our time and commitment. These hopes need to be practical—that is, rooted in actual existential conditions, which include actual individual and social habits. While it lacks a concrete end relative to which we can determine existential conditions necessary for its realizability, hopefulness has as its means and conditions habits of hope that foster its openness and connectedness to other agencies and so to increasingly meaningful possibilities. Such connectedness is itself practical in the sense of energizing as well as expanding the limits of our selves.

We must now begin to develop more carefully these dimensions of the life of hope.

CHAPTER *One*

The Practicality of Particular Hopes

THIS chapter presents the basic themes of a pragmatic theory of
hope, focusing on the most familiar dimension of the life of hope:
particular hopes. I will thus examine the activity of hoping as it
relates to specific ends or ideals. As noted in the introduction, we can
only *abstractly* separate particular hopes from hopefulness and habits of
hope; we will see traces of both throughout this chapter. Nevertheless,
our focus here is upon the nature and genesis of the particular ends for
which we hope. Subsequent chapters will treat habits of hope and
hopefulness as fundamental means to hoping.

Just as particular hopes need to be related to the other dimensions
of the life of hope to be properly understood, so too must hoping itself
be situated in the broader context of human life. Consequently, our
preliminary task is to consider the interactive nature of human beings
and the kinds of contexts in which hopes arise. Central to this discussion are habits (understood as our primary tools of interacting), as well
as desires, intelligence, and imagination, all of which play important
roles in reconstructing habits. Since the interweaving of habits, desires,
and intelligence is largely the operation of the self and has a potentially profound effect upon it, I also sketch a pragmatic view of the self.

The second half of the chapter focuses upon the general nature of the ends for which we hope. The goal of this chapter, though, is not merely to uncover basic features of particular hopes, but also to begin developing the first sense of hope's practicality—that is, its dynamic relation to actual conditions and powers. In particular, I will explore characteristics of the desirability and realizability of hoped-for ends which justify our commitment to them. Typical of pragmatic justification, action and habits (whether individual or social) play a central role. In the next chapter, I will expand on hope's first sense of practicality by highlighting those habits of hope which function as vital means to maintaining commitment and developing our ends.

The Generative Context of Particular Hopes

Our theory must not abstract hope from its generative context, for only in such a context can we adequately understand its function and meaning in human life. From a pragmatic perspective, proper treatment of hope's genesis presupposes that we understand the primarily interactive and developmental nature of human beings. Traditional theories of human nature recognize that humans interact with an environment and undergo development; to do otherwise would run counter to ordinary experience. But while they acknowledge these facts, traditional accounts do not give them the central role pragmatists give them. Typically, humans are thought to possess an essential nature antecedent to and independent of their engagement with the world. While interaction provides the occasion for developing that nature, it does not play a vital role in defining or constituting it. Pragmatists argue, by contrast, that the human organism is what it is in virtue of its engagement with the environment. Humans do not possess an essential nature formed independently of our experience; rather, our nature is interwoven with and a *result* of our interaction with the world. It is constituted of dynamic relations. The nature of the human organism, both generally and particularly, depends on its concrete history in specific contexts.

Included among these contexts is the natural environment with which we must successfully interact if we are to survive and grow.

Pragmatists understand humans as fundamentally biological organisms. This does not mean we are exhaustively described in physical or biological terms, but it does mean that properly understanding human life and activity requires situating them in biological contexts. This consideration applies to hope as much as to any other human activity. Equally pervasive in human life are social contexts. Humans are social as well as biological, for we continually and characteristically form common modes of interaction based on shared activities, values, and meanings. Social contexts condition, foster, and at times impede our individual activities, truths, and values. Consequently, pragmatists consider the view of an individual as an isolated being, possessing its own nature apart from and prior to interactions with the larger world, to be a misleading abstraction. Individuals may seek to transform and at times reject certain modes of social conditioning, but they cannot escape them altogether.

In addition to recognizing these general contexts within which we live and act, a pragmatic theory of human nature also emphasizes the interweaving of two primary features of our interaction.[1] First, the human organism is always situated in, and so conditioned by, its environment. It must thus adjust to conditions and demands imposed by a changing and often precarious world. These adjustments presuppose it has a plasticity in virtue of which it *can* be conditioned and changed. No organism is completely plastic, however, for each interaction leaves a residue that conditions (both positively and negatively) its abilities and shapes its nature. James thus notes that "[*p*]*lasticity*, then, in the wide sense of the word, means the possession of a structure weak enough to yield to an influence, but strong enough not to yield all at once" (PP 1: 110). Second, the human organism is not merely passive or condition*ed*, but also active and condition*ing;* it is a dynamic center of energy. Interaction between organism and environment involves more than the former's adaptation to the latter, for as Dewey notes, adaptation "is quite as much adaptation *of* the environment to our own activities as of our activities *to* the environment" (MW 9:52).[2] Humans not only respond to changes but also initiate them, both adjusting to antecedent environmental changes (creating a two-step between organism and environment) and deliberately attempting to refashion the environment to make it more conducive to fulfilling purposes and realizing ideals. While our conditioned nature presupposes we have plasticity, our activity indicates that we have energies and abilities we seek to exercise and expand. Consequently, much of our activity is directed at finding modes of interaction that promote development of our capacities and increase our energies.

At the heart of interaction are the habits we develop in response to our environments. A common conception of habits (and their close cousins, customs) is that they are onerous things, impediments or largely limiting modes of behavior. This view is due to the fact that we usually only think of habits when they get in the way of what we want or need. Their most notable characteristic in such situations is their stubborn tenacity; a well-worn habit is a terribly difficult thing to discard or even transform. Though this view has its element of truth, it fails to capture the heart of habits. Rather than being *liabilities*, pragmatists argue, habits are our greatest *abilities*, making complex interaction—including control and creation of environment—possible. Instead of being inherently restrictive, they are expansive powers of development and growth. Most generally, habits are patterns or ways of dealing with external forces and organizing internal energies in our interplay with the environment. They direct, channel, and give structure to our energies. We develop habits *through* our interaction with the environment. Engagement with the environment shapes and structures human plasticity into powerful, purposive modes of activity. Dewey explains that our plasticity makes possible "the ability to learn from experience; the power to retain from one experience something which is of avail in coping with the difficulties of a later situation. This means power to modify actions on the basis of the results of prior experiences, the power to *develop dispositions*. Without it, the acquisition of habits is impossible" (MW 9:49). Possessing plasticity thus means that we can learn, grow, and develop; yet our capacities develop *through* our interactions. As we noted above, the human organism is primarily energetic. Energies flow; that much is given. What defines an individual organism's specific nature are the details of its interactions, which check, test, modify, and expand its energies.

Once developed, habits are vital resources ever ready to spring into action. Dewey thus describes them as "assertive, insistent, self-perpetuating" (MW 14:43). Habits prepare us to act, indicating modes of interaction that have worked in the past and so can be relied upon in the future. They signify those strands of past experience that have generated patterns of response which prepare the organism to act. In channeling our energies, they projectively structure the world. Habits thus map out paths of meaningful action we can travel. They spread out *horizons of meanings*, rich matrixes of goods and actions defined by our abilities and projects and so contoured by the means and ends we have successfully pursued. To the extent that they do not require conscious attention or effort, habits become especially efficient means of engagement with the environment; once we can rely upon them, we direct our effort and attention elsewhere. This efficiency makes possible, and is itself nurtured by, more complex modes of activity. On the solid basis of established habits, we can form habits of habits, or habits nested within other habits. Most complex human behavior is of this kind. For instance, my ability to type this paragraph requires the coordination of typing habits with those of critical thinking and sentence construction. Together these make possible this complicated mode of communication. Thinking itself is a habit of habits insofar as it employs the effective use of habits to solve problems. C. S. Peirce describes habituation as "the power of readily taking habits and of readily throwing them off,"³ and identifies it as perhaps our most effective habit. So understood, habituation signifies not the operation of inflexible routine, but rather the power of forming and transforming successful modes of action and interaction. Such a habit increases our ability to respond to changing circumstances.

This efficiency and increasing complexity extend beyond the individual human's habits insofar as they are nested within broader social habits which condition and give them meaning. We learn habits by modeling the behavior of others; our horizons of meaning are thus funded by their experience as well as our own. My habits of writing utilize a language and various utensils not of my own creation; their power derives in part from the larger, shared context in which they have their use. Indeed, nearly all individual habits are developed and employed within the broader context of social habits; driving habits governed by traffic signs illustrate the manner in which particular habits are invested with meanings defined by social norms. Even those habits we identify as primarily personal are not cut off from their surrounding environment. Not only are they developed through interaction with the environment, but they also arise through our use of objective materials in that environment. As Dewey notes, habits "give control over the environment, power to utilize it for human purposes" (MW 9:57). They do not belong solely to the organism, but incorporate and transform the objective conditions to which they are responses.

Habits constitute the primary basis of our ability to interact with environments by providing us a complex network of alternate responses to the various changes, demands, and needs that arise. Unfortunately, however, not all habits are equally adept at meeting changing circumstances, for many become rigid repetitive ways of acting. Although common wisdom holds that the heart of habit is repetition, such a perception mistakenly identifies a capacity made possible by habits with their essence. The key to development and subsequent employment of habits is not repetition but successful and efficient action. Dewey tells the story of a dog, locked daily in a pen, which repeatedly nudges at the latched gate trying to get out. One day the dog hits the latch with his nose and opens the gate. On subsequent days, he learns to directly hit the latch with his nose, eliminating all other forms of nudging as unnecessary. Some would say that the dog developed the habit of opening the gate through repetition. Dewey points out, however, that if this were the case, the dog would still be nudging at the gate as he initially did.[4] We do not form habits by repetition, but "by eliminating the excessive activity of our first attempt, and emphasizing that particular activity which leads in the direction we want to go" (LW 17:301). *Selection* of ways of acting, then, is vital to the formation of habits. Two significant consequences follow. First, selection of a particular way of acting *precedes* the consolidating effect which results from repeated performance; such selection itself aims at success in getting what one needs or wants. Second, all habits are purposive in nature; successful completion of a task, and not simple mechanical repetition, is their proper function.

Of course, success in developing habits can be of varying degrees. Imagine that our fabled dog, in trying to get out of his pen, simply howls until his owner lets him out. If this secures the desired effect, howling would then be developed into a habit. But, of course, opening the gate with his nose gives the dog the greater freedom to leave the pen whenever he likes. While perhaps not what the owner desires, it would be a more successful habit in producing what the dog wants. Similarly, suppose I have greatest coordination in two fingers; I may then develop the habit of typing with those fingers alone. While my habit may enable me to type, it is unlikely that it will be as powerful, quick, and efficient as one which allows me to use all my fingers. If, upon discovering one successful means we no longer seek alternatives, our achievement may be partial and tentative at best. We limit ourselves to the extent that we do not attend to and evaluate the success of our habits. Humans are capable of great flexibility in the formation of habit, since they have intelligence. Pragmatically understood, intelligence marks the operation of thought as it functions, not primarily in representing the world but rather as a complex instrument of adaptation. Most generally, intelligence is our ability to attend to and evaluate relations between ourselves and the environment, between means and ends; it thus enables us to direct and redirect our energies and abilities as we interact with the environment. By its means, we are capable of evaluating and improving the success of our habits.

Habits are coordinated behaviors that can be repeated until they cement into routine, but this is neither necessary nor the essence of all habits. Though they can be routine, habits can also be intelligent. Mechanical repetition is the heart and soul of routine habits. Whenever they *may* be employed, they *are* employed regardless of their effectiveness. Routine habits indicate that the original plasticity from which habits were formed has been frozen into solidity and permanence; rigid boundaries line the channels of these habits. By contrast, intelligent habits are, as Dewey describes them, "fused with thought and feeling" (MW 14:51) such that they are adaptive to changing circumstances. These habits are flexible and sensitive to particular conditions, retaining their plasticity so they can be adjusted or modified to serve more varied ends. Intelligent habits, as the name suggests, employ intelligence in the adjustment of habits to new needs, purposes, and ends. Peirce's notion of habituation, noted above, provides an excellent example of this. Indeed, the more complex the organism, the greater the flexibility of which it is capable in its habits.

While every habit is a readiness to act in certain ways formed through prior interactions with the environment, this readiness can and should be responsive to new situations. When it is, habits are truly master skills or tools which enable us to adjust sensitively (with benefit of intelligence) to changes in the environment. Though they still structure our activity, habits are then dynamic structures conducive to developing new habits and attaining new ends. As such, they constitute our ability, rather than liability, to grow and further develop. But whether routine or intelligent, habits are our primary tools or means of acting. We do things by means of them; they are, in essence, our agency, our ability, our primary resource in acting.

So far, we have emphasized that the human organism is embedded in and conditioned by its environments. Equally important, though, is the fact that it does not simply react to external exigencies; it also actively, dynamically, directs its own behavior and transforms its environment. This is a general consequence of the fact that the organism has energies which it seeks to express. Our activity is manifested not only in the responsivity of habits, but also in our quest to fulfill desires and realize ideals. Having sketched the former, I now turn to the latter, addressing the genesis and function of desire in the context of a problematic situation. This discussion provides, as we shall see, the blueprint for hope.

A habit's career is usually fluid and dynamic and only rarely stable and static. We rely on habits so long as they work—that is, secure successful interaction—but environmental alterations often interrupt their smooth operation. Changes in our surroundings can make habits, especially those rigidly employed, ineffective or obsolete. When a favorite bar or restaurant moves, we may find ourselves delivered by means of habit to the old location—even though we know of the move. Future interaction can also bring habits into conflict with one another, further disrupting their easy employment; the college student's late night socializing habits frequently collide with productive study habits. When it interrupts habits, the changing scene of interaction generates a problematic situation requiring adjustment or modification—on the part of the organism or the environment—if activity is to be restored. Impulse or desire is the initial result of interruption and also the first step in restoring activity. Dewey characterizes desire as follows:

> When the push and drive of life meets no obstacles, there is nothing which we call desire. There is just life-activity. But obstructions present themselves, and activity is dispersed and divided. Desire is the outcome. It is activity surging forward to break through what damns it up. The "object" which then presents itself in thought as the goal of desire is the object of the environment *which, if it were present,* would secure a re-unification of activity and the restoration of its ongoing unity. The end-in-view of desire is that object which were it present would link into an organized whole activities which are now partial and competing. (MW 14:172)

Vital to restoring fluid interaction is the formulation of an end-in-view relative to which we can generate means capable of resolving the problematic situation. The interruption of habits releases energy previously structured by those habits; this is the source of the "activity surging forward" to which Dewey refers. If it is to restore interaction, however, such energy needs some sort of focus; otherwise, it will likely dissipate, leaving the organism even more frustrated, out of sync with its environment, and relatively powerless to do anything about it. Focus is provided by ends-in-view, included among which (as we shall see in the next section) are particular hopes.

While traditional philosophy frequently pits desire against thought (and intelligence), pragmatists like Dewey understand the two as working in tandem as responses to the environment. Thought is not independent of desire, as rationalists often contend, nor a slave to it, as some empiricists hold; rather thought *clarifies* desire. Though habits structure the flow of energy, their interruption leaves that energy unchanneled. The office of thought is to help find or construct new channels for that energy. Thought clarifies desire by giving it direction or an objective. As Dewey notes, "[i]n this case desire and thought cannot be opposed, for desire includes thought within itself. The question is now how far the work of thought has been, how adequate is its perception of its directing object" (MW 14:176). When thought is applied to desire, desire is given focus and definite form so it can be integrated with the pattern of habits the organism has developed. As a consequence, thought also makes possible the reconstruction of habits, wedding them to the renewing energy of desire in a way that restores successful interaction with the environment.

The imagination plays a vital role in this process. Traditionally, the imagination has been variously understood as a deficient mode of perception (a mode of false representation—typically at odds with rational structures of thought), a mysterious but powerful access to the extraordinary, or simply an instrument of escape and fantasy. By contrast, pragmatists treat it as an integral part of the process of resolving problematic situations. As such, it is interwoven with the operation of intelligence in finding and wedding means and ends. Most generally, the imagination is a mode of our ability to abstract, to go beyond what is presently available to us and to play amid possible relations not yet realized in fact. Pragmatists view the imagination as our ability to see the actual in light of the possible.[5] This ability contributes to simple acts of deliberation as well as the creation of complex works of arts, functioning not only in the context of specific problems but also in the wider arena of our quest for meaningful lives. To begin resolving a specific problematic situation, we must first formulate an end-in-view as well as the means which will realize it; we employ the imagination in doing both. We typically draw ends and means from the vast reservoir of experience (both our own and that of others), though we must creatively adjust them to our present situation if they are to successfully resolve the problematic situation. It is the imagination which explores and attends to possibilities, considering them in adequate detail to anticipate their value or meaning to us in resolving the problematic situation and also contributing to the larger activities and meanings of our lives.

Consequently, imaginative operations do not simply peruse possibilities that are neutral; they explore *meaningful possibilities.* Dewey, for instance, argues that "the only meaning that can be assigned the term 'imagination' is that things unrealized in fact come home to us and have power to stir us" (LW 9:30). Imaginative exploration considers and creates possibilities that are meaningful, that are continuous with the larger horizon of meaning. Imagination is *rearrangement* of possibilities in *thought* in *meaningful* ways. It contributes to the discovery and pairing of means and ends and so assists in reconstructing habits and rechanneling unleashed energy. By allowing us to see the actual in light of the possible, the imagination ties a present situation (whether problematic or not) to broader contexts of meaning, which are supported by habits and guided by ideal ends. Thomas M. Alexander aptly describes imaginative activity as "a *creative* exploration of *structures* inherited from past experience which thereby allow[s] the future as a horizon of possible actions, and so of possible meanings, to guide and interpret the present."[6] Imaginative exploration is not some random, dispassionate, unstructured exercise of our mental capacities, though it does, of course, have an element of play about it. Being able to imagine means being able to abstract from present conditions, temporarily severing existential conditions and relations in our minds to create new connections and so possible new realities. Sometimes we generate ends not yet experienced or means never before tried. While such possibilities may be discontinuous with present actualities, they only stir or motivate us, and thereby engage our attention and energies, to the extent that they are or can be made continuous with some portion of our horizons of meaning. Imaginative creations entice us to explore possible means that might establish the needed continuity with meaningful real conditions. Consequently, the imagination generates both ends and means, freely relating them in light of the different possible meanings they have for us.

Even uses of the imagination to sketch out fantasy worlds or destructive scenarios demonstrate that its object is exploration of meaningful possibilities. Flights of fancy are possible, but even these have ties with reality whereby they become meaningful. Consider a recent movie, *Little Voice.*[7] The protagonist is a shy young woman who lives alone with her crass overbearing mother now that her beloved father has died. Little Voice, as she is called, frequently retreats from the real world to a world defined by the music of her father's records. She keeps him alive and finds comfort by singing his favorite songs, imitating the original artists with remarkable precision; she imaginatively generates a world in which she is Judy Garland or Shirley Bassey, singing to a captivated audience on a brightly lit stage. When she occupies this world, singing in her room, her shy reserved demeanor fades away and is replaced by that of a confident, dynamic star. Here in this world of music her father still lives, visiting her occasionally and giving her comfort and advice. Moreover, here she can thrive. Even though this world is fantasy, its meaning to Little Voice is rooted in the real world. Its solace and power derive from its connections to her father's favorite music. This world is rooted in achieved meanings, even though it sadly remains disconnected from the rest of her present life.

Destructive uses of imagination also show this link to meaning. Those who conjure up scenarios where they kill their enemies and show the world what they can do seem to find in such imaginings release from the pain of humiliation or torture by others, as well as the creative rush that comes from putting together a complex plan to solve a problem.[8] Thankfully, such scenarios are typically discarded intelligently when their authors realize that any meaning secured by such possibilities is quickly outweighed by negative consequences—that is, by the alternate goods and meanings destroyed in the process. While fascinating because liberating and consummating in limited contexts, such images are judged destructive and meaningless when considered in light of real conditions and consequences. The great merit of the imagination is that we can detect such limits to seemingly meaningful possibilities in thought rather than in deed.

Indeed, performing explorations in thought both increases our resources and enables us to avoid sometimes severe costs we might otherwise face. Dewey explains that in such cases "[t]he trial is in imagination, not in overt fact. The experiment is carried on by tentative rehearsals in thought which do not affect physical facts outside the body. Thought runs ahead and foresees outcomes, and thereby avoids having to wait the instruction of actual failure or disaster" (MW 14:132). Consequently, the imagination proves an invaluable resource to us in improving interaction. Though able to break free from the bonds of present reality, it need not be cut off from or at odds with it. Our own experience provides the basic materials of the imagination, only loosened from the bonds of reality so that we may uncover or create new relationships. The imagination can spin its own worlds so fully that some people prefer to live there rather than in the "real" world. This frustrates the full employment of the imagination, for its function is to engage in practical matters, enhancing reality with a touch of creativity.

Consequently, three general related forces condition the formulation and realization of an end-in-view. The first is the problematic situation to which the end proposes a resolution and restoration of activity. Such a situation signifies that activity has been frustrated. Some change or resolution is demanded; otherwise, the organism will likely be harmed or crushed by its environment. Each end-in-view arises in response to the *particular* need or desire wrought by this situation. Ends do not simply appear out of nowhere, but function relative to real conditions. Each end represents a good to be achieved in a particular context and so is a *conditioned* good. Its actual value is determined by how well it meets the original need. An end-in-view is not simply given by the problematic situation. Instead, we must imaginatively consider and create ends, projecting and selecting them in light of their likely success in solving the original problem. Nevertheless, the nature of an end-in-view is partially determined by the context out of which it is generated; otherwise, it would not be a response to *that* need and a restoration of *that* activity.

The second factor conditioning ends-in-view is the organism's other ends and undisturbed habits. Frustration of interaction in a problematic situation does not leave the organism completely without resources, for other habits typically remain intact. If I break or sprain one of my two typing fingers, for instance, I can perhaps revert to habits of writing by hand. Also consider a scenario in which I find myself temporarily confined to a wheelchair because of an accident; my habits of mobility certainly will be impaired. Though I will not be able to walk freely as I am accustomed, I can still use my arms to move the wheelchair; I can also seek assistance from those with whom I interact. Interruption of one habit does not neutralize all others. Consequently, a complex network of habits (both social and individual) conditions the formulation of an end-in-view. The other purposes and ideals we have at any given moment also have an effect. Only rarely are we pursuing but one end; the value of each end must be weighed in light of that of others. Although any end promising to fulfill a need or bring satisfaction is a good and so is *desired*, further consideration of it in relation to other goods is necessary before it can be judged *desirable*. We value ends to the extent that they not only fulfill present needs but also do not impede the satisfaction of other, perhaps larger, needs, goods, and meanings. As complex organisms possessing habits, purposes, and ideals (some of which may require supporting habits we currently lack), the very integration of our habits and ideals may be a dominant ideal conditioning all other ends. Indeed, ideals concerning the very nature of the self tend to be vested with special value, not because we are inherently selfish, but rather because realizing such ends generally lies most fully within our own powers. As I will explain below, these ideals are living to us, and so we invest our resources in them. An end-in-view gains in attractiveness and desirability when it fosters or at least does not impede larger, more personal tendencies and ends.

The third force conditioning our ends-in-view is intelligence, aided by imaginative explorations. The difference between a desired and desirable end is marked largely by the operation of intelligence. Intelligence functions to evaluate competing desires, matching means with ends and assessing the relation between various ends. Each end as a desired good is conditioned by both its generative context and the means required for its realization. But since ends belong to the means-end continuum, they are also potential means to other ends or consequences. We employ intelligence in evaluating imaginative possibilities, considering both conditions and consequences of selected means to determine whether they are the most desirable of those possible—that is, desired or good in relation to other goods as well.[9] In the process, means are proposed and assessed in light of their suitability in realizing the end-in-view. But the end-in-view is itself open to assessment, especially should there be no means to its realization, or should it be found to generate unwanted consequences. Ends whose realization either requires unacceptable means or results in unacceptable consequences are ruled out. By contrast, ends which foster and reinforce other desired ends are judged more valuable, more desirable, than those which do not.

A striking example, drawn from the horrors of one person's real life, illustrates both the expanse of the imagination and also the difference between the desired and desirable. Martha Manning provides a thoughtful autobiographical account of her own battle with depression in *Undercurrents*.[10] A therapist herself, Martha takes all the recommended steps in dealing with her depression. She sees a psychopharmacologist as well as a psychotherapist, experimenting with medications and confronting her growing depression openly. Nothing, though, seems to work. As the depression gets worse and worse, she finds herself thinking about death and even suicide. While in the past she would have quickly discarded (if even considered) such thoughts, she now finds herself imaginatively exploring them in detail. Martha notes that "[r]ather than feeling the revulsion and fear that would have resulted from thinking about these things several months ago, now I find them strangely comforting" (93). When her doctor asks if she has been thinking about suicide, requesting that she explain what she imagines, she responds with the following specifics: "I think about pills, but I'm afraid I'd botch the job. I've thought about hanging. I think I know the basics of it, but I'm afraid I could screw that up too. Now I'm thinking about guns" (105). Each of these possibilities is considered in the context of her abilities and its likely consequences—and so in light of means and ends; each takes on its own degree of meaning in light of such contextual features. Ultimately, though, Martha decides that no course of suicide is really a viable option. She tells her doctor, "I can't leave Keara. . . . I can't do this to my child. She is the only thing that stands between me and dying" (105). Here we see vividly illustrated how we consider ends in light of possible means, and how the complex of each is gauged in terms of other meanings and other goods. While each path to suicide might be meaningful in providing an escape from the hell of Martha's depression, each becomes meaningless when considered in light of the effects on her daughter. Though perhaps desired in a limited context, suicide is not desirable against the backdrop of meaning in her life. To kill herself might mean escape, but it would also mean certain failure and cruelty to her daughter. We will return to Martha's story below.

While past events and achievements direct and shape the human organism and what it will do, purposes and ideals are means of projecting ourselves into the future. This is obvious in Martha's case; her own projects include overcoming depression and being a good mother. It is in light of our ends, in particular, that we guide our own activity, not just in accommodating ourselves to the world, but also in making the environment friendlier to our special goals. Generated in the fire of experience, these ends have the power to elicit our commitment and energies, whether individual or social. They find root in and enrich our horizons of meaning, existing at first in thought or imagination and later, if we are successful, in reality. Consequently, humans are incomplete not only in that we always face new challenges, but also in that we are constantly engaged in projects whose completion lies beyond the horizon of the present. Development and completion of these projects requires continuity with future states. Every manner of ideal—whether a wish, dream, hope, or plan—thus entices us to extend a part of ourselves into the future. Motivated to fulfill not only needs generated through external exigencies but also its own purposes and ideals, we constantly reach for completion or satisfaction. Though realization brings satisfaction, fulfillment is only provisional, since we are always temporal, always in process. New satisfactions will be called for or desired as we reconstruct ourselves through interaction with a changing environment. Provisional though they may be, satisfactions are vital in developing our abilities, for they provide lures which focus and call forth our energies.

Consequently, the human organism is not only conditioned but also open and projective. Both features play a significant role in defining the self. I end this section with a sketch of a pragmatic view of the self, for it brings together our discussions of habits and ideals; it also lays important groundwork for later discussions of hopefulness and despair (see chapter 3). I noted above the possibility that integration of our habits and ideals may itself be an end awaiting realization; this is the domain of the self. The self is that dimension of the human organism which integrates the various episodes of its history, both actual and prospective, with one another. Habits and ideals each play significant roles in our interaction with the environment. Without past habits we are helpless in navigating the changing currents of the world. Without purposes we have no direction and so are reduced to being mere reactors to external conditions. The self is conditioned by past activities, and so by past integrations, yet it is an active integrating or reintegrating of these in light of changing circumstances, needs, and goals. The self is thus the *reconstructive dynamic* of the human organism.

Traditional philosophy typically identifies the self with consciousness, with that part of the organism that is aware of its activities. While consciousness does play a vital role, it does not exhaust the self. Dewey argues that the self consists just as much, if not more, in established habits. Bad habits in particular teach us "that a predisposition formed by a number of specific acts is an immensely more intimate and fundamental part of ourselves than are vague, general, conscious choices. All habits are demands for certain kinds of activity; and they constitute the self" (MW 14:21). Anyone who has tried to modify a habit has struggled with the tension between the desire to change and the enormous weight of an established habit, particularly as it interweaves with other habits. Importantly, habits are the vital abilities which enable us to act and interact successfully; they are the seat of our agency or will. Though rooted in habits, however, the self is more than a set of habits. The tension experienced when attempting to change a habit reveals the self's complex dynamic nature. The self consists not only in habits, but also in desires, purposes, and ideals. More accurately, the self is the active and ongoing interweaving of the organism's different dimensions, including habits, desires, intelligence, and ideals. Each of these dimensions typically enjoys some influence from social conditions. Consequently, the self is the integration of multiple habits and desires, both actual and ideal, both individual and social.[11]

To properly understand this pragmatic view of the self, we must be clear about what we mean by *integration*; it is here that the role of consciousness becomes clear. We might think that the goal of the self is the unification of its interactive episodes. But *unification* typically suggests preserving all antecedent elements when, especially in the case of interactive biological organisms, not all elements should be preserved. Adaptation or more successful interaction is the primary directive of the biological organism, and so unification should be subordinated to it. Some habits are stubborn relics of bygone days; others may still be useful, but not without modification. Similarly, desires and purposes may be misguided or grossly out of touch with current conditions so that their pursuit is a waste of energy. As the organism seeks satisfactions, the role of the self is to select those ends which merit expenditure of energy and then to *direct* that energy toward them. Selection and direction are operations of intelligence, rooted in consciousness. Though integration may at times occur habitually, ideals and habits frequently conflict and generate awareness. Sometimes conflict arises from an incompatibility between social and individual habits, as when duties due to a job or social role clash with habits of pursuing hobbies. It may also arise from a tension between a powerful ideal and dominant habits, whether social or individual. Mere awareness of conflict does not establish the link between consciousness and the self; rather, what is needed is the recognition of these elements as *integral parts* of a *larger project*, the project of the *self*. Habits form the basis of its abilities, and ideals enticingly draw it toward new possibilities that fulfill and expand it. When habits and ideals conflict, awareness that both play a natural and vital role in the self intensifies their conflict and heightens the need for its resolution. With this comes the opportunity to intelligently evaluate and integrate these different dimensions of the organism. Both cannot be readily preserved as they are; if they could, they would not conflict. Instead, habits must be reconstructed to better serve as means to the ideal—or an ideal may be revised or perhaps abandoned in light of another which disrupts fewer habits. Consciousness thus links together habits and ideals, means and ends, by embedding them in the larger context of the self. As such, the self can aim at, and so be directed by, the growth of increased breadth and richness in the ends achieved and enjoyed.

Consequently, the goal of the self is best understood not as unification, but rather as *creative integration*, with explicit acknowledgment of selective emphasis and the inevitable loss that comes with it. Integration can take a variety of forms. Just as habits can be routine and repetitive or intelligent and adaptive, so too can the self be oriented toward conservation or growth. For instance, the self may be dominated by familiar habits; resistance to changing these indicates that novelty is all but selectively discarded. At the other extreme are individuals who shun regularity and pursue everything that challenges their abilities. In each case, some dominant or regnant habit guides and structures the process of integration. This habit can be intelligent, routine, productive of growth and expansion, or supportive of the status quo. It can even cripple us by shrinking the sphere of our concern and the extent of our ability, as occurs in the case of a despairing self dominated by habits of fear and hopelessness. By contrast, the regnant habit of a hopeful self is that of hopefulness rooted, as I will argue, in habits of hope.

While our regnant habit determines the goods we pursue, the self need not be only concerned with its own immediate goods, for it is conditioned by the natural and social contexts it inhabits. It may, of course, purposefully embrace social connections, nurturing them and successfully executing social roles. It may also seek to ignore or minimize others' goods and activities, drawing itself into an isolating cocoon. Numerous modes of integration are possible; indeed, we may exhibit several in succession at various points in our development, or a mixture at one stage. Though the self is always conditioned by the larger context of interaction, how it deals with that context—adjusting or abandoning habits and ideals—can take multiple forms; this is what accounts for the endless variety of selves we encounter.

Creative integration is an ongoing project, frequently marked by experimentation—especially for individuals whose goal is further growth and whose primary habits are intelligent. In most cases, the human organism strives to develop itself in different contexts and to find further satisfactions.[12] Since we face a variety of things we *could* become, life is itself an experiment. Whether our primary goal is establishing basic compatibility with the environment or finding activities in which we flourish, experimentation promotes both. In the former case, external pressures with which we *must* deal typically dictate the course of our exploration. By contrast, our endeavor to flourish is more a matter of productivity than necessity, and so is conducive to more leisurely experimentation. In each case, though, we creatively reach out for new possibilities, testing and seeking to expand our capacities to act and interact.

Insofar as it actively seeks the integration of past achievements with future goals, the self is an achievement—that is, an active and ongoing transformation of purposes and powers generated through greater and more complex integration. Consequently, the self is best understood not as an entity, but rather as an active and creative *relating*. It is a project or a continuity of projects, a continuous journey marked by both successes and failures. The self is that dynamic of the organism which creatively reconstructs the organism in ongoing efforts at adaptation to and of the environment.

Where do particular hopes fit into this understanding of the human organism? Clearly, hopes are among the various ends or ideals we seek to realize. As such, they arise in particular situations and so meet specific needs. Realizing them requires drawing on social and individual habits already possessed, as well as reconstructing and developing others. As I argued in the introduction, the pursuit of hopes must be justified in terms of their desirability and realizability, especially as these are affected by the particular conditions of their genesis. In the next section, I address the specific features that define hopes, in order to more fully address the first sense of hope's practicality.

The Nature of Hope in Relation to Its End

In the preceding section, I provided a pragmatic account of how ends are formulated and pursued in the context of problems that arise when interacting with our environment. This account applies to many activities, hoping among them. As I noted in the introduction, hoping is largely continuous with other activities such as wishing, dreaming, and planning; successful hoping can lead to planning and to subsequent realization of desired ends. Hoping differs from other activities largely because of special circumstances attending its ends. Particular hopes are remote blocked ends which we nevertheless consider both desirable and realizable enough to merit our time and commitment. We justify them primarily by assessing *how* desirable and realizable their ends are. Such justification thus requires that we attend to the specific nature of hope's ends and the conditions which give rise to them. I take my lead from St. Thomas Aquinas's general description of hope. My primary goal in using Aquinas is not to identify a pragmatic account with his view, for the two differ in significant ways. First, Aquinas does not view the human being as a primarily interactive biological organism. Instead, he argues that we have an essential nature which is tied to God. Unsurprisingly, then, Aquinas's theory of hope posits supernatural ends with a supernatural ground; our pragmatic account has neither. Nevertheless, Aquinas provides a clear generic sketch that highlights what is unique about hoping, particularly with respect to its end. I thus begin my discussion with his account.

Aquinas defines hope as a future good that is arduous and difficult—but nevertheless possible—to obtain (I-II.40.1). Four distinctive features characterize its end: it is future, good, arduous, and yet also possible. Though each feature has special significance, none should be severed from its relation to the others, or else we will fail to properly understand hopes. Generally, the second quality (goodness) determines the desirability of the end, while the other three characterize its realizability. Importantly, though, the realizability of a hope affects its desirability. To persist in pursuing an end that appears desirable but is, by all accounts, impossible to bring about is a foolish waste of time and energy. Similarly, few of us are willing to commit resources to the realization of an arduous end that is not sufficiently desirable, even if it is possible. We can make the same point in the language of means and ends. Futurity and goodness primarily characterize the end (or end-in-view) for which we hope, and arduousness and possibility are conditions of its means. Of course, an end-in-view plays a significant role in the selection of means; moreover, ends and means are revisable in light of one other. So while each of hope's features is distinct, none can truly be isolated from the others. I here treat each individually for special emphasis.

Futurity

To say hope's end is a *future* end is rather obvious, but its significance should not be overlooked. We do not hope to attain what has already happened or what we already possess. In the former case, the end is already a settled fact, while in the latter, we do not hope for but rather enjoy the end. As already possessed or achieved, it is remembered and judged in terms of its fecundity. As presently enjoyed, the end is perceived. Of course, if its continuation is desired but also threatened, *then* we may quite plausibly hope for such. We may also hope that an end presently possessed will give rise to further ends and so develop into even greater riches, as when we hope that current success at work fosters further productivity. In no case, however, do we presently possess the ends for which we hope.

The futurity of hopes signifies that they *may* happen, that they ride on the crest of the wave of time and creativity, that they are or may be in the making. This indeterminacy accounts for both the blessings and curses of hope. Hope's futurity signifies a certain remoteness about its end. Many ends are yet to be achieved, but ends for which we hope are unique in not being readily obtainable. Closely related to hope's futurity, then, is its arduousness. Typically, a hope's remoteness is due to some problem concerning the means to its realization. Means may be nonexistent or simply out of reach, either because of our limited abilities or because of some definite obstacle which stands in the way. In either case, this remoteness is the source of an indeterminacy which plagues hopes. For any hope to be worthy of my time and attention, it should not only be possible, but really possible *for me*. Knowing this, however, is no small feat. Consider the case of a cancer patient. Many have successfully undergone chemotherapy, securing either temporary or permanent relief from cancer. Though promising, their success does not guarantee my own. Will I enjoy similar results or nothing at all? Will relief come soon, or only after I have expended virtually every vital resource I have? Especially because of the future's indeterminacy—signifying the abode of the unpredictable—pursuing hopes carries all the dangers catalogued in the introduction.

This indeterminacy also accounts, however, for part of hope's power: though a hope has not yet been realized, it still *might* be. While hopes arise from present problems and so have one foot in reality, they would fail to live and grow without the indefinite expanse of the future; its openness and variety provide fertile soil in which we can plant ideal ends. Consequently, hope's futurity, difficult to confront though it may be, elicits one of our greatest human capacities: the ability to attentively await, to invest in what is presently unseen. Importantly, what we do may itself contribute to hope's realization, though there is no guarantee of this. Especially since hopes are yet to be, part of the process of hoping involves discovering whether we can contribute to their determination. We see what is possible not in advance, but rather subsequent to acting, to trying. In the language of means and ends, a particular hope functions as an end-in-view, an end yet to be achieved, and an end around which the self can mobilize itself. This calls forth our resources and creativity. The indeterminate future thus proves to be a source of not only hope's infamy but also its fame.

Goodness

Despite its remoteness, an end for which we hope has the power to attract, to draw our attention and energies to it. In other words, the end is a future good, promising some sort of satisfaction. This is the second feature of hope's end, generally, and of its desirability, specifically. When hoping, we aim at something desired as good; if the end were thought to be a future evil, we would not hope for but rather fear its realization. Instead of moving toward it, we would seek to avoid it. As I argued above, whether a desired good is also *desirable* depends on its relation to other goods, especially as judged in light of its conditions and consequences. If the conditions needed for its realization are impossible or too costly—preventing the pursuit or enjoyment of other goods—we wisely reject an end. If we judge its conditions possible, we must then also consider the likely effects it will produce. Consequently, the desirability of the end cannot be fully assessed apart from considering its realizability.

Before exploring salient features of the goodness of hope's ends, it will help to sketch some concrete hopes on which we can draw. The first is the story of young Cedric Jennings, recounted by journalist Ron Suskind in *A Hope in the Unseen: An American Odyssey from the Inner City to the Ivy League.*[13] When Suskind begins his tale, Cedric is an African American teenager growing up in the dangerous world of Washington, D.C.'s inner city. Living with his mother—his older sisters now gone and his father imprisoned for dealing drugs—Cedric's main hope in high school is to make it to the Ivy League. Such an end is clearly a good for him. He is an intelligent, quiet young man with talents and ambitions which would be squandered if he took the route traveled by most of his peers: aim low, get out of high school without drawing attention to yourself, and either find a job or attend a local community college. Though clearly desirable to him, most of Cedric's classmates judge his end to be impractical, not signifying a legitimate hope but rather expressing his excessive pride. Things are different from Cedric's position. His pride is his drive, and realizing this hope promises a way out of the inner city and into a productive world populated with like-minded people. Cedric's specific hopes range from graduating high school at the top of his class, to getting into an Ivy League school, to finding a place in society where he feels like he belongs. To say that he plans to do all these things would be to underestimate the challenges he faces. Even the most straightforward goal of graduating at the top of his class is fraught with peril; Suskind catalogues the numerous forces which threaten to drag him down. In addition to dangers of violent peers and the trials of belonging to a poor one-parent family, he must contend with distracted teachers and unsupportive colleagues. Suskind explains how many of Cedric's classmates punish him for his aspirations, demonstrating what some educators call the crab/bucket syndrome: "when one crab tries to climb from the bucket, the others pull it back down" (Suskind 17). Consequently, realizing his end will require everything Cedric has to offer—and more.

Though perhaps less prominent than his hope to escape the inner city is Cedric's hope to make friends. This hope is, of course, common to both the rich and poor, the young and old. Few doubt the good such companionship brings; with friends we share values, interests, and activities, as well as the joys and sorrows of everyday life. Aristotle notes that a full life requires friendships in which both parties share a similar character (and so habits) as well as a concern for the other's good.[14] Making friends, especially good friends, is not an easy task. It depends on finding kindred souls who are open to investing in new relationships, as well as having the time and energy to nurture them. Cedric, for instance, repeatedly finds himself feeling alienated from others. In truth, many extend the hand of friendship, yet his dominant hope—and at times crutch—to realize his own academic ambition sometimes gets in the way. We can, of course, take measures to meet new people and foster new friendships, but since our success is contingent on the desires and efforts of others, we hope rather than plan to make friends.

As our next example, consider the hopes for recovery that arise in the various contexts of debilitating and life-threatening illnesses. Whether the illness is AIDS, cancer, or depression, these hopes take numerous forms. We have already encountered one in Martha Manning. As noted, Martha does everything that experts advise and yet her depression only gets worse. She experiments with many forms of medication (with her doctor's guidance) and searches for answers by undergoing psychotherapy and attending a religious retreat, but nothing halts the drag of depression that is taking control of her life. She has enormous trouble sleeping, finds her own abilities shrinking, thinks of death and suicide, and becomes basically paralyzed. Her depression gets so severe that she finally undergoes electroconvulsive therapy (ECT). Her hope throughout is to recover from depression, especially in a way that does not threaten her own sense of self: her self-reliance. When I later discuss the discoveries she makes, we shall see how this is transformed in a surprising but meaningful way.

Other examples of people hoping for recovery from illness can be found in Sherwin B. Nuland's insightful book *How We Die*. His numerous examples demonstrate how cancer patients hope for a variety of different ends: that they can find treatment which successfully rids them of the cancer; that they can prolong life as long as possible to see their children grow; or that they, like Nuland's patient Bob DeMatteis, can endure with dignity the likely pains of advancing cancer. Some, such as ninety-two-year-old Miss Welch, hope that cancer takes them quickly, so that they will be freed from the trials of this world and, perhaps, delivered to a new existence. Obviously, some of these ends are compatible (for example, the hope for prolonged life and the hope to endure with dignity), such that we may concurrently hope for both or utilize one in realizing the other. If one end increasingly proves unpromising, we may retreat to another. Which end, or set of ends, we hope for depends largely on contextual conditions of our past and present states. For instance, if our lives have been rich and productive, we will probably hope for complete or partial recovery; if they have been miserable, we more likely hope for release.

Finally, consider two examples of hopes that focus on the good of another. Cedric's mother, Barbara Jennings, provides a rich example of a parent who invests herself in her son's hopes. Like most parents, she actively hopes her child will grow to be a strong, productive member of society—even in the face of apparently slim odds. Typically, we cannot really plan the realization of such an end, since a child's development and maturation depend on many forces other than their parents. Members of the extended family, friends, teachers, and the media also exert considerable influence on our children. Nevertheless, Barbara recognizes and takes advantage of the fact that she is in a prime position to give clear, strong direction to Cedric. When he was an infant, she quit work and lived on welfare so she could personally ensure Cedric had all the love and attention he needed during his vital years of development. Once he reached school age, she returned to work but continued to be self-sacrificing, working hard to secure material conditions that nurtured healthy emotional and physical growth as well as opportunities to develop his talents. Barbara is ever aware of the influence of family (especially Cedric's father), friends, teachers, the church; she knows all too well how their effects, as well as Cedric's own abilities and purposes, can strengthen, mitigate, or all but counteract her efforts. She perseveres in her hope, though; indeed, the story of Cedric's hope cannot be told apart from Barbara's hopes for him.

As our last example, consider those all too common and frightful instances when we discover a loved one has been involved in an accident whose consequences remain unknown. Whether the accident is at sea, in the air, or on the ground, our first hope is typically that our loved one survived or at least died a relatively painless death. In either case, we are generally unable to do anything to directly affect the outcome. Though no planning that will immediately help the loved one is possible in such cases, this does not make our investment in hoping meaningless. Hope can still give us the strength to support one another, or to prepare to help the loved one should he or she survive. It can keep us open and oriented to the various *possible* goods still available to us, even if the worst of our fears should prove true.

These examples illustrate three salient features of the goodness of hope's ends. First, they highlight the way context conditions what counts as a good to be pursued. We already noted how Martha was shocked to find herself comforted by thoughts of death and suicide, things she normally would not consider good, but which nevertheless *did* offer *some* good to her in the depths of her depression. More generally, the very hope for recovery from cancer, rather than quick release from this life, is a good primarily in a society which places a premium on continued earthly existence and which also possesses possible means of recovery. Similarly, none of the goods presented in our examples is abstract or imaginary in the negative sense. Each represents a concrete end pursued and realized by real persons in our society. Others have successfully made it to the Ivy League, made new friends, recovered from cancer, raised healthy children, and enjoyed a loved one's return from a disaster. As we shall see, a good's contextual conditions help justify our commitment to particular hopes, especially when it comes to the fourth condition of hope's end, its possibility.

The second point our examples illustrate is that we can rank our ends in terms of relative value, thereby creating a hierarchy or nesting of hopes. Unsurprisingly, since ends are embedded in the means-end continuum, hopes gain in value to the extent that they contribute to the realization of other goods or hopes. Cedric's hopes are living illustrations of the means-end continuum, with each end (graduating high school at the top of his class, getting into an Ivy League school, finding a place in society where he feels like he belongs) serving as a means to further ends. Similarly, before we can recover from cancer, we must develop habits of endurance to undergo therapy. I will argue in the next chapter that hopes become more practical when coordinated and pursued step by step. Larger, more distant hopes can be more readily achieved by pursuing more immediate hopes which expand our agency. One does not play in Carnegie Hall without first developing skills that are not only reliable but also musically expressive.

The life of hope is, however, capable of considerable complexity, often exceeding simple hierarchies and straightforward step-by-step progressions. While Cedric hopes to find kindred spirits, he tends to subordinate this hope to his larger hope of making it into the Ivy

League, pouring himself into the latter hope and all but ignoring the former. One of the beauties of Suskind's account is that he shows how intricately complex the life of hope can be. Cedric's primary goal may be in the area of academics, but it is sometimes fueled by, and at other times a means to promoting, his desire to belong. Hopes can interweave in productive ways so that we only artificially designate one the dominant end and the other the subordinate. Overlaps in multiple paths of progress toward different hopes can not only complement one another, they can also impede or distort each other. Since a plurality of ends, sharing multiple relations to one another, can foster valuable alternatives that keep hope alive, intelligence plays a considerable role in tracing and promoting productive relations among our ends. A cancer patient, for instance, may prioritize the hope for recovery but also acknowledge the benefit of hoping to meet adversity (including death) with dignity. Should the former hope prove unrealizable, the latter will become increasingly valuable.

The third point our examples illustrate is that the goodness of hope's ends tends to be salvific or extensional. Salvific ends are perhaps the most familiar. These are good insofar as they free us from intolerable situations. They promise emancipation from the bonds of a problem and so implicitly promise a way around an obstacle. ECT, though largely frowned upon in our culture, liberates Martha from the grip of her extreme depression. The cancer patient's hope for recovery represents the elimination of the original diseased condition. Other salvific hopes include release from an emotional or physical prison and overcoming an addiction or undesirable character trait. Equally important, though, are hopes which extend or develop our capacities. These are positive ends that promise progress, growth, and further fulfillment. Working to graduate at the top of his class stretches Cedric's abilities; making new friends helps develop his interests, insights, and character.

Salvific and extensional hopes have at their heart the promise of some improvement, whether it be liberation (from pain or fear or indeterminacy), growth (of one's talents and capacities), or even mere change (from the deadening repetition of past tendencies). Relative to the original situation which generates them, hopes promise the introduction of some novelty which improves upon whatever goods (if any) the original situation possessed. The ends for which we hope are never merely future *possibilities*, nor even merely *meaningful* future goods, but rather future goods *promising improvement* relative to our present state. Though typically the heat of hope arises directly from the flames of a specific problematic situation, perceived *possible* problems that are capable of affecting us can also generate or foster hopes. All too frequently, productivity lapses or people follow undesirable paths. Cedric sees both occur in his classmate, Phillip Atkins, who forgoes academic promise for social acceptance. His desire to avoid sharing Phillip's fate adds fuel to Cedric's own hopes. Consequently, even when nothing directly threatens our current state or actually blocks activity, we may still genuinely hope for continued success and fulfillment.

Though possessing goodness, hope's end must also be evaluated in terms of its overall desirability. As a remote end in competition with more readily obtainable goods, a hope must have added force to both attract our attention and warrant commitment of our resources. Its end must be *living*, such that we take a vital interest in it. As William James explains, an end's *liveliness*, its power to tempt and animate us, depends more on conditions of its acquisition and use in specific contexts than on any property belonging to the end per se.[15] Consequently, an end (for example, recovery from a disease through medicinal means) may be living in one context (the modern hospital), but not in another (the Christian Scientist community). This provides yet another illustration of the contextuality which pragmatists emphasize. The liveliness of hopes contributes to their desirability. For a remote end to win our attention and energy, its allure must be intense enough to overcome that of more immediate ends. Ends promising salvation or extension of the self usually harbor such intensity, as most of our examples readily demonstrate. Admission to the Ivy League represents to Cedric not only an important academic achievement, but also a significant step into a world in which he believes he will be more at home. His own sense of self is wrapped up with this hope. Similarly, recovery or release from cancer means termination of painful incapacity. A future good sparks vital interest in us especially when its realization or absence significantly affects our future integration. In such cases, a remote end becomes desirable because of its projected enhancement of the self.

The very nature of hopes often generates this vital liveliness, for the difficulty involved in their realization can intensify our commitment to them. Aquinas, for instance, argues that "the thought of [the hoped-for end] being difficult arouses our attention; while the thought that it is possible is no drag on our effort. Hence it follows that by reason of hope man is intent on his action" (I-II.40.8). Dewey and James make similar points, though with pragmatic backing. Interest in an end, Dewey argues, depends on whether it awakens and meshes with our active tendencies. When this does happen, arduousness tends to actually increase interest, for "if the self is deeply concerned with, thoroughly committed to, its object, each successive obstacle will deepen the sense of the importance of the object and increase the *effort* expended in behalf of its realization" (MW 7:255). In "The Energies of Men," James contends that *"as a rule men habitually use only a small part of the powers which they actually possess and which they might use under appropriate conditions"* (MS 240, italics in original). Trying circumstances often call forth our "second wind," bringing to light the hidden reaches of our abilities.

Chief among the live ideas or ends which tap into our reservoirs of unused energy are those *ideals* that serve us most in social and biological contexts. Recovery from cancer has both biological and social significance, for it shows the life force surging forth with the assistance of our collective efforts and intelligence, refusing to give up without a fight. Though defeating a disease is a mundane necessity if we are to pursue our own purposes, it also signifies a triumph of human strength and ingenuity over destructive forces. Raising productive children has both the biological and moral force of beating the odds and moving upward. Shared social ideals, in particular, exert a powerful presence which guides and structures our behavior. Acceptance into the hallowed halls of the Ivy League requires scholastic and creative ability and confers on those who attain it a special status in our society. James notes the social contagion that attaches to certain ideas (for example, liberty and patriotism), so that when they are espoused by those with whom we already identify, we find ourselves drawn to them as well. Parents or loved ones can ignite in us passions similar to their own, whether because of simple proximity or our own investment in their well-being and way of life.[16] Whatever spurs our effort, the general process is the same: a live idea attracts our attention, generates interest and subsequent effort, and taps into our often unused abilities. Accessing these hidden resources has two significant effects. First, every exercise of an ability affords an obvious opportunity to develop it, thereby securing our command of it and expanding its efficacy in the world. Second, tapping into reservoirs of energy produces its own unique satisfaction; because of our energetic nature, we flourish in the exercise and expansion of our abilities. Consequently, lively ends prove to be productive in being efficacious and fulfilling.

Sometimes, of course, we incorrectly gauge the desirability of ends. Though lively and promising much that is vital to the self, an end may nevertheless still be undesirable for a variety of reasons. Its realization may require means that are unacceptable to us, as when cancer treatment drains us physically, financially, and emotionally. It may lead to consequences we cannot tolerate; some could not endure the social stigma of having undergone ECT. The end may simply be unrealizable, as when we hope a loved one already killed in an accident survives. Sometimes the allure of a hope is so strong that we too quickly overlook the impossible conditions it requires. Hoping then becomes a matter of wishful thinking. In assessing desirability, we must thus be attentive to a hope's realizability.

Arduousness

In examining the remoteness of hope's end, we already saw indications of the arduousness that plagues hope. Hoped-for ends lie in the future largely because of the impediments that surround their realization. We neither possess them, nor can we readily attain them. Their means may be nonexistent, obstructed, or simply beyond our present capacities. Of course, hope's ends need not lie in the *distant* future to be arduous to realize. I can hope to pass a test or hope for the rescue of a loved one by day's end, without the limited time frame in any way minimizing the obstacles characteristic of hopes. Similarly, arduousness can be increased by indirect circumstantial factors; even though ECT helped Martha begin her recovery, social prejudices against it compounded her troubles. What is common to the ends for which we hope, though, is that *some* difficulty attends their means and indicates the limits of our agency in realizing them.

Aquinas rightly highlights arduousness as a significant dimension of hope, since we do not hope for what we can secure by our present powers or abilities. Typically, we plan rather than hope to have breakfast each morning, unless following our morning routine proves ineffectual in achieving this. If, for instance, we are in a hurry, traveling in an unfamiliar country, or are homeless and penniless, then getting breakfast may be problematic and so become a hope. By contrast, since recovering from cancer is something few of us have achieved before—at all or with any ease—it is something for which we typically hope rather than plan.

Consideration of the relation of means to ends illuminates the difference between hoping and two closely related activities, wishing and planning. Each of these activities has some end as its focus; their differences depend on the extent to which the means to that end are specifiable and accessible. When no means can be specified, because they either do not exist or are so indeterminate we cannot think of them, we are more plausibly said to wish than hope for the end. Most of us only wish we had a million dollars, for virtually none of our normal occupations yield such amounts of money. Since the ends for which we wish are generally judged unrealizable (and to that degree undesirable), we only foolishly commit ourselves to and invest our energies in them. At the other extreme, when an end's means are not only conceivable but also directly within our grasp, it makes most sense to say we plan or simply act to realize the end. Transferring a million dollars from my account to yours is something I may plan (or simply do), if I have the funds and nothing impedes completion of a normal bank transaction. Hope's ends lie between these two extremes.[17]

Hope shares much with both wishing and planning. Like wishing, it involves yearning for some unavailable good which has the power to at least capture our attention. Like planning, hoping consists in trying to connect (sometimes through forming) means or abilities with ends. Hoping is closer to planning than to wishing in that its ends have potential real means; this combination of means and ends has the power to focus our energies and summon our abilities. Hoping and planning also both involve experimental exploration and refinement of ends and means. Their primary difference consists in the degree to which realization of the end lies within our grasp. Hoping involves recognition of the limits of our agency, *either* because of some indeterminacy which attends its means *or* because of a deficiency or limitation in our own abilities. Hope's arduousness arises in part from our limitations and so indicates a certain vulnerability in our pursuit of an end. We remain vulnerable so long as we remain open and committed to ends whose realization depends on forces beyond our present control. Our susceptibility, however, is not complete but rather conditioned by the activities we take to pursue our ends (especially by the habits of hope discussed in the next chapter); it manifests itself in patience, in *awaiting*. I will discuss these points more fully in the next chapter when considering habits of patience.

Difficulties surrounding hopes thus tend to fall into one of two general categories. In the *first*, means prove problematic to identify or create. For instance, we may have formulated an end, such as finding a cure for AIDS, and yet lack a definite sense of the actual means which could secure it. While it is true that we have successfully discovered cures for other deadly diseases, even today we still do not know what, if anything, will cure or prevent AIDS. The *second* kind of difficulty occurs when means, though identifiable, lie beyond the reach of our current abilities and so are hard to secure. This usually happens when we have formulated an end whose realization is contingent upon a complicated set of means; Cedric's hope to enter and succeed in the Ivy League is one such example. Another scenario is that some determinate obstacle stands in the way of realizing hope's end, as when our children befriend delinquents and subsequently get into trouble. Or, finally, we may hope for an end, such as the survival of a loved one in a plane wreck, when its means, though conceivable, are almost entirely out of our hands.

A brief look at the kinds of indeterminacies that plague means is instructive in better understanding hope's arduousness, especially in its first category. Means may be difficult to identify because they are either nonexistent or epistemologically indeterminate—though a fine

line is sometimes all that separates the two. Consider our hope to develop a cure for AIDS. Since many diseases once thought incurable
have now been eradicated or successfully treated, we might conclude
that an AIDS cure exists but remains epistemologically indeterminate.
We simply have not discovered it. Note that *discovery* of a cure suggests
that some substance *already* exists, though its potency as a cure remains
epistemologically indeterminate to us. It may also be, however, that ingredients still need to be synthesized or manufactured, and so the cure
has yet to be created. In either case, its antecedent existence is largely
irrelevant so long as it remains epistemologically indeterminate to us.
Moreover, we must also acknowledge that it is also possible, though
perhaps difficult to accept, that a cure is impossible.

Arduousness can be due to indeterminacies concerning hope's ends
as well as its means. Difficulty in formulating or accessing means may
itself result from an indeterminate end. Recall that an end-in-view provides a focal point relative to which appropriate or adequate means can
be selected. Consider, for instance, a young child having difficulty realizing the hope to make friends at a new school. If the end which guides
his behavior is simply to make friends, he may not know where to start.
Patterns or habits relied on in the past may work; consequently, he may
rush to the nearest jungle gym to find like-minded playmates. But at
the new school, there may be no jungle gym, or the jungle gym may be
the domain of the rough kids rather than the athletic ones. So long as
his end remains as general as "to make friends," our youngster will not
know how to find the appropriate means. But, especially after discovering that past habits are not appropriate means, he can make that end
more specific: he can hope to find friends who enjoy athletic activities.
Having refined the end, he will be able to seek new playmates apart
from looking to the jungle gym. Even if the new end leads him to the
athletic kids, it may not realize his hope, for there is no guarantee that
these kids will be his friends. They may be athletic, but they also might
be so because they are economically privileged. If our new boy is
rather poor, they may exclude him from their activities. In that case, he
can give up his hope or revise the end again and seek new means.

My point is not that numerous indeterminacies beset the realization of every end, but rather that ends-in-view function best when they

are clearly defined. The more general the end, the less it guides us to a specific end. In addition, as the previous example shows, we can revise ends *through the process of pursuing* a hoped-for end. Indeed, here we see a dialectic between means and ends which indicates that the process of realizing an end involves making *both* means *and* ends more determinate. Of course, it is quite possible that though an end is carefully formulated *no* means could promote its realization. I may, for instance, hope to converse with Plato at the Academy in 380 BCE about the nature of practical knowledge. I might even have formulated means to this end, having designed a machine requiring an alloy that can withstand traveling through so-called wormholes in the space-time continuum. The only problem may (and is likely to) be that no such alloy exists. (Of course, we *might* create such an alloy in the future; the history of invention demonstrates the dangerous limitations of arrogance.) What we have here, then, is an elaborately developed end whose means are unavailable. We have a wish rather than a hope.

A similar point can be made via our cancer example. Upon receiving a diagnosis, most patients at first hope simply to recover. Whether or how they will is initially rather indeterminate. The first step is typically to *plan* to consult with doctors about possible forms of treatment, hoping to discover one that will succeed. This plan, though rather mundane in itself, will likely possess vital meaning for such patients, since it may be a means to realizing their more general hope of recovery from the cancer. Here, hope thus guides and gives special meaning to plans. Consequently, we can foster hope's development by formulating and realizing a series of hopes in which each is a potential means to some other. The series may consist of a mixture of hopes and plans, with more proximate steps being plans, and more distant ones being hopes. The general hope for recovery guides the process, but it also becomes refined and made more concrete. Patients do not simply hope for recovery, but hope that the combination of surgery and chemotherapy successfully rids them of the cancer. Here we see the value of nested hopes, discussed in the previous section.

So far, we have explored that category of hope's arduousness that is due to indeterminate means or ends. Though perhaps more usual, the second kind of difficulty—when means are specifiable but beyond our current abilities—is largely derivative from the first. Hope's arduousness increases as the realization of its end depends less on our own abilities and becomes contingent upon forces well beyond our agency. The significant qualification to this point, however, is that our agency can often be developed or expanded in the process of hoping. Consider what Cedric discovers once he actually enters Brown University. At this point, he has successfully realized his hope of getting into an Ivy League school; this hope in turn serves as a means to the further ends of securing academic success and finding like-minded colleagues. Although Cedric has already developed discipline, concentration, and the basic intellectual skills needed to be admitted, he soon realizes that success at Brown will require much more than this. He lacks basic knowledge of the classic texts and history which most of his white colleagues take for granted. Moreover, though his math skills are competitive, his critical thinking and writing skills—though adequate to get him through his high school—are underdeveloped. Consequently, Cedric lacks some of the vital means needed to foster his hope for academic success; these limitations define the arduousness of realizing his hope to succeed at Brown.[18] All is not lost, of course, as Cedric himself recognizes that he can acquire and hone these skills. Though he lacks these means, his hope to succeed motivates him to develop them. Necessity, ever an effective prompt, summons the appropriate resources.

Our own contribution to hope's realization varies across a rather broad range of cases. At one extreme are hopes for which our own agency, limited though it may be, is the primary force of realization. Consider, for instance, my hope to complete this book. Whether and how I finish depends mostly on what I in fact do; my own resources and abilities are the chief means. Of course, the interference or love and support of others can have contributing effects, as can natural (or in this computer era, technological) disasters and the like. Realizing my end is beset with hardships typical of hopes: though I am invested in the project, its success depends on my ability to clearly grasp and present the ideas, to solve unforeseen problems that arise in the process of writing, and to successfully devote the needed time and energy to completing the project. Even if I presently lack the insight and stamina to complete the book, I can develop them in the very process of writing. Moreover, if I cease hoping for this end, I will surely not realize it. My own commitment and subsequent investment in the end make the vital difference here. My agency, limited and in need of expansion though it may be, proves to be the factor that will determine whether or not my hope is realized.

In Cedric's case, success at Brown is at first beyond his abilities; yet he recognizes that his own discipline and hard work—complemented by taking advantage of available tutoring—can change this. Realizing this hope chiefly depends on—indeed is impossible without—Cedric's contribution, on the expansion of his own agency. By contrast, his success in making friends is far trickier. Even if he pursues friendship by intelligently seeking like-minded comrades in places they are most likely to congregate, there are limits to his success, since it also requires the willingness and efforts of his colleagues. This dependence on others adds a level of difficulty absent from our previous examples; individual agency (whether real or potential) plays but one role among others in realizing the hope.

In our other examples, personal commitment and agency carry less weight, thereby increasing the arduousness of those hopes. As Barbara Jennings vividly knows, her own voice is but one of the many Cedric hears. His father also threatens influence, and Cedric has to spend his days in high school dealing with often combative colleagues who find his hope a threat to their own identity. Parents can do their best to nurture and provide their children with opportunities, and yet the influence of other people (or their own misguided goals) can lead them into destructive ways of life. The fragility of Barbara's hope increases as it depends on, and is confronted by, external forces. Likewise, Martha does everything she can and should do, trying medicine after medicine and seeking cure after cure. ECT does help in the end, though the whole process of undergoing it proves to be almost entirely out of her control. Indeed, one of the special challenges of her hope is that its realization requires her to acknowledge the limits of her agency, something she is reluctant to do. Similarly, while a patient's commitment to the hope for recovery from cancer can contribute to its likely realization, other forces make it more arduous. But even summoning the strongest of resources is not always enough to win the battle. Sometimes the cancer has spread too far or resists even the most aggressive treatments. Diseases tend to be oblivious to the hopes of their hosts. At the far extreme of our continuum, our own agency can be all but irrelevant to our hopes. If we are presently in another country, there is little we can do to affect the actual outcome of a plane wreck.[19]

As we move beyond our present abilities, hope's realization becomes ever more difficult to achieve. In our first examples, hoping itself proves the crucial factor that either summons untapped energies or further develops current abilities and so extends us beyond present limits. Our last example demonstrates the greatest impediments not only in achieving but also in maintaining our commitment to such ends. To the extent that no means are available for affecting the survival of a loved one a continent away, such a hope becomes indistinct from a wish. Nevertheless, rather than concentrating on the desire that a loved one survive, we may instead hope to deal well with the outcome, whatever it may be. In other words, we need not restrict ourselves to a single hope common to such situations; we can creatively consider alternatives or focus on the power of hoping in general. If the loved one survives, hope may still play a significant role in determining how we help him or her recover. Unlike wishing, hoping is an active orientation capable of sustaining us and promoting the search for better ends.

When we discover that means are not possible or cost us too much, we need to change our original assessment of an end's desirability. Ends whose means drain us preclude realizing other goods. Pursuing hopes we cannot justify not only wastes our resources, but also threatens to lead us to despair. This is especially true when we invest in hopes whose liveliness and desirability are rooted primarily in how they affect the self. The failure of such hopes usually exhausts and disappoints us so thoroughly that it is not simply the hope which fails, but we ourselves. Investing in hopes that cannot be realized, no matter how desirable they may appear in limited contexts, sets us up for the sorts of disappointment that lead critics to argue we are better off without hope. Consequently, even when ends are lively, continued commitment may not be justifiable. Means and ends should be modified in light of one another, as should desirability and realizability. The process of justifying a hope involves a dialectic of both conditions.

We can summarize by noting that when means are determinate and within our reach, hoping is closest to planning. By contrast, it shades into wishing when means are largely unavailable (if not impossible to acquire) or wholly dependent on forces other than our own. Similarly, when personal involvement is more efficacious, hoping focuses on acting; when it is less effective, hoping becomes primarily a matter of wishing. We should not, however, seek to fix too finely the distinctions between hoping, wishing, and planning; surely the edges blur. How we categorize an activity matters less than attending to means to see whether or to what degree they are accessible. This, in turn, translates into judging whether the end is really possible.

Possibility

No particular hope can be realizable, and hence deemed truly desirable, if it is not a real possibility with some link to existential conditions. No one willingly invests her time and energies in pursuing a hope she knows to be impossible; to do so is a foolish waste of valuable resources. There are no means to my goal of conversing with Plato at the Academy in 380 BCE, if that goal is taken literally. I can realize that end, however, if I take it figuratively; in this case I can "converse" with Plato through the large body of his written works which remain. Surveying and imagining alternate possibilities thus increases our ability to revise, and so realize, our hopes. Indeed, hoping itself is an orientation toward possibilities. Of course, even the undesirable can be possible; hope thus seeks out possibilities that promise something good, especially as liberating, regenerative, or fulfilling. Hope's ends must be not only conceivable (or logically possible) but also able to entice and move us. Unless those ends are really possible so that they can be realized by us or those able to affect us, however, hoping produces little more than false promises and wasted energies.

When we hope, then, we must face the challenge of knowing what is and what is not really possible. Hope's arduousness arises because we know neither whether its end is possible nor how to achieve it. The

often fuzzy line separating existential and epistemological indeterminacy only exacerbates the difficulty. Technological and medical advances illustrate how what was once thought to be impossible *really*
was possible, once the appropriate means were found and applied.
Individually, we commonly discover that we are capable of more than
we once thought, as when persistence at a task ushers in a second wind
of energy. Sometimes, though, even our best efforts come up short.
Knowing what is possible is complicated not only by the limits of our
understanding but also by the changing tide of events. What once was
impossible can later become possible, as the ceaseless waves of time
wash fresh possibilities onto the sands of reality.

Our primary resource in differentiating the possible from the impossible is factual knowledge—that is, knowledge of the actual. A known
fact represents a settled and determinate situation or set of conditions.
Insofar as something is known to have happened or existed as a matter
of fact, we know it was possible at least once, for everything actual was
once possible. Of course, a significant function of factual knowledge is
not only to report what has occurred, but also to indicate what is likely
to occur. Facts are determinacies that help us gauge what is possible in
the future. Understanding recurring patterns (especially causal ones)
increases our ability to predict what is possible under certain conditions and so gives us a greater grasp of possibilities pregnant in current
situations. For instance, doctors' knowledge of the dynamics of human
health provides them a basis for determining what methods of recovery
will most likely work in specific cases; understanding thermodynamics
enables engineers to design bridges capable of withstanding a variety
of stresses. Knowledge is thus one of our most powerful instruments of
control and so an invaluable means in every endeavor. Without our
knowledge of the actual, we would have no basis for projecting the
possible.

We should not, however, overestimate the bearing of factual
knowledge on possibility for a variety of reasons. First, as James notes,
possibilities outrun actualities; the possibilities that have been actualized are selections from a far broader field of possibilities.[20] James
argues at length to show that while this position embraces an ineradi-
cable element of chance or indeterminacy in the universe, it does not

signify that *anything* can happen. Rather, it means that *more than one* possibility is continuous and so compatible with any given state of affairs. In reporting what is or was the case, then, factual knowledge gives us but a slice of the realm of possibility. Of course, it also provides us an important bearing, since possibilities realized in the future will occur largely in compliance with the conditions set down by present actualities. Possibilities do not pop into being from nowhere; there must be means to their realization. Nevertheless, actualities do not exhaust possibilities.

Moreover, factual knowledge proves a limited guide in canvassing possibilities, since the past provides a necessary but ultimately insufficient basis for the present and future. Conditions change, opening up new possibilities and extinguishing others. The drifting of continental plates once limited migration by foot to a single continent. Of course, transcontinental travel is now possible within a single day by aircraft, but discovering virgin territories, unsullied by human civilization, has become increasingly impossible. Moreover, some possibilities make only a momentary appearance on the screen of life. Consider the burst of energy people sometimes get in emergencies; some have been known to lift objects far beyond their capacity in order to save a loved one who is trapped. While really possible at that particular time, such energy can rarely be summoned later at will.

A third limitation to our knowledge of fact is the role it can play in closing, as well as opening, us to possibilities. Experience teaches most of us all too quickly how cruel people can be toward one another. Once we have this taste of "the real world," it becomes impossible to regain our former innocence. On the one hand, factual knowledge gives us a record of past successes and failures, and so helps define the boundaries of sensible and foolish action; it thereby forms an indispensable guide in forming habits and customs. This knowledge, however, threatens to blind us as readily as it offers us foresight when it generates complacency or dogmatism about what can or cannot happen. Whether they are primarily individual or also social, habits of thought which have become rigid both blind us and make us resistant to the currents of rising new possibilities. Adults often contrast youthful idealism with the realism they have forged through experience. Yet, inexperience can be a good thing, for it leaves us open to reach for new possibilities. Aquinas, for instance, notes that the lack of experience in the young tends to be a source of hope; not having encountered many limits to their pursuits, they tend to have an "unrealistic" sense of the extent of their own abilities as well as of what is possible. While this may lead to reckless pursuit of hopes, it can also be a spring to exploring and generating new modes of acting. Without the taste for adventure, our customs grow rigid to the point that we cannot even conceive of their alternatives. Unsurprisingly, Dewey argues that one of the challenges and benefits of education is to blend the guidance of well-worn habits with the youthful zest for adventure, thereby revitalizing the former and productively channeling the latter.

The wealth of knowledge and abilities developed through experience need not, however, blind us to alternate possibilities. Indeed, it can actually foster a certain humility and respect for the vast reaches of unforeseen possibility. Our own century has witnessed tremendous technological advance and teaches any who will listen that much of what was once thought impossible wasn't really so. Creativity has transformed our world to such an extent that it is arrogant to assume we can achieve more than a tentative grasp on what is possible or impossible. Moreover, the awe we feel when watching a jumbo jet soar into the sky signifies both pride in human achievement and also wonder at what further world-changing innovations lie on the horizon. Progress and the growth of experience, then, can foster a sense of humility, so that we realize we only dimly perceive what is possible.

Though the determinate past provides means—whether bodies of knowledge or active skills—for dealing with the indeterminate present and future, those tools need to be tested and revised. Conditions change enough that we must always be sensitive to how they affect our action and interaction. Our success requires attending to the new possibilities which arise, even as we rely on the past. Especially in hoping, though, we must also grapple with the difference between an end that is possible per se and one that is a real possibility *for us as individuals.* Knowing what is or is not generally possible often proves insufficient in determining whether or not an end is realizable for me—that is, whether it is possible relative to my abilities and the situation. What has been possible for others may not be possible for me. Others have successfully completed books, recovered from cancer, raised healthy productive children, had loved ones survive horrible crashes—and so may I. But I also may not. The fact that there are determinate and available means to an end may justify my hope, but it provides no guarantee. Chemotherapy may ravage my system as well as the cancer, or I may simply lack the needed abilities to complete the book. Moreover, what was not possible for others may be possible for me. Stories of great inventions constantly teach this lesson. Many people hoped to create a machine that could fly; many tried and failed. The Wright brothers, however, pursued their hope diligently; they endured repeated setbacks and also suffered considerable ridicule, especially for defying conventional wisdom in their design. Eventually, however, their efforts proved successful. The creativity and persistence of genius, coupled with the ability to see and nurture possibilities where others only see sterile ideas, accounts for much of our progress.[21]

At the basis of any exploration of possibilities are imagination and also our habits. Habits create a zone of our abilities which marks out specific possibilities, providing a basis for what we may expect to occur (either to or by us) in the future. They indicate patterns of behavior that we have successfully employed and that should be available for future use. Indeed our habits offer focal points relative to which we gauge things as possible or impossible for us. The fact that we or others have successfully secured some good via habitual action gives us a basis for believing the same good to be a real possibility in the future. Nevertheless, neither a habit's future applicability nor its success in mapping possibility is guaranteed. As circumstances change, some will likely become ineffective and obsolete. Habits may, of course, be modified to meet changing circumstances, especially when infused with imagination and intelligence; they then make possible new, perhaps more complex forms of activity. Consequently, though they define the familiar, habits need not circumscribe the possible. In addition to transforming our habits to access new possibilities, we can also always creatively imagine possibilities that transcend their reach. In the process we formulate new, perhaps more inclusive ideals that sketch out a background in which our activities have special meaning. Even so, the function of intelligence is to explore such possibilities by attempting to wed them, through experimentation in thought and in deed, to present conditions. Included in these conditions are, of course, our habits.

While factual knowledge, imagination, and intelligence open catalogs of possibilities, we often cannot determine what is *really* possible, especially for ourselves, apart from acting. A special value of the imagination, as noted above, is exploring and testing possibilities in thought without suffering their actual consequences. Such testing occurs against the background of our common knowledge drawn from past experiences, whether others' or our own. But since the past is necessary but not sufficient for determining the present, the final test of an idea comes in acting on it. Acting both uncovers conditions of possibility and also generates them. Given the tenuous line between epistemic and existential indeterminacy discussed above, it is clear that sometimes our own actions are the very factors which determine what can actually be realized. In some cases, factual knowledge accurately reports all the relevant possibilities. With the passage of time, we may learn that a loved one has not survived cancer or a plane wreck. Once the die is cast, our hope for the contrary state of affairs must be given up or replaced with another. But so long as the matter has not been settled (and this is often difficult to determine), so long as an end dances before us as even a remotely real possibility, acting plays a vital role, whether simply in discovering that there are genuine means to it or by creating and making determinate conditions which bring it to fruition.

Suppose, for instance, I find myself buried beneath the rubble of a building that has just been bombed. My hope for survival and rescue is likely rooted in the fact that bombed buildings are usually scoured for survivors. This social habit provides a basis for my hope. But though some survivors are rescued, surely not all are. Some die before help can arrive. Consequently, simply waiting to be rescued is not my only, or perhaps even best, option. Hoping to survive this situation, I can actively seek to remove myself from the confines of the rubble. First, I clear away a little debris, then some more, and so on until I reach my limit. This limit may be rooted in my own injuries, in the rubble's resistance to removal, or perhaps both. I cannot discover this limit, however, apart from active exploration, guided of course by caution and intelligence. Action is experimental.

In addition to revealing limits, acting also generates new conditions and abilities. By seeking to remove myself from the rubble, I not only discover my limits but also may in fact alter conditions such that I increase my chances of rescue. Noises caused by readjusting the rubble may alert others to my presence. Of course, they may also lead to nothing or to more precarious circumstances. This is a danger inherent in such action, and so it must be counterbalanced by proceeding intelligently, both drawing on and being ready to modify that common stock of truths and habits generated through past interactions. But additionally, changing conditions afford new applications of our habits *and so can reveal new potentialities within them.* Habits, especially intelligent ones, can retain their original plasticity; the extent to which we can mold that plasticity to current conditions is discovered only through acting. Although hopes involve recognition of the limits of our agency, active exploration of those limits and limiting conditions (especially as concerns their malleability or obduracy) can open new paths to desired ends.

Consequently, acting *as if* an end is realizable—that is, as if there are means which will make it a reality—plays a vital role in both testing and promoting its realizability. There is really nothing extraordinary about acting in such a manner, nor is acting as if unique to hoping. We act as if on a regular basis to determining the truth or likelihood of beliefs and ends. For instance, we act as if conditions in a familiar but darkened room remain unchanged when we follow a habitual path across it to turn on the light. Every habit harbors a tendency to act as if something were the case. Nevertheless, we require greater awareness and intelligent guidance when acting in cases such as hoping where habits are undeveloped, limited, or impeded.

Acting *as if* means believing something possible and acting upon that belief to determine its veracity. At its heart is a certain form of faith indispensable to the activity of hoping. Pragmatically understood, faith is not some weaker alternative to knowledge, possessed by those who turn their back on science or conventional knowledge. It is not a competitor for rigorous modes of thinking or the employment of intelligence, but an integral part of them. James explains that "[f]aith means belief in something concerning which doubt is still theoretically possible; and as a test of belief is willingness to act, one may say that faith is the readiness to act in a cause the prosperous issue of which is not certified to us in advance" (WB 76). Rather than the conviction that something is the case, faith is a conviction about what *may be* the case, borne out or determined by acting *as if*. As Dewey argues, "[c]onviction in the moral sense signifies being conquered, vanquished, in our active nature by an ideal end; it signifies acknowledgment of its rightful claim over our desires and purposes" (LW 9:15). Such conviction prompts us into action.

Faith, then, indicates a willingness to act on a belief or in pursuit of an end, even in the face of risk or doubt. What tempers this risk is the fact that faith, pragmatically understood, is tested through acting, making adjustments as conditions arise to determine the veracity or desirability of a certain belief. Indeed, faith requires courage, understood as intelligently informed and guided risk taking.[22] James aptly describes faith as a working hypothesis, a means of orienting ourselves and acting in certain ways to determine whether a hypothesis is truly workable. Having faith does not require blind adherence to a belief; rather, it indicates *readiness or willingness to act on a belief in order to test it.* Acting demonstrates a belief's compatibility or workability amidst actual conditions. Should the belief prove wrong or misguided, we can modify or eliminate it. Consequently, faith does not oppose or conflict with knowledge, but rather provides *a preliminary step toward it.*

In most of the examples we have considered, faith functions as a formative factor in fostering what it projects. Our action generally orients us toward ends, but faith, manifested through acting *as if*, helps create the conditions needed for their realization. If I act as though I have or can develop the resources required to finish the book, I test my belief that I do in the very process. I may tap into hidden energies, as when getting a second wind; one never gets a second wind apart from acting. I may also develop the needed resources as I proceed. Similarly, acting as if we can make friends, especially when rooted in past success at doing so, means we approach others in a friendly manner and are more inclined to develop possible shared interests. James notes that

central to building trust is acting as if we trust other people and showing ourselves to be trustworthy as well. Vital to this process is our faith
that trust is possible. Apart from it, no one would develop trust.
Consequently, faith is a formative element in creating trust. In both of
these cases, acting on the hypothesis or faith that some end is really
possible, that our abilities (individually or combined with those of
others) can meet or overcome the difficulties we face, enables us to discover and perhaps push beyond our present limits. Assessing the realizability of an end is problematic, but in a potentially productive manner,
since the limits of our agency are *not* determinately fixed for all time.
Each act can further develop habits and expand our abilities, thereby
making possible for us what was once barely conceivable or out of
reach.

As we noted in the previous section, personal involvement sometimes has very little impact on the realizability of a hope. Consider our
final example concerning a loved one involved in an accident. How
can acting *as if* meaningfully contribute to or test the realizability of
hopes in such cases? Much depends on the particular form we give the
end. If our hope is that the loved one survives, all we can do is wait. In
this case, hoping does not contribute directly to the end of survival.
But recall that hopes need not be isolated ends; often they cluster together, at times nesting within one another. We can also foster related
hopes, such as aiding in our loved one's recovery, should she survive, or
coping with personal loss if she does not. Consequently, hoping (or, as
I shall explain it later, remaining hopeful) in the face of this tragedy can
prove productive, even if it does not promote the most obvious end of
survival. In hoping we prepare ourselves by imaginatively canvassing
our options and so orienting ourselves to various possible ends; *hoping
means we invest ourselves in developing a horizon of meaningful promising possibilities.* Should one end prove unrealizable, we will be able to invest in another. So even when personal contribution is unlikely to directly
realize a hoped-for end, hoping can nonetheless make a difference, especially by opening us to other related ends.

In sum, acting *as if* plays a vital role in testing and developing hopes.
We discover our limits and what is really possible for us, find our second wind, expand present abilities, or create needed conditions—all

through acting. Of course, doing so carries the risk of wasting energy or creating a dangerous situation, but acting *as if* need not be a blind groping in the dark. It can be infused with intelligently directed experimentation, marked by the definition and revision of means in light of ends and ends in light of means. Our last example, though, reminds us that there are limits to our agency and to acting *as if*. Patience, coupled with an attentiveness to changing conditions, is a vital part of hoping, as it is in testing any belief or faith. In the next chapter, I will explore the fundamental roles habits of patience and attentiveness play in hoping. We may have already established these habits, or we may need to develop them; often, we can do so even through pursuing our hopes. Without these, we quickly lose our faith or fail to properly invest in justifiable hopes. Indeed, habits of hope help foster realizable hopes, thereby making hoping more practical. They provide us with the vital resources we need to face and overcome impediments to promising but remote, obstructed ends. Before turning to these points, however, I conclude this chapter by considering the special meaning of hope we can glean from the general nature of its ends.

Hope's Meaning in Light of Its End

Our analysis of hope's end has helped us identify justifying grounds of hopes in virtue of which they can be practical (in the sense of being realizable). We have defined hope as the active commitment to the desirability and realizability of a certain end. The fact that its end is a future good highlights conditions of its desirability. But its realizability, which can in turn affect its desirability, is tempered by the fact that, though arduous, it is nonetheless possible. That hope's end is both good and possible signifies that we await and anticipate its realization. But its futurity and arduousness make that realization questionable or problematic; they indicate both our disconnection from the end and our subsequent need to justify the commitment of our energy and resources. Though difficulties attend its realization, either because of indeterminate means and ends or because of our limited capacities, our belief that it is possible, tested through acting, can actually prove to be a contributing cause. Committing to a hope indicates our willingness to promote actively, in whatever way we can, realization of its end. Because it is not within our reach, some degree of patience is needed. But in hoping, patience is coupled with an active orientation toward the end, an orientation which includes acting *as if*—testing our beliefs about the end and its means—to see what we can contribute to its determination. As is typical of pragmatic justification, we discover and promote the practicality of particular hopes through experimental activity guided by intelligence.

Hopes are certainly meaningful to us because of the specific goods that they promise. Yet what can we learn about the larger meaning of hope by focusing upon its end? My claim is that our examination of particular hopes, especially the conditions of desirability and realizability required for their justification, enables us to better understand the nature of hope as conditioned transcendence. Hopes arise in problematic situations, their arduousness signifying a disconnection between ends and those who hope for them. Each end transcends its originating situation, attracting us with some good which is salvific or extensional. It nevertheless lies at or beyond the limits of our agency, whether social or individual. It is disconnected from present conditions, including our abilities. Arduousness thus indicates limits; but of course there is more to hope than arduousness. There is also the lure or promise that we can transcend such limitations and not be locked in their grip.

Whether we tap into unknown energies or develop new capacities, hoping signifies the possibility of transcending current limitations and problems. To hope is to commit to the desirability and realizability of an end even though it presently transcends our current conditions and abilities. Such commitment involves more than having an intellectual apprehension or a certain feeling (for example, warmth or enthusiasm) about the end; it also requires actively searching for means or conditions that bridge the gap between organism and end. Hoping is an activity of pursuing an end by promoting the growth of agency, whether individual or social. We grow, either by expanding our own abilities (as when I develop new capacities in writing the book) or by connecting with other agencies (as when the cancer patient turns to her physician as healer). *Hope thus signifies the transcendence of limits through the growth of agency.* This is hope's larger meaning. It involves transcendence, but a transcendence rooted in actual conditions, chief among which is our own agency. Hoping is no passive or merely intellectual retreat from current conditions of the world; it is an active engagement with and reconstruction of them. Agency, though, is a matter of habits, and so to fully understand hope we must explore those habits that are integral conditions of and means to the activity of hoping.

CHAPTER *Two*

Hope's Habits

T HOUGH friends, Andy Dufresne and Red, the central characters in Stephen King's novella *Rita Hayworth and Shawshank Redemption*,[1] share little in common. Both are inmates serving life sentences at the Shawshank prison, Red for a murder he did commit and Andy for one he did not. Though thoughtful, quiet, and patient, Andy maintains activities that enable him to retain continuity with his previous life. A former banker, he at first offers financial advice to the guards and warden; on the basis of the clout he thereby acquires, Andy subsequently transforms the prison library into a source of learning and contact with the outside world for all the inmates. By contrast, though he is a man who can get things like cigarettes and posters, Red feels cut off from the outside; his primary goal is to stay out of trouble by keeping a watchful eye on things. While Andy is an active planner and doer, Red observes and goes with the flow.

These differences largely account for the manner in which each participates in the life of hope. Fearful of hope to the point of rejecting it, Red admires Andy but shuns his propensity to hope. When Andy shares his hopes for a better life, Red dismisses them as mere pipe dreams. King's novella is an account of Andy's time in prison as seen through Red's eyes. As Red narrates the story from Andy's entry into Shawshank's restricted and seemingly hopeless life to his surprising escape, his awe and respect for his fellow inmate becomes apparent. At first Red is amazed that Andy was able to escape. But after pondering the situation carefully, he comes to understand the power of hope, which not only sustained Andy in prison but also fueled his escape. He realizes Andy has what I call *habits of hope*—that is, abilities that maintain his commitment and pursuit of his particular hopes. Though Red has his own habits which enable him to survive prison, they allow no room for hope.

Ma Joad and her daughter, Rose of Sharon, present a similar contrast in John Steinbeck's novel *The Grapes of Wrath.*[2] Driven by the hope for a better life, the Joad family moves from the dustbowl of Oklahoma to California, the promised land of milk and honey. Linking Steinbeck's classic to the theme of hope is controversial, since the Joads' grapes of hope eventually turn into grapes of wrath. Indeed, the book appears to chart the demise of hope and to show its futility; the Joads leave the desperate conditions of Oklahoma only to lose their remaining income and family cohesiveness in California. Hope then appears to give way to fear, anger, and despair. I will argue, however, that we can find the dynamics of hope operating throughout the book, especially if we view hope pragmatically. Central to understanding Steinbeck's message of hope is the rich relationship between Ma and Rose of Sharon. Ma plays the pivotal role of anchor to her family, providing stability throughout their journey. Rose of Sharon, by contrast, is a pregnant teenage bride whose hopes are high, though her abilities are limited. Throughout the course of their journey, some family members die and others run off, abandoning the family hope for a better life. But Ma and Rose of Sharon remain steadfast, exhibiting to varying degrees their participation in the life of hope. While Ma more clearly exemplifies the practicality of hoping, Rose of Sharon nevertheless develops her own ability to hope until, in the book's last scene, she becomes the central figure of hope by nursing a starving stranger. An analysis of her development, both in contrast and in conjunction with Ma's, illustrates the importance of acting through habits of hope.

These examples vividly illustrate hope's development, especially by presenting us with rich characters at different stages of progress. The initial contrasts between their characters, in particular, illuminate the means—the habits of hope—which foster the development of both particular hopes and hopefulness. In this chapter, I explore our primary habits of hope; in the next, I explore their relation to hopefulness. As we shall see, while it is Andy and Ma who actively pursue hopes, Red and Rose of Sharon are beneficiaries, brought into the life of hope through their association with these active hopers.

Habits as Means

While the focus of the last chapter was the ends at which particular hopes aim, in this chapter I shift from hope's ends to its means in order to flesh out more fully the life of hope. I have argued that hoping is an activity; here I will emphasize how organizing a complex array of habits fosters its *development*. Indeed, we misunderstand the nature of hoping if we think it simply requires exercise or implementation of skills and abilities already possessed. Pursuit of hopes frequently fosters these skills; as argued in the previous chapter, hoping itself can be a formative element in the realization of its own end. Consequently, we must understand our participation in the life of hope as a developmental process.

Of course, no account of means can be separated properly from that of ends, and vice versa. We thus glean the means required by particular hopes from the general nature of hope's ends and the commitment necessary for their realization. Such means are as integral to hope's realizability as ends are, for ends are realized, of course, through means. The particular nature of these means, however, is conditioned by the specific features of the ends. While each end requires means whose specification is best carried out in a particular context, we can nevertheless identify hope's general means by focusing upon the generic features of its end articulated in the last chapter.

Since its end is a future good that is arduous but possible, hoping involves commitment to the desirability and realizability of that end. The end transcends current conditions and abilities, and so we must build connections to it. If hoping is to bring about ends in a practical

manner, we must be capable of justifying conditions of the desirability
and realizability of its ends. As we noted, however, conditions of realizability in particular are usually indeterminate and frequently depend
on the very actions we take. Faith, then, as a working hypothesis or belief on which we are willing to act, lies at the heart of hoping. Recall
that such faith is conviction not about how things are, but rather about
how they may be. Faith means acting *as if*, testing a belief or ideal by
acting under its guidance to see whether it successfully brings—usually
through reconstruction of existing conditions or means—the desired
good that it promises. Apart from such faith, there is no *pursuit* of the
end. Acting on a belief, however, does not ensure its ready confirma-
tion (or disconfirmation), for as James notes, "while some [working]
hypotheses can be refuted in five minutes, others may defy ages" (WB
79). Especially because of the arduousness and futurity of its end, hoping frequently extends over an indeterminate amount of time. Since its
end transcends current conditions and abilities, hoping requires not
only that we be able to discover or build connections to that end,
but also that we can sustain and direct our efforts in the process.
Commitment to the pursuit of a particular hope thus requires sustenance and direction over time.

The locus of such support is our habits. Our various abilities constitute hope's primary means, and since agency is a matter of habits (capable of intelligent direction), I will focus on those habits aimed at
realizing hopes. Habits are central to any activity, providing structures
which direct energy and enable more complex modes of interacting.
Hoping itself sustains us as we pursue an end, thereby functioning as a
complex means to its own realization.[3] It is also, however, developed
and made practical by habits. Of course, not all habits contribute to
hoping. Some, such as responding to problems with denial, undermine
it; others, like habits of eating and sitting, prove largely irrelevant to
hope's development. Yet since hopes arise when habits are frustrated or
break down during interaction, some of our habits are among the limiting conditions we seek to transcend. Nevertheless, not all habits are
blocked or fail at once. Moreover, though they may sometimes prove
obsolete, impaired habits frequently can be transformed or expanded
in order to realize hope's ends. Undisturbed habits, especially insofar as

they are reserves of directed energy, remain our primary resources in reconstruction.

Habits play a vital role in hoping for two central reasons. First, hoping requires supporting structures, both individual and social. Especially given their self-propagating and insistent nature, habits provide such structures, enabling us to persist in hoping and preparing us to act when conditions are appropriate. They channel energies unleashed by both the original problematic situation and the enthusiasm resulting from attraction to the promising ends; apart from habits—especially intelligent habits which foster growth—these energies would otherwise dissipate without producing any product. Second, habits enable us to do things with ease so that we may focus our attention elsewhere and develop new, more complicated modes of acting. They thus not only direct but also help to develop and expand energies, thereby contributing to the growth of agency which lies at the heart of hoping. Agency grows as patterns of acting become more complex. As interactive organisms, we always have some habits on which we can rely; they have already been developed and spring into action whenever possible. But especially when faced with an end difficult to realize, we must expand other abilities. Consequently, we must think of our habitual life as always in process, with potential for further possibilities for expansion.

Habits of hope are those habits by which we pursue—that is, seek and nurture—the realization of hope's ends. They are vital and integral dynamics in developing hope, particularly in maintaining our commitment to its ends. In the remainder of this chapter, I will provide a pragmatic account of the central habits of hope. These habits either build connections between hope's end and our current agency or, when agency is limited, expand it generally. In pursuing hopes, commitment to its end is vital. We require, then, habits which sustain and guide our endeavor to discover or create appropriate means, whether direct or indirect, through either our own agency or that of others. Chief among them are persistence, resourcefulness, and courage. Habits of persistence sustain us, while habits of resourcefulness guide our active exploration and attempts to transcend our limitations. Courage undergirds our ability to persist and to explore by enabling us to face arduous tasks. These three habits represent hope's most general means; they are the chief habits of hope. Each, however, is a complex coordination of other habits; persistence, for instance, consists in patience and atten-tiveness. Moreover, though each habit has its own independence, habits of hope can reinforce one another; indeed, they can be deliber-ately coordinated to develop a disposition or character best described as hopeful. In the remainder of this chapter, I explore the nature of each habit and its contribution to the activity of hoping. This will com-plete our discussion of particular hopes and will furthermore provide a hinge to the final dimension of the life of hope: hopefulness.

Persistence

Persistence performs the important function of sustaining us as we hope. Without it, we are unlikely to maintain commitment to our end, especially in the face of trials posed by its arduousness. As Cornel West notes, "one of the qualities of hope is that it's not a one-day show" (West 48). Rather, it extends over time, such that consistency and com-mitment—both of which are components of persistence—are required. Persistence does not aim primarily at the realization of an end; its chief function is to sustain us as we await or develop the necessary means. Those who persist patiently stay the course and continue in their activ-ity. Persistence then functions to provide structures that not only en-able us to continue to wait, but also to explore and act when appropriate. Like the little leaguer who keeps getting up to bat even though he has repeatedly struck out, persistence marks our determina-tion to keep trying and our refusal to give up.

Early in his book, Steinbeck provides a vivid image of persistence when describing a turtle that crosses Tom Joad's path. On his journey home at the story's beginning, Tom spots the turtle moving with great determination toward some unknown destination. He at first picks it up, then puts it back down. Promptly, the turtle resumes its journey, contin-uing to move in its original direction. Tom then puts it in his pack, where it struggles but fails to escape. When he later releases it many miles down the road, the turtle hurries back in the direction of its origi-nal destination. This turtle, despite repeated human efforts to derail its quest, constantly returns to its original path in order to reach its intended destination. Steinbeck uses it as a metaphor to illustrate how humanity, even when oppressed, pushes forward toward its desired goals.

Persistence proves useful to activity generally, but we especially need it when immersed in lengthy processes where nothing definitive happens to confirm or disconfirm our commitment to an end. In such cases, we must decide whether to continue on our present course or to revise and perhaps abandon our end. Persistence makes possible the former option; it indicates the ability (or the *developing* ability) to keep energy focused for extended periods of time. Consequently, it prevents the lagging of spirits and the loss of commitment. We can, however, persist in ways contrary to hoping, so persistence is not always a habit of hope. An early scene from *The Grapes of Wrath* illustrates this point. Former preacher Jim Casy has joined Tom in his journey home. When they reach their destination, they find the family home abandoned. The Joads's neighbor, Muley Graves, arrives shortly thereafter and explains that, like other families, the Joads have been forced off their land; they are now staying with Uncle John while they prepare to leave for California. Muley's own family has already left for California, but he remains, wandering around "like a damn ol' graveyard ghos'." Casy sympathizes with Muley's plight, noting that a "Fella gets use' to a place, it's hard to go. . . . Fella gets use' to a way a thinkin', it's hard to leave" (Steinbeck 53).

Leaving the familiar, whether it be a place or a way of acting, proves especially difficult for some people.[4] Persistence in old ways is often easier than facing change, especially since courage is required to face the harder task. Unless coupled with intelligence and so with a willingness to adapt, persistence transforms habits into entrenched routines, thereby impairing its usefulness as a means to hoping. What hoping needs is not fixed tenacity or stubbornness, but the active dedication of energies to its pursuit. Continued commitment to a fruitless way of acting or to impossible means indicates not a dynamic force creatively moving toward future goals, but a recalcitrant adherence to past patterns of behaving. Consequently, habits of persistence need to be aimed at hopes and so interwoven with habits of resourcefulness. I will address the relation of persistence and resourcefulness later, but first I will explore more fully the nature of each.

Hope's persistence is a complex habit constituted by habits of patience, attentiveness, self-control, and the ability to keep active. Together these interweave to create the ability to persist. The role of patience is rather obvious. Since hope's end is future and arduous, lying at or beyond the reach of our agency, we must wait for appropriate help from others or for conditions to arise which we can control. Biblical references to hope frequently couple it with patience. Paul, for instance, explains that "hope that is seen is not hope. For who hopes for what is seen? But if we hope for what we do not see, we wait for it with patience" (Rom. 8:24–25). Again, the general message of Revelations is to urge true believers to endure patiently in their commitment to Christ, for in that activity lies salvation.[5] We frequently think of patience as passive, since it entails that we postpone acting. Nevertheless, patience has an active component, for it requires that we postpone acting without losing our focus. To persist in hope, we must patiently await the arrival of the specific means needed to realize a specific end (or ends). Consequently, patience indicates the ability to *maintain a focus* without losing commitment or being distracted. It is, then, an active waiting or an *awaiting*. It is a habit which conserves energy, preventing its dissipation and keeping it in reserve until the time for its proper release arrives.

By contrast, impatience demands that things hurry along. Unwilling to wait for events to unfold or conditions to arise in their own time, impatience frequently drives us to ultimatums: *either* proper means arise *or* we abandon our hope. As impatience undermines our commitment, we become easily distracted and so shift allegiance from our original end to another usually more immediate good. Hope's end is then given up for something more readily attainable. Moreover, the loss of focus leads to the dissipation or untimely release of energy. Hope without focus, then, usually turns into despair; in such cases, hoping drains us of energy and so robs us even further of resources for responding to the original problematic situation. Patience, on the other hand, gives things time, allowing them to develop. It awaits the moment when expenditure of energy contributes to pursuit, if not realization, of an end. Hope is patient for the *right* time. Patience, of course, has and should have its limits. When continued commitment to an end threatens to spread our resources so thin that we will likely be unable to respond even if the desired conditions arise, we more wisely modify or abandon our end than continue awaiting its means.

Red describes Andy as one of the most patient men he has ever known, so patient that he could chip away at a cement wall for an unknown number of years. Andy's hobby of carving rock sculptures fits in well with his interest in geology. Red surmises that studying geology "appealed to [Andy's] patient, meticulous nature. . . . Andy told me once that all of geology is the study of pressure. And time, of course" (King 92). All prison inmates have plenty of time. Their use of it differentiates them from one another, especially with regard to patience, persistence, and hope. While Andy uses his time to expand his resources, eventually realizing his hope, Red simply endures his sentence. He lives from one day to the next without any focus or sense of connection to a future, so much that he claims he does not even worry. Time signifies not opportunity, but rather the primary means of his punishment. Red confesses that looking at Andy's rock sculptures makes him "think about what a man can do, if he has time enough and the will to use it, a drop at a time" (King 72). Nevertheless, Red continues to simply endure, while Andy patiently awaits development of conditions which realize his hope.

While patience as a form of awaiting focuses on a particular end, it also attends to its means. Though I will discuss attentiveness more fully below when exploring resourcefulness, it also functions as a significant ingredient in patience.[6] Patience requires attention to actual conditions and to their pregnancy; in other words, it attends to both relevant actualities and their corresponding possibilities, whether hidden or obvious. If we misunderstand or overlook actual conditions, patience will likely result in a waste of time; the proper means might be near at hand or altogether impossible to produce. Since our own abilities and limitations are included among these conditions, awaiting without attending to our ability to *use* proper means should they become available amounts to awaiting to no avail. We need not forgo patience when we lack such abilities; rather we should seek to develop them *as* we wait. We can allot some of the energy conserved through patience to their growth.

Attention to our limitations reveals our vulnerability in hoping, thereby highlighting the role of humility and trust in hope's patience. To the extent that our ends lie beyond our own abilities, we are dependent on other forces for their realization. Both Cedric and Martha have to depend on others to realize their hopes. Cedric needs the love and unwavering support of his mother as well as the financial assistance of his benefactor, Dr. Benjamin Korb, a Boston optometrist who regularly provides money for basic school needs. Martha has to acknowledge the fact that, though herself a therapist, she needs to accept others' help in order to overcome her depression. Such vulnerability finds expression in a humility which proves to be an ally of both patience and hope. While we frequently think of humility in predominantly negative contexts where it denotes weakness or self-debasement, these characteristics do not exhaust it. Humility can also indicate the healthy and realistic recognition of our limitations. Without considering the limits of our ability, we resist being patient and boldly proceed as though we can accomplish whatever we desire. Such moves are all too frequently checked by the obduracy of existential conditions; even though they are malleable to some degree, failure to note their resistance to even the most determined human efforts leads to the loss of energy.

Human destiny, as Dewey notes, is intimately interwoven with forces beyond human control (LW 9:17). Hoping progresses actively, but it should not do so blindly or without caution. Recognizing limits to our knowledge means realizing that our own perspectives are not the only ones and, hence, that possibilities exceed the scope of our vision. While impatience demands determinacies of things before their time, patience without humility assumes them *where they may not exist.* Humility can then actually promote hope, especially when it comes to assessing possibility and impossibility. If we lack humility, our judgment of determinate conditions is just as likely to blind us to hidden possibilities as it is to provide guidance for our action. Humility then fosters the recognition that possibilities outrun actualities, such that we cannot be completely certain that a hope is possible or impossible, especially not apart from acting *as if.*

Of course, while keeping us open to hope, humility can also invite paralyzing uncertainty. We must complement it, then, with the recognition that limitations are not absolute. I may be unable to see a salvific possibility in a trying situation, but that does not mean others cannot. Similarly, though unable to realize an end via current habits, I may be able to develop my abilities or coordinate them with those of others. Consequently, humility fosters patience and hope by making us receptive to contributions due to time as well as the insights and abilities of others. Hope's humility, however, does not produce an *unconditioned* openness. Instead, it fosters a natural piety which recognizes but does not thereby simply accept limitations; it also seeks to expand them. While our limitations reveal our dependence on others for the goods we desire, this need not incapacitate us or make us fearful. Dewey argues that "our dependence is manifested in those relations to the environment that support our undertakings and aspirations as much as it is in the defeats inflicted upon us" (LW 9:18). Dependence does not mark absolute limits of ability, but denotes interconnection and possibilities for coordinated efforts. A cancer patient may depend on the doctor for knowledge and administration of medication; but of course by allowing the doctor to contribute to her healing process, she thereby moves that much closer to her goal.

Recognizing our limitations should not thereby limit us. While we need to acknowledge our limits, we must not neglect or underestimate our abilities. Dewey captures the unique character of natural piety when he explains that it "may rest upon a just sense of nature as the whole of which we are parts, while it also recognizes that we are parts that are marked by intelligence and purpose, having the capacity to strive by their aid to bring conditions into greater consonance with what is humanly desirable" (LW 9:18). Consequently, hope's persistence sustains our pursuit of ends by enabling us to patiently await appropriate means and, with humility, to accept (indeed, seek) help. Hope needs humility and it needs help. While investment in an arduous and future good may open us up and make us vulnerable, this vulnerability has an active basis which renders it a conditioned openness.

Jim Casy illustrates piety early in *The Grapes of Wrath* when he explains his view of human interconnectedness. He tells the Joads how his religious explorations have given him an expansive, more inclusive understanding of humanity. He explains that

I got thinkin' how we was holy when we was one thing, an'
mankin' was holy when it was one thing. An' it on'y got unholy
when one mis'able little fella got the bit in his teeth an' run off
his own way, kickin' an' draggin' an' fightin'. Fella like that bust
the holiness. But when they're all workin' together, not one
fella for another fella, but one fella kind of harnessed to the
whole shebang—that's right, that's holy. (Steinbeck 83)

Casy's piety—his recognition of our interconnectedness and the subsequent power of acting in concert with one another—provides the basis
for his later involvement in the labor movement. Additionally, its effect
on Ma becomes increasingly apparent as the story unfolds. Though she is
at first most concerned with her own family, near the book's end Ma extends her concerns to embrace the human family. She broadens her conception to include the Wainwright family and, later, even strangers like
the dying man in the book's last scene. Much like Casy, Ma explains that
"Use'ta be the fambly was fust. It ain't so now. It's anybody. Worse off we
get, the more we got to do" (Steinbeck 444). This transformation plays a
significant role in Ma's development as a hopeful person. She now acts to
foster others' needs and desires, making their hopes her own. She thereby
invests herself in the hopes of the larger human family.[7]

Natural piety, as described above, indicates a kind of trust or faith
which supports patience specifically and hope generally. When we
delay action or refuse to abandon an end lying beyond our current
means, we indicate trust in our own abilities or in the compatibility of
other powers with our own. To await realization of a hope, to commit to
an end which requires remaining open and vulnerable to forces beyond
our control, is to trust that agencies *can be found* which make such realization possible. It is to trust that we will be *able to use* appropriate means
should they become available. Even more generally, it is to trust that the
universe is *friendly* (or at least not unfriendly) to our goals.[8] Each form of
trust is, of course, a faith, a willingness to act *as if*. When we are patient,
we act as if the conservation of energy will be productive. As any form
of faith, of course, patience needs to be tested in light of its actual productivity in contributing to desired ends. Otherwise, our trust is care-
less, and we merely wait rather than await.

Though attentive to limitations, patience also attends to the pregnancy of actual conditions. Awaiting signifies giving things time to develop and seeking the right time for action. Knowing when conditions have matured, or call for the directed release of energies rather than their temporary suspension, requires attending to how emerging conditions might function as means to our ends. As we shall see shortly, patience is tied to an active exploration of possible means-end relations, typically performed in thought or imagination before attempted in overt action. Without the ability to see possible future means in present conditions, patience becomes a matter of merely waiting rather than awaiting. Patience awaits in two senses, then. It conserves energy for expenditure in relation to a particular end. It also awaits by attending to means likely to realize that end. In each case, patience prepares us for realization of an end.

Andy vividly illustrates this attention to possibility. In an early scene, he, Red, and some other inmates are tarring a prison roof. Though unspoken prison custom dictates that inmates show no evidence of overhearing the guards' conversations, Andy offers unsolicited advice to one guard having financial troubles, advice grounded in his own past as a banker. The guard is at first angered by the presumption of a lowly inmate, but quickly warms to Andy's advice. Andy soon earns a special status in Shawshank by becoming a tax consultant to the guards and warden; he then becomes indispensable to the prison administrators.

Andy's action demonstrates his refusal to simply endure his time at Shawshank; it also serves as a likely basis for his eventual escape. Near the end of the story, Red surmises that Andy did not enter Shawshank with the specific hope of fleeing through a hole in his cell wall. Certainly he was a "methodical cuss," as Red calls him, but we see no evidence that he came into prison with such a goal. After all, he served twenty-seven years of his term before escaping. Upon discovering the wall's weakness, however, Andy saw a possible means of escape. Breaking out of Shawshank required that he know the lay of the prison, since boring a hole through a cell wall only promises freedom *if* that hole leads to a way out of the prison. Red assumes that Andy probably got access to the prison blueprints as a consequence of his special status. Again, he does not think Andy *originally* sought a privileged position in prison *in order* to escape (King 95). Instead, it seems more likely that Andy's special status resulted from his desire for some continuity with his life outside, some hint of normalcy in a cold and desolate environment. As Andy tells Red at one point, "Better to have Sunday expeditions here [in the prison yard] than no Sunday expeditions at all" (King 29). Andy's special status not only secured such continuity, but also opened doors of opportunity which he was perceptive enough to see. As he gained greater freedom in the prison, he was able to see his new privileges as possible means to his eventual escape. These means included his freedom from having a cellmate, exemption from regular inspections of his cell, and also his likely access to the prison blueprints. Andy's patience would not have contributed to his escape if he had not seen potentialities in his special conditions. He had to recognize and take advantage of them.

In order to patiently await as Andy did, we must be able to control and temporarily suppress energies which seek expression. Awaiting thus depends on self-control—that is, ability to direct and determine the release of one's energies. Obviously, self-control and attention can mutually reinforce one another. Attending to the limits and possibilities of actual conditions allows us to formulate possible means or plans toward which we can and should direct our energies. If we cannot control our energies, we will probably lack the time and energy needed to be attentive to appropriate conditions. We then will not be able to properly sustain and prepare ourselves as we await arrival of necessary means. The ability to await, to *actively* wait, depends upon the ability to maintain focus and delay expenditure of energies. Without self-control, then, there can be no patience and no persistence.

Even though it possesses an inherently active element, patience alone does not suffice to sustain and maintain our commitment to an end. To persist in maintaining our commitment also requires that we remain engaged, continually trying to realize our hopes. The little leaguer and Steinbeck's turtle do not simply await realization of their ends; they actively pursue them. Since attentiveness to our actual current abilities (as well as our potential for growth) often reveals their need for development, persistence indicates that we actively create or nurture them whenever possible. Persistence, then, is perhaps best characterized as an *ongoing* commitment or a *re*-commitment; it carries the sense of moving forward toward our goals. For sake of simplicity, I call this movement *keeping active*. It has two chief effects. It exercises our agency, thereby keeping our energies flowing—albeit under our control. Consequently, dispersal and unwanted diversion of energy are avoided. Further, keeping active develops our abilities and explores possibilities both in thought and in deed.

Ma and Andy illustrate these effects. Ma repeatedly preaches the gospel of keeping active, especially to guard against draining forces. She faces her difficulties by doing something rather than fretting and encourages others to do the same. Her primary response to problems is, "Hush. Don' worry. We'll figger somepin out" (Steinbeck 453). Ma aims to avoid whatever threatens to waste her energy. Her belief in the power of keeping active is most apparent in her relationship with Rose of Sharon. Numerous times she sees Rose on the brink of crying about her situation; Rose is upset when the family dog is killed, when Grampa and Granma die, when Connie leaves her, and when a stranger lectures her on the dreadful effects her sinful behavior will have on her baby. In each case, Ma refocuses Rose's attention by giving her a task. She quickly puts Rose to work, typically by getting her to help others. Rose of Sharon would otherwise quickly give in to the paralysis of fear. Keeping active, then, functions as an indispensable protective measure against the draining effects of fear and distraction. Without it, fear and loss would replace hope and growth.

Andy's constant activity also has significant bearing on his hoping. Unlike Ma and Rose of Sharon, though, keeping active not only helps him avoid the malaise of his plight but also directly increases his chances of escape. At first, the relation of his general activities to his hope is unclear and indirect at best; but especially since he attends to their potential effect on his end, their contribution becomes clearer and more powerful. We have already noted how Andy courageously offers his services to a guard, thereby retaining continuity with his past and exercising his financial expertise in a context where it has precious few outlets. He thus maintains his agency, an important indication of his ability to persist. Moreover, Red notes that "Andy kept up on the tax laws and the changes in the stock market, and so his usefulness didn't

end after he'd been in cold storage for awhile, as it might have done"
(King 96). In the process he secures privileges among the guards and
prison administrators. His favorable status gains him the freedom to
seek external funds to expand the prison library. This, in turn, produces
numerous benefits, the most important of which is the access he presumably gained to books about concrete and the actual blueprints of the
prison. One courageous effort to use his abilities led to further opportunities, all of which contributed to the growth of conditions which enabled him to realize his hope.

Hope's persistence, then, consists in a complex interweaving of
habits of patience and activity which sustain our commitment to an end.
Patience functions primarily to conserve our energy for proper release
when conditions arise which contribute to that end. We will not be able
to await such conditions, however, if we are not attentive to actual conditions, including our own abilities and limitations. Recognizing our limitations produces a form of humility that, if a dimension of piety, does not
incapacitate us. Piety indicates our interconnectedness with other forces
and so provides a ground for the trust in others that is needed if we are to
be patient. In addition, patience requires attention to the pregnancy of
actual conditions; apart from this we do not await proper means, but simply wait. Since energy must be conserved and its release properly timed,
being patient depends on our ability to control our own energies.
Keeping active provides opportunities to exercise and expand such control as well as to develop our abilities. It also protects us from the debilitating effects of fear and restlessness, thereby keeping us focused.

Persistence has, then, a significantly active core. It focuses and
contributes to abilities needed if we are to pursue hopes. But though it
moves us toward our hopes, fuller consideration of agencies required to
realize our ends is needed. I now turn to habits of resourcefulness,
whose primary function is to support, direct, and expand our abilities
to pursue hope's realization.

Resourcefulness

Recall the Athenians' claim, recounted by Thucydides (123), that hope
is less detrimental to those who have "many other advantages" than to

those who risk everything on it. The greater our resources, both mate-rial and human, the more practical our hoping will be. Since habits of hope aim to make hoping practical (especially in the sense that hoping itself contributes to the realization of its ends), they must include not only those habits which foster continued commitment but also those which promote movement toward the hoped-for end. Hoping requires that we actively explore alternatives and develop abilities needed to meet its arduousness and to gauge its possibility. We especially need to expand our abilities so that we will be better able to use means once they arise. In addition to habits of persistence, then, hoping requires habits of resourcefulness, for these are the chief means of guiding and developing our efforts. Indeed, resourcefulness is itself a means to means, so to speak, since resourceful people are those capable of find-ing or expanding their means.

A quick sketch of the parameters of our resources shows them to range from native to acquired abilities, from individual to collective agencies, and from physical tools to scientific knowledge. Material ob-jects function as resources when used to secure desired ends, but our resources also include "spiritual" or human means such as the habits of persistence discussed above. While habits of patience and attentiveness sustain hoping, they also function as resources that foster development of other abilities, even as they conserve energies. Andy's attentiveness to the means hidden within his privileges must rate as one of his prime resources in formulating an escape from Shawshank prison. Addition-ally, sophisticated knowledge proves a valuable asset to hoping; our hope for a cure for cancer is rooted in extensive bodies of knowledge about how the body works.

Any material object or ability is a resource if it can contribute or be applied to a desired end. Resourcefulness is thus the ability to *connect* means with ends, both in thought and in deed. As such it is a habit which indicates our ability to pursue means intelligently and imagina-tively. Hope's resources then are quite simply those materials and abili-ties utilized in the realization of its ends. The primary habits which foster more practical hoping can be divided into those abilities that help us *focus* and those that enable us to *expand* our energies. On the one hand, focusing requires habits that enable us to successfully utilize experience, factual knowledge, and imaginative thinking in formulating and adapting means and ends. Because circumstances as well as our own needs and abilities change, we must be flexible in our commitment to an end, recognizing the potential productivity of pursuing related alternatives. On the other hand, since realizing hope's ends involves transcending limitations, we also need to be able to draw on, develop, and expand needed resources. A vital expansive resource is our ability to foster connection between our own ends and abilities and those of others. Seeking to realize ends that lie beyond our own agency requires us to seek and accept help, especially in the face of our own limitations. The social dimension of hoping thus becomes especially clear in this context. In sum, hope's resources include both cognitive and growth-oriented habits.

We draw resources appropriate to hoping from a variety of areas. While some prove most relevant to focusing our energies and others to expanding our abilities, some promote both. Our most readily accessible resource is our own agency, including our talents and native abilities. As creatures of habit and intelligence, however, we are capable of building on and making more complex our basic abilities, developing new responses through ongoing interaction. Our funded experience, then, proves a vital asset in hoping. A related resource is our imagination, especially as it enriches our horizon of meaningful possibilities and promotes adaptable means and ends. Education, both in schools and beyond, serves as a fundamental site for nurturing human agency. Finally, we will see how vital basic social dynamics of love and cooperative interaction can be in promoting the growth of hope's agency.

Rather obviously, realizing our hopes depends to some extent on our native abilities. If we lack the proper talent or physical prerequisites needed for a particular hope, its pursuit is likely to lead to frustration. Talent can mark the difference between mere dreams and realizable hopes. We need only think of the many opportunities schools provide students to explore the limits of their abilities. Teenagers, so often impatient to attain full maturity, frequently discover their limits as they reach for the stars in athletics, academics, and the arts. Of course, many of them overshoot their abilities, hoping to be captain of the football team, the lead in a play, or concertmaster of an orchestra. Upon failing to soar to such heights, some give up their dream. Others continue in their activity out of simple love for it; they thus modify their hopes to better match their abilities. Still others push on, seeking to develop the needed skills. As a common saying has it, the way to get to Carnegie Hall is to practice, practice, practice. Even native talent needs to be developed to determine its full range; pushing out toward one's limits can lead to discovery of previously unknown capacities.

Successful hoping requires that we recognize that we develop our abilities and discover our limitations in medias res. Cedric, for instance, learns that he is a natural when it comes to mathematics, but he lacks an affinity for critical writing. Especially since its ends lie at or beyond our limits, hope's practicality depends not only on natural talents or already established skills, but also on our capacity to develop needed abilities. Further abilities are nurtured best through proper training and education. Cedric himself seeks tutoring (graciously funded by Dr. Korb). Moreover, the coordination of our efforts with those of others nurtures hoping, as when Martha finds guidance and the assistance of fellow psychologists in confronting her depression.

Of course, acquiring, testing, and developing abilities occur through experience, our most general resource. Indeed, past and present experiences can richly fund hoping, providing us a vast store of knowledge and insight embedded in personal and collective history, literature, and memory. Undergoing life's trials brings with it not only knowledge and insight into the workings of the universe, but also demonstration of our own abilities. Aquinas rightly notes that "by experience man acquires the faculty of doing something easily" (I–II.40.5). Trying and successfully achieving something gives us confidence in our abilities and allows us to direct our attention elsewhere. Moreover, with each act we take a step toward developing a habit. As James notes "nothing is easier than to imagine how, when a current once has traversed a path, it should traverse it more readily still a second time" (PP 1:113). Indeed, the primary virtue of habits is that they can make ongoing interaction smoother and richer. Of course, habits can render an act second nature and yet also impede our ability to adapt to changing circumstances. Cedric, for instance, frequently falls back on his tendency to withdraw from social settings, thereby hindering realization of his hope to fit in and find friends. Especially when habits need to be reconstructed to realize a specific end, *intelligent* habit formation proves more important than mere possession of habits developed through experience. Routine habits rarely afford the flexibility needed to transcend current limitations. Since experience can be more or less intelligently directed, it can be more or less useful in hoping.

Though a likely resource, experience thus varies considerably in its contribution to hoping. Aquinas recognizes that experience can cause both hope and despair, for we gauge what is possible or impossible largely on the basis of experience. In considering the grounds for hope, he identifies two categories: "a thing may be a cause of hope, either because it makes something possible to a man: or because it makes him think something possible" (I–II.40.5). The latter includes whatever makes us believe ourselves capable of realizing an end: teaching, persuasion, or experience. Teaching and persuasion both tend to convince us of what can and what cannot occur on the basis of others' purported expertise.[9] To a great extent, however, our own experience and actions prove the highest court of appeals. Aquinas argues that "experience is a cause of hope, in so far as it makes [one] reckon something possible, which before his experience he looked upon as impossible" (I–II.40.5). A single successful attempt at an act can successfully dispel even the most compelling arguments that something is impossible. By contrast, the practice required to develop virtually every skill is frequently attended by failure and frustration. Repeated unsuccessful attempts to attain a certain end or develop a specific ability can lead us to conclude that the end or act is impossible—even when all that is needed for success is a change in our approach. Experience thus bears a complex relationship to hope. While it can promote hope, it can also lead us to despair.

Similarly, though it sometimes impedes hoping, a lack of experience can also inspire it. As Aquinas notes, "inexperience is a cause of hope, for the same reason as experience causes lack of hope" (I–II.40.5). Especially when young people have experienced relatively few obstacles to their ends, they tend to believe everything good or desirable is possible if only they try hard enough. The future stretches out before them, giving them a sense of unbridled opportunity. This attitude is not confined to the young; Martha, intent on demonstrating the force of her own determination and willpower, tends to think she can overcome her depression if only she puts her mind to it. She needs, and gains through her struggle, the sort of experience which teaches us to be more cautious and sensitive to what is actually possible. Valiant attempts can fail or fall short of their intended goal, bringing with them an increased sense of the limits of our agency, a fact Martha glimpses during the early stages of her depression. After coming down from an exhilarating rush to meet the deadline for a grant proposal, she sadly reflects that "I have done another of the crash-and-burns that are the price of my blitzes. I am grounded, heavy, and slow. I have overdosed on effort, and the hangover is horrible. I guess this is what I get for flying too close to the sun. Unfortunately, I never remember this part when I am aloft" (Manning 5). Experience can thus both increase and decrease our sense of what is possible and so variously affect hoping.

Consequently, we must not be content to identify experience per se as a vital resource; rather, what matters is the *specific kind* of experience we have. Past and present experiences clearly condition how we hope and that for which we hope. Anyone who ignores the lessons of her past is, as Santayana noted, likely to suffer them again. Direction comes not from experience in itself, but rather from the way in which experience fosters *intelligence*—that is, the ability to identify, connect, and assess means and ends in light of one another. As we noted above, the principal distinction between routine and intelligent habits is the flexibility of the latter. Routine habits foster repetitive experience and entrench us in our limitations. Experience that fails to promote the growth of intelligence provides, at best, a haphazard resource for hoping.

Thought and intelligence prove vital resources in our pursuit of hopes by helping us focus and prioritize. Though we noted the centrality of maintaining focus in our discussion of attention as a habit of persistence, attention also functions as a significant resource in pursuing hopes. To be realized, an ideal must have some continuity with actual conditions, for it is out of these conditions that we find, develop, and utilize its means. Dewey argues that the discovery of how things *do* occur makes it possible to conceive of their happening at will, and gives us a start on selecting and combining the conditions, the means, to command their happening. . . . there must be a most realistic study of actual conditions and of the mode or law of natural events, in order to give the imagined or ideal object definite form and solid substance—to give it, in short, practicality and constitute it as a working end. (MW 14:162)

Both when formulating and pursuing our hoped-for end, we must attend to knowledge of fact, whether specific or general. Otherwise, our end will lack appropriate connection to actuality and so generating means will become more difficult.

Every end needs to be formulated and pursued with attention to past experience, knowledge of actual conditions, and insight into alternative possibilities. An end which has no continuity with actual conditions and our own abilities belongs to the realm of wishes and dreams. In such a case, means are wholly lacking, leaving us with literally nothing to do and so promoting a sense of disconnection and helplessness. Rose of Sharon's ends, for instance, tend to be dreams rather than hopes, for though she yearns for their realization, they have no connection to actual conditions. Her most general end is to have a family life rich in material and spiritual goods—all of which she thinks is possible once the family arrives in California. She is wise enough to articulate specific ends: she wants a nice house, a good job for Connie, and a healthy home for the baby. Yet apart from the general promises of the flyers advertising work, neither she nor Connie (nor anyone in the family for that matter) knows what real opportunities California has to offer. Her own youth and inexperience complicate matters, for she possesses little ability or knowledge of how to attain her ends. Lacking resourcefulness generally, Rose teeters on the brink of fear and despair whenever something goes awry. As we noted above, what prevents her from tumbling down dark paths is the ever-resourceful Ma, who stabilizes Rose by assigning her productive tasks.

Not only ignorance but also denial of actual conditions seriously undermines formulating practical hopes. In dealing with his brother

Harvey's cancer, Sherwin Nuland learned the hard way the devastating
effects denial could have. Though acutely aware that we develop complicated stratagems to avoid acknowledging the fact that we all die,
Nuland engaged in his own when he refused to share with his brother
the real prognosis of his cancer. He explains that he "became con-
vinced that telling my brother the absolute truth would 'take away his
only hope'" (Nuland 226). Nuland refused to tell Harvey the truth,
thinking he was enabling Harvey to hang on to hope. The unfortunate
consequence was that, fueled by false hopes, Harvey underwent procedures which led to greater pain and suffering without forestalling his
death. Nuland admits, with obvious remorse, that

> Harvey paid a high price for the unfulfilled promise of hope. I
> had offered him the opportunity to try the impossible, though
> I knew the trying would be bought at the expense of major suf-
> fering. . . . Thirty years earlier, when there was no chemother-
> apy, Harvey probably would have died at about the same time
> that he eventually did . . . but his death would have been with-
> out the added devastation of futile treatment and the misguid-
> ed concept of "hope" that I had been reluctant to deny him and
> his family, as well as myself. (231)

Here we see the sort of hubris which blinds us to alternative hopes.
Though Nuland knew what the actual conditions were, he assumed
that acknowledging them meant succumbing to them. Hope's humility,
however, embraces our vulnerability and patiently allows time to reveal
other conditions and other possibilities. Nuland's best resources told
him Harvey's cancer was terminal, yet he refused to accept this fact and
thereby denied his brother an accurate picture of his actual state.
While he thought he was protecting Harvey, helping him hold on to
hope, he confesses that he really robbed him of forming and pursuing
alternate hopes. Recovery is not the only end for which we can hope in
the face of cancer. Bob DeMatteis, another of Nuland's patients, shared
Harvey's plight, but lacking faith in medicine and doctors, chose to
hope to die on his own terms. Nuland explains that "Bob knew he
was going to die of cancer, and he planned to let it happen without

interference. He was not a religious man, but he had an abiding faith in himself, which at this point became the gyroscope that stabilized his remaining time" (236). Though driven to this hope largely through his fear of medicine, Bob found an alternative which, though less common than the desire for a cure, nevertheless provided an appropriate focus for his hoping. Nuland himself notes that we can all hope—and should foster the hope in one another—that we will not suffer or die alone; this powerful hope provides a meaningful alternative when other hopes wither.[10] Nuland overlooked this possibility with Harvey, restrictively thinking recovery was the only hope his brother would or could pursue. Failing to grasp the reality of his situation, Harvey lacked the needed resources to formulate a hope he could have realized. Denial of actuality, then, proves an enemy of hope.

We should not understand too narrowly the ability to focus, for it requires attention not only to the past and present, but also to the future. Indeed, hoping draws from all three temporal dimensions. Formulating and pursuing ends requires attention to actual conditions and also to the possibilities they present. Knowledge of fact provides an important basis for selecting or developing practical ends for which to hope. Yet attention to alternatives, especially in light of existing conditions, increases our ability to formulate the right hope for ourselves. It also leaves us with other options should our chosen end fail or need revision. Thus attention to ends should be richly funded and explored.

While experience may condition our sense of what is possible, our imagination can richly expand it. In the last chapter I explained the pragmatic view of the imagination as an integral phase of intelligent activity which adjusts means and ends in light of one another to promote better interaction. As such, it is neither divorced from nor opposed to intelligence. Flights of fancy are possible, but even these have ties with reality whereby they become meaningful. Through imaginative exploration, we consider and creatively *rearrange* possibilities in thought in preparation for meaningful action. Such possibilities need not be novel, nor need they be the most desirable, though they may be both. The possibilities with which we play may be discontinuous from actuality, yet insofar as they stir or motivate us, they foster the exploration of means which might establish the needed continuity. Before they are connected in act, means and ends are related in imaginative experimentation. The imagination generates possible matrixes of ends, painting horizons of meaningful alternatives. Sometimes this means sketching ends that are simply alternatives to one another. I may hope medical treatment allows me *either* to recover *or* to at least ward off excessive pain and degeneration into incapacity. At other times, though, imaginative exploration and experimentation reveal connections between ends so that they can be linked and prioritized, thereby forming a chain of means and ends. The merit of such exploration is that it helps us build bridges between previously distinct options. Though pain is something about which we are passionate to avoid, the imagination helps us see how doses of it can play a role in the larger context of recovery.

Unfortunately, we often think of the imaginative process as a primarily private affair. Its sometimes common association with fantasy (especially in the minds of "practical" people who value the truth) tempts us to locate it wholly within isolated minds seeking a reprieve from the challenges of reality—even though such cases are themselves hedged by the social and environmental conditions which make ends attractive and meaningful to us. (We saw this in the case of Little Voice.) The social dimension of the imagination is even more obvious in the very social activity of telling stories. Indeed, stories, whether fictional or not, tend to be among the most common and fruitful products of our imaginative capacities. Closer examination of them illuminates how very valuable a resource the imagination is to hoping.

To show the power of imagination as a dominant resource for hoping, I will focus on the crucial role *stories* play in developing this resource. Much attention has recently been devoted to the nature of narratives and their role in our moral life. Alasdair MacIntyre, Robert Coles, Martha Nussbaum, Richard Rorty, and Mark Johnson have all critiqued traditional moral theories, criticizing the picture of our moral life as a process of articulating and following absolute moral laws.[11] These authors argue that our moral development occurs in rich, complicated contexts which force us to acknowledge the process and contingency of our temporal lives. Narratives—whether written, spoken, seen, or simply thought—provide the larger setting within which we acquire, develop, direct, and transform our character and identity. We weave the various dimensions of our lives (past, present and future, actual and ideal) together into the unity of a narrative fabric; some function as beginnings of our narratives, others as middles, still others as ends. Seemingly isolated events or behaviors then take on their special meaning as obstructing forces, contributing means, or consummating achievements. While moral laws are possible guides to action, these authors argue, they must be understood within the fuller context of our character, of both personal and social habits and ideals.

On the most general level, the narrative structure of stories provides a rich context for presenting illuminating examples. Every teacher knows that conveying a point or lesson is rarely successful in terms of highly abstract ideas; students need examples which give them flesh and bring them to life. The more abstract the idea, the more its meaning depends on our ability to connect it with more concrete meanings. Participants at a science conference are not exempt from this; rather, they are sophisticated enough to have already developed connections between abstract symbols and rich meanings (whether of things or activities); they do so automatically. Examples stimulate the imagination and demonstrate its power to *make new things meaningful*. It does so by bringing possibilities into new relations (with each other or with more familiar things); when continuous enough with achieved goods to stir us, these possibilities attain their own special meaning and thereby expand our horizons of meaning. Examples may be of the order of anecdotes. Yet lengthier stories, with complicated dramatic structure and detail, prove most valuable in showing and fostering hope's imaginative resources. This is largely due to the isomorphism between the narrative structure of most stories and that of hoping.

Stories typically (though not always) establish an organic continuity between events that is temporal and purposive, with progression from beginning through middle to end. Mark Johnson describes this structure by means of the schema of SOURCE-PATH-GOAL. He explains that "[t]his image schema underlies the structure of stories that typically *start* at some point in time, *move through* a series of more or less connected intermediate events, and *end* with some culminating event" (Johnson

166). Johnson argues that the combination of this schema with BAL-
ANCE schemas (which define what counts as a restorative harmony) accounts for the basic structure of the prototypical narrative (169). Such
a structure reflects the temporal nature of human existence and captures the contingency and meaningfulness of starting points. (Our own
existence begins amidst a world that we did not create and that still
conditions and has value to us.) It thus parallels both the genesis and
pursuit of hopes. Born out of problematic situations, we structure our
action as a journey governed by specific hopes that function as ends-
in-view. Stories, then, are isomorphic with our interactive nature and
experience, both generally and in respect to hoping. This makes them
among our most valuable resources for learning and maturing. As
Johnson argues, since our lives themselves have a narrative structure,
"[i]t is in sustained narratives, therefore, that we come closest to observing and participating in the reality of life as it is actually experienced and lived" (169).

Indeed, a special value of such stories—whether fictional or real—
is that they do not merely inform or entertain but also have the power
to stir us by spinning out prototypes for meaningful action. Typically
stories initially move us because they bear some continuity with our
lives, which gives us entrance into new domains. A character suffers a
similar plight, values the same things we do, struggles with what we do,
or must deal with the same sort of people we do. Robert Coles in *The
Call of Stories*[12] tells how Phil, a young fifteen-year-old polio patient,
finds great comfort in Mark Twain's *Adventures of Huckleberry Finn* and
J. D. Salinger's *The Catcher in the Rye*. None of the characters in these stories shares Phil's own trials, yet he is drawn to their way of stripping
away "phoniness" and confronting reality. These stories comfort him
and give him a new voice with which to speak. Coles sees him change
from one whose future is little more than a "black space" to someone invested in his further development, wondering what sort of education
he wants in light of his special difficulties.

Whatever the hook, the story's original continuity allows us to be
drawn into entire new worlds of meaning, values, and action which we
store in our memory as possible alternate modes of acting in novel situations—just as we do with our memories of our own experience. Stories

thus provide the imagination living possibilities with which it can play, giving us prototypes for new ways of thinking and behaving. Coles also tells the story of Ben, a white junior at Harvard whose encounter with Ralph Ellison's *Invisible Man* deeply affects how he sees himself, the world, and his education. Ben used to think of himself as somewhat invisible, prone to falling between the cracks; this probably accounts for his initial attraction to Ellison's book. Yet he discovers more than a compatriot here; he finds a new lens through which to view the world. His view of both himself and his education changes. Ben explains the effect of reading *Invisible Man* as follows:

> once I was with Ellison, I stayed with him; I mean, I "connect-ed" with the invisible man. I think, after a while, I began to see people the way he did: I watched people and tried to figure them out. I didn't want to be an outsider, but I was—the way black people are for us, for lots of us. The more I looked at people through my outsider's eyes, the more I felt alone and ig-nored; it was no fun—and it made me understand not only my own social problems, my trouble getting along with people, but how black people must feel in this world. (Coles 69)

Ben recognizes how he himself is blind to numerous people he regular-ly sees, like the guard who checks student identification at the library. He also considers the invisibility of the homeless and even lives on the streets for a short time to better understand their plight. Ultimately, Ben finds himself questioning the value of his Ivy League education, es-pecially the way it primarily challenges the intellect (through discus-sions, papers, and exams) and not the conscience. In a conversation with Coles, he expresses his newfound passion by explaining that edu-cation should truly matter; it should, he argues, not only make us smarter but also better.

In a similar way, stories of hope move us by expanding our sense of what is really possible. Martha's story, for instance, not only lets us know that ECT can help someone overcome depression; it also gives us insight into the steps needed to endure such a process. Moreover, a special value of stories is that they give us insight into characters; they show us habits in action so that we can see both the conditions necessary for them as well as their consequences (including possibilities of change and transformation). We see how Andy's patience was rooted in such little acts as giving investment advice and carving rocks. We see what tempts Rose of Sharon to despair and how Ma actively intervenes to turn her around. Stories thus prove informative as well as inspiring. They help us *concretely* envision both the ends and possible means needed to realize hopes.

In learning stories, we are also presented the opportunity to develop not just insights, but skills—including attending to and discriminating what is morally relevant, patiently awaiting the turn of events, and fostering our own projections of what we want or think it best for characters to do. First, our encounters with stories can help us develop moral sensitivity to the relevant features of diverse situations. Ben learns how looks and bodily comportment can be means of making others invisible; he consequently seeks to not only be aware of such behavior in himself but also actively to curb it. Steinbeck's tale shows us both the power and difficulties we face when family solidarity takes priority over personal ambition, especially in the midst of hunger and poverty. Similarly, stories can also teach us to recognize, as Nuland eventually did, that recovery is not the only or most desirable hope a cancer patient can have. These lessons involve more than simply acquiring new information; they change how we prioritize values and structure the problems we face.

Finally, and partly as a consequence of the previous skills, our engagement with stories can foster habits such as patience and active awaiting. Whether we watch Andy's story unfold on the movie screen or on the screen of our own mind, we cannot help but anticipate what will happen or wonder what means of escape might arise. We watch for details, signs we can seize upon to predict a resolution to Andy's (and Red's) struggle to be free. Of course, we do not have to wait as long as Andy does, nor do we actually suffer the vagaries of prison life as he does. But even sharing his journey imaginatively opens up the opportunity to actively await the arrival of conditions conducive to his hope. Stories, then, can provide a training ground for developing patience by helping us learn to detect patterns as well as to anticipate, await, and watch events unfold in a meaningful way.

The power of imaginative explorations explains why I have given stories such a prominent place in this book. Anecdotes and abstract examples, of the sort with which professors sprinkle their lectures, are suggestive but rarely carry us very far. Especially when dealing with the life of hope—which is so interactional, temporal, and purposive in its roots—stories prove vital in illuminating dynamics of struggle, our habits and resources, and the process of developing means and ends in pursuing our hopes. Habits and character, in particular, need to shine through, for they play a central role in the life of hope. If we cannot observe them in their complexity, we fail to see how fully they are operative in our lives, generally, and in hoping, specifically. A mere anecdote that fails not only to identify the dominant habits needed and possessed by characters but also to show their transformation in the context of the dramatic situation cannot begin to foster the insight and moral sensitivity needed when pursuing hopes. By contrast, the complicated structure of a story, bolstered by details about the motives, goals, and actions of characters, helps make new situations living to us, thereby giving us alternate meaningful possibilities. If hoping is to be productive, we must carefully formulate our ends, yet they linger in a realm of impotent ideas when disconnected from habits. Intelligence demands that we understand hopes as they live, as they inspire and move us.[13]

Stories, then, show how our imaginative capacities can foster the growth of agency by providing inspiration, blueprints of possible means-ends matrices, and an opportunity to develop some of the resources needed in hoping. Details prove the key ingredient in promoting all three ends. By their means, we imaginatively place ourselves in foreign worlds and so expand our own horizons of meaning. Stories inspire us by setting up precedents, broadening our conception of what is possible. They give us patterns to follow in dealing with new foreign experiences. They help us discover means, especially when they are spun with sufficient care so that we can see what habits operate and what individual objects, acts, or people have special meaning to us. They also give us new ends to consider, not simply as abstract possibilities but rather as living options which we can pursue. Stories are sustained employments of imagination, educating and expanding by means of the genuinely living alternatives they sketch.

Imaginative exploration also proves a vital resource in hoping by promoting adaptability. As circumstances change, we need to be ready and able to adapt. The imagination assists us by spinning out alternative matrices of means and ends. Though we need to be committed to hope's ends, we must also be willing to alter them to better fit existing conditions. Identifying one's well-being or ultimate fate with just one end only makes hoping more risky than it already is; should it prove unrealizable, we will likely be seriously weakened. Without Ma's support, for instance, Rose of Sharon would have been completely devastated by the death of her child. Though abandoning a particular hope can be draining or even demoralizing, we should not overlook the possible infusion of new energy that can come from pursuing a new end. Just as the sight of the original hoped-for end can inspire, so too can the revision. It can even possess more power than the original by offering a *new* way out of a problem in which we have already invested ourselves. If its power is not to disappoint us, though, this new end must be continuous with real conditions and tied to our habits. Indeed, this is precisely what is meant when talking of making an "adaptation": it is a revision rooted in improved knowledge of conditions and so in firmer grounds.

Adaptation variously requires us to alter means in accord with ends, and ends in accord with means. Andy and Martha illustrate the first option. The hallmark of Andy's resourcefulness is his ability to fit current means to his desired end. Martha similarly proves able and willing to try new means. When medication after medication proves useless in combating her depression, she follows the guidance of her doctors by undergoing ECT, even in the face of the dangers and social stigma attached to it. Nuland, on the other hand, demonstrates the significance of altering ends in light of means. He is particularly sensitive, as a doctor, to encourage his patients to consider multiple hopes. Though recovery from cancer through treatment might prove the most attractive option initially, hope's ends, like all other ends, should be tested and appraised as we pursue them. When treatment becomes debilitating without producing much improvement, we more wisely shift our focus from treatment to some other end. Bob DeMatteis's case illustrates another viable alternative should other ends fail to be desirable or realizable. Creativity and imagination operate in both cases. Shifting ends, though, is facilitated by having already mapped out possible alternate ends. While persistence is an integral part of hoping, it must be balanced with the ability to change our ends should they prove unrealizable.

If we are to promote adaptable hopes, though, we must first recognize what can make us resist adaptation. Sometimes we invest so heavily in certain hopes that they become means of protecting ourselves from the harshness of reality. We have already seen this in the case of Little Voice. Similarly, a character on a recent television program refused to visit the grave of her mother who had died three years earlier. When pressed for her reasons, she finally explained that doing so would add reality to her mother's death. So long as she avoided the gravesite, she could keep alive the hope that her mother might come back. She was unwilling to sacrifice that hope, recognizing how it buoyed and protected her from facing something she feared, even though on one level she knew her mother was dead. When hopes protect us in such a manner, we may be reluctant to alter or abandon them. Hope, then, becomes an instrument of denial, shorn from attentiveness to conditions of both reality and possibility. Overcoming such resistance can be aided by two of the resources discussed in this section: imaginative exploration of alternatives and the power of human connection (to be discussed below). We can pursue the former option by telling stories which teach that the mother's presence is more alive when it fuels our daily living (and pursuit of other hopes) than when it simply cushions us from reality. Even more efficacious, though, is the latter option, whereby we show such persons that they are not alone in facing reality, that hopes which have public lives shared by the living and aided by intelligent habits are more nurturing and protective than an isolating hope could ever be. Hopes which generate their own self-contained worlds may protect us from fears, but they cripple rather than empower us.

Furthermore, adaptability requires practical sensitivity, for it stands in tension with our commitment to an end. If we are always willing to shift our devotion from one end to the next, we will undermine both our habits of patience and also our persistence in realizing that end.

There are no easy guidelines or set rules that determine when an end should be given up and when we should continue to pursue it. Rather, we must rely on the sort of moral sensitivity that experience and imaginative explorations foster. Surely, when an end is intelligently judged to be impossible, we should seek alternatives. When its realization lays close at hand, we should stay the course and resist the temptation to change our allegiance. But in between these two extremes lies a continuum of cases. Surely, the more resources we have invested in an end, the more unlikely we are to turn from it. Yet, as our discussion of resistance shows, such investments should not blind us to other possibilities or to the actual state of affairs before us. Our attentiveness to and knowledge of real conditions, both environmental circumstances and our own abilities, prove the most valuable resources in gauging when to give up and when not to. Surely, part of the equation depends on the obduracy of reality as well as our own limits. Neither of these is easy to determine, especially given the indeterminacies which plague interaction. New attempts may stretch our abilities or uncover new potencies in existential conditions. The key is intelligent exploration of both. I shall say more about this when I discuss Martha's decision to undergo ECT in the next section.

Adaptability and other habits of focusing and attention are bolstered by the *expansion* of abilities that comes with the development of means necessary to realizing hope's ends. While pursuing hopes usually requires transcending antecedent conditions, among which are our own limitations, we may find that our own capacities cannot be stretched enough. Subsequently we may either alter or abandon our end; we may also seek others' assistance in attaining it. Especially when our own labor contributes little to an end's realization, an important resource is the ability to draw on and coordinate the abilities of others. This too can expand individual ability; after all, we must be able to solicit, receive, and put to use these other resources. Yet by acting in concert with others, new agencies are developed which do not belong solely to a single person. Technological advances may be spearheaded by an individual, but they are rarely tested and developed apart from a larger community. Consequently, the expansion of agency occurs on both individual and collective levels.

Whether formal or informal, education fosters the growth of individual agency through a social medium. For Cedric, education is the primary means to not only escaping the turmoils of life in the ghetto but also developing his abilities and finding his place in the world. Broadly conceived, education aims at the transmission and intelligent transformation of a range of habits, whether they concern information gathering, exploration techniques, healing, production, or social interaction. Aquinas notes that "hope is caused by everything that increases a man's power; e.g. riches, strength, and, among others, experience: since by experience man acquires the faculty of doing something easily, and the result of this is hope" (I–II.40.5). Money and power increase our access to means; but, again, these are impotent unless we have skills to properly employ them. Similarly, experience provides us the opportunity to develop habits, though these can be either routine or intelligent. While routine habits increase our ability, by their nature they also tend to frustrate further growth and adaptation. Consequently, the chief means of expanding individual abilities is through intelligent formation of habits—which is, or ought to be, the primary goal of education.

Education should, then, promote the development and control of habits. Dewey, for instance, defines education as "the enterprise of supplying the conditions which insure growth, or adequacy of life, irrespective of age" (MW 9:56). It thus aims at nurturing and organizing the powers that foster growth. Since these powers are our habits, education functions to direct habit formation by nurturing skills for careful formulation and intelligent pursuit of ends which maximize the flexibility of habits. James preaches a similar message when discussing habits. He argues:

> The great thing, then, in all education, is to *make our nervous system our ally instead of our enemy.* It is to fund and capitalize our acquisitions, and live at ease upon the interest of the fund. *For this we must make automatic and habitual, as early as possible, as many useful actions as we can,* and guard against the growing into ways that are likely to be disadvantageous to us, as we should guard against the plague. The more of the details of our daily life we

can hand over to the effortless custody of automatism, the more our higher powers of mind will be set free for their own proper work. (PP 1:126)

An education of this sort does not require the institution of a school; it simply needs thoughtful development of our habits.

James offers four maxims we can follow in developing habits; these apply to habits of hope as much as any other. The first admonishes us to be decisive when forming new habits: "We must take care to *launch ourselves with as strong and decided an initiative as possible.*" The second reinforces the first: "*Never suffer an exception to occur till the new habit is securely rooted in your life*" (PP 1:127). Each performance of an act can further contribute to or distract us from forming a chosen habit; continuity, as James notes, proves the key if we are to build upon our first decisive step. (Both of these maxims embrace as well as promote development of habits of persistence.) The third maxim follows from the first two: "*[s]eize the very first possible opportunity to act on every resolution you make, and on every emotional prompting you may experience in the direction of the habits you aspire to gain*" (PP 1:128). Far too often, we delay a change in behavior, postponing it until tomorrow. The effect of such, though, is to allow our other habits to continue their domain; the ruts of routine habits in particular get deeper and deeper.

James's final practical maxim focuses on our need to retain mastery of our habits. He urges us to "*Keep the faculty of effort alive in you by a little gratuitous exercise every day*" (PP 1:130). So acting, he argues, provides insurance of our abilities. Control of our habits, meaning our ability to use and transform them at will, requires regular daily practice. Consequently, James urges that we

be systematically ascetic or heroic in little unnecessary points, do every day or two something for no other reason than that you would rather not do it, so that when the hour of dire need draws nigh, it may find you not unnerved and untrained to stand the test. . . . So with the man who has daily inured himself to habits of concentrated attention, energetic volition, and self-denial in unnecessary things. He will stand like a tower

when everything rocks around him, and when his softer fel-
low-mortals are winnowed like chaff in the blast. (PP 1:130)

James's fundamental insight is that we can and should be masters of our
habits. Yet especially once they become second nature, we rely on
them without thinking. It is then that they can take control of us,
rather than vice versa. If we are to develop intelligent habits and remain masters of them, we must be attentive and remain sensitive to
their conditions and their effects. While patience is developed by
being patient, we are unlikely to do this without effort and concentration. Keeping active similarly demands our attention.

      While control of habits provides stability, it does so primarily by
expanding our capacity to transform or reconstruct our habits. Peircean
habituation, then, is a chief resource in expanding agency. Recall that
for Peirce, habituation does not mean the irrevocable entrenchment of
habits, but rather "the power of readily taking habits and of readily
throwing them off" (Peirce 189). So understood, habituation is the
habit of making habits fluid—that is, the power or ability of forming
and transforming habits. As such, it maximizes our ability to respond to
changing circumstances. We can foster it by following James's recom-
mendation to regularly exercise our faculty of effort. Without some element of this sort of habituation, I would be unable to develop new
habits needed for writing a book, the cancer patient would be incapable of adapting to the rigors of treatment, and parents would impose
rigid norms and goals on their children. Whether in reconstructing
failed habits or expanding the reach of others, hoping moves forward
through habituation.

      Though education and habituation may have individuals as their
focus, they do not occur in private isolation. Indeed, Dewey argues
that education aims at transmission of knowledge and abilities to ensure the continuation of community.[14] Expansion of personal abilities
thus occurs within the broader context of expanding collective agency.
Collective agency includes, and expands by means of, both material
technologies and human means. Indeed, among our chief human resources are social agencies as well as simple human capacities to trust,
nurture, and love one another. While developing material technologies

requires an abundance of material goods, it also requires ability to use those goods without exhausting them, developing means which liberate rather than incapacitate us.

Technology generally increases our means by giving us greater access to a broader array of possibilities. Computer technology, for instance, has opened up new avenues of communication with people across the globe. Generally, technologies are but an extension of habituation; they are instrumentalities that give us greater control of our interaction with environments. Nuland recognizes how the new biomedical technologies have given once humble doctors the power to play not only healer but also God. A chief triumph, of course, has been development of vaccines which prevent diseases. No longer must we hope for a cure from smallpox; we have all but eradicated it from the planet. While we lack cures in many other cases, we have nevertheless developed sophisticated treatments that enable patients to live longer with as little discomfort as possible. Chemotherapies help cancer patients, protease inhibitors extend the lives of AIDS patients, and ECT helps some fight depression. Hope for remission thus accompanies hope for cure.

Of course, greater access to more means does not ensure better hopes. Bob DeMatteis feared the new technology and so was driven to explore alternate hopes. In the process, he avoided the debilitating route Harvey Nuland traveled. Nuland also tells of his ninety-two-year-old patient, Miss Welch, for whom technology was a burden rather than a source of liberation. Miss Welch was alone in the world and ready to die. When she became ill, Nuland recognized that recovery through an operation was likely, so he ignored her protests and operated on her. After the operation, she cursed him, since she did not value survival for survival's sake. Nuland learned that though he had the technology to save her, he overlooked her own very understandable hope. She had lived a full life and had no reason to prolong it. Yet Nuland was blinded by his own power and so deprived her of what she longed for: "the hope that she could leave this world without interference when an opportunity arose" (253).

Nuland thus uncovers the darker side of technologies. Surely they have expanded our control and liberated us from previous limitations.

Nevertheless, technologies can become the focus of our attention to such an extent that they mask the ends they make possible. Nuland explains:

> In this high-tech biomedical era, when the tantalizing possibility of miraculous new cures is daily dangled before our eyes, the temptation to see therapeutic hope is great, even in those situations when common sense would demand otherwise. To hold out this kind of hope is too frequently a deception, which in the long run proves far more often to be a disservice than the promised victory it seems at first. (233)

Steinbeck voices a similar criticism of technologies in his novel, noting that by themselves they are just as likely to curse as to save us. Early in the story, he acknowledges the central role the family truck plays in enabling the Joads to realize their hope for a better life. Apart from the truck, they lack the proper means to escape the wasteland of their home and to journey to the promised land of California. Young Al Joad's role in the family is defined by his knowledge and skill in mechanics. Steinbeck is thus sensitive to technology's promise. But in a late chapter which vividly illustrates the book's title, he recognizes not only the greatness but also the limitation of our technological advances. Steinbeck writes that by means of knowledge and technique we have transformed the agricultural world; we have developed plants that will "resist the million enemies of the earth: the molds, the insects, the rusts, the blights" (Steinbeck 346). We have grown new plants that produce both more and new fruits. But social technologies to unify people with these new means and ends have not developed in sync with agricultural advances. Steinbeck bemoans the fact that "[m]en who can graft the trees and make the seed fertile and big can find no way to let the hungry people eat their produce. Men who have created new fruits in the world cannot create a system whereby their fruits may be eaten" (348). This failure "topples all our success" (349), thereby turning the grapes of hope into the grapes of wrath.

By themselves, then, technologies are no more means to our ends than anything else is. They must be used appropriately, and such use itself presupposes our ability or access to them. Material goods and technologies enable us to realize our goals. Indeed, technologies are more than material tools; they are techniques—that is, abilities to use material goods to realize ideal ends. Consequently, though they increase our agency, technologies must be intelligently assessed in light of our chosen ends. Otherwise, their application and expansion become ends in themselves; they are then abstracted from the means-end continuum and lose their proper function. Appropriate use of technology means understanding and evaluating it as embedded in concrete contexts of living purposes.

Steinbeck shows that without appropriate *human* resources technological advances can prove either ineffectual or burdensome. Social and political structures are thus technologies vital to the growth of agency just as are sciences and material tools. In addition, though, personal and interpersonal resources nurture the expansion of agency required in hoping. Self-control and ability to focus are important resources in discovering and attempting to transcend our limitations. Yet beyond these, human contact provides both direct and indirect aid in fulfilling hopes. The ability to connect with others, seeking their help and coordinating our efforts, enables us to overcome personal limitations. Whether in writing a book, attempting a recovery from cancer, or hoping a loved one survives an accident, others can provide comfort as well as additional means in realizing ends. Their contact can renew our energy and commitment, especially when their perspectives uncover new means and ends. Moreover, sharing our trials and hopes with those we love and trust brings comfort, support, and the contribution of insights and abilities of those who care. Human relations are not mere means; they are dynamic bonds, rich with meaning, which have and continue to nurture us.

Connection with other humans, such that a sharing of concerns and abilities is possible, is important both in persisting and in pursuing hopes. Our own investment in others proves invaluable in this context. Early in grappling with her depression, Martha looks on as her daughter and her girlfriends sleep, and she is filled with the promise a young life can hold. She still feels connected enough to her daughter, Keara, to feel peace and also hope. She explains that "[a]s lousy as I feel, it is a comfort to know that the pleasures of children can still penetrate my darkness. This chance to watch them sleep, these ring-around-the-rosy girls, full of promise and possibility, gives me a hope for the future, however, fleeting" (45). Later on, she finds solace in her grandmother's rosary beads. Though she herself does not wholeheartedly share the Catholic faith in their power, the beads form a link with one she loved dearly and so she holds onto hope through them.

Similarly, the ordinary goodwill of others makes pursuit of hopes easier. In return for his financial advice, Andy only asks that the guards give him and his buddies a cold beer. Though seemingly meager, Red notes that Andy is actually paid in perhaps the most valuable currency in prison: "simple good will" (King 51). This goodwill earns Andy privileged status among the guards and his fellow prisoners alike. Cedric similarly benefits from the contributions of many people. While some of his classmates threaten to drag him down, he enjoys the support and special privileges of his teachers Mr. Govan, who opens the computer center early for him, and Mr. Dorosti, the computer science teacher who takes on an independent study with Cedric, which gives him free access to a computer at all times of the day. There is also Mr. Taylor, the chemistry teacher who provides Cedric with constant interaction, intellectual challenges, and also moral (and spiritual) encouragement.[15] And, of course, Barbara Jennings invests virtually all of her energies into helping Cedric realize his hopes.

Similarly, Ma frequently recognizes the importance of both offering and accepting help. Early in the story, the Joads meet the Wilsons along the side of the highway. Both families suffer specific limitations; the Joads' truck is overloaded and the Wilsons lack any knowledge of cars. They pool their resources and travel together. That way some of the Joads can ride in the Wilsons' car, and Al and Tom can help Mr. Wilson with any mechanical problems he encounters. In response to Mr. Wilson's fear that his family will prove a burden, Ma quickly reassures him, "You won't be no burden. Each'll help each, an' we'll all git to California" (Steinbeck 149). (Jim Casy, as we noted, shares this cooperative spirit; it leads him to join forces with the union later in the book.) Ma repeatedly invites others to join the family, whether the Wilsons, the Wainwrights, or the starving man and his son at the end of the book. As Mrs. Wainwright tells Ma, "No need to thank. Ever'body's in the same wagon. S'pose we was down. You'd a give us a han'" (Steinbeck 444). Ma responds affirmatively, including others within her family of concern. Hope needs help—in some cases, the help of others in similar circumstances.

We must, of course, be thoughtful about the help that we give. Martha observes with dismay how readily so many people offer her advice for overcoming depression. She endures their good intentions, even as they make her feel increasingly isolated. Martha notes that others' presumption that since they have felt down before, they have some expertise in the matter, just shows how few of us know what severe depression is really like. It is only with her husband, Brian, that she is perfectly frank. When he tells her he does not know how to help her, Martha responds pointedly, "I don't want you to help me. I want you to be with me" (Manning 77). Sometimes the most powerful thing we can do to help another is to simply *be with* them, acknowledging the reality of their situation without the distancing comfort of platitudes. After she begins recovering from her depression, Martha acknowledges that she never could have made it without the companionship of her family and doctors along the way. Sometimes the most effective mode of cooperation is the simplest act of being there.[16]

Cooperation, whether complex or rudimentary, thus helps overcome individual limitations by developing new collective agencies. Close relationships with family and friends play a particularly important role in the growth of agency. Especially when vulnerable, we turn first to those whom we love and trust. An obvious reason for this is that we share with such people habits which make communication and concerted action easier. We more readily identify with and act together when we have common abilities (embodied by habits) and values (embodied by hopes and ideals). Consequently, expansion of agency occurs most readily in personal and interpersonal relationships. We build communities of hope out of these shared habits and hopes. Ma provides an anchor for her family generally, but she plays a special role in helping Rose of Sharon pursue her hopes. We have noted Rose's youth and inexperience. As the story progresses, we can chart her development, largely under Ma's guidance. Mimi Reisel Gladstein notes that we repeatedly see Ma teaching Rose "through precept and example nourishing and reinforcing behavior patterns."[17] Both Ma and Rose share similar hopes for a rich family life. Rose of Sharon, however, largely lacks the necessary skills. Rather than focusing exclusively on her own needs or events beyond her control, Ma teaches Rose to tend to the family in whatever immediate ways she can. Rose's final act in the book, nursing the dying man, demonstrates her growth under Ma's tutelage. In the next chapter, I will argue that this close family relationship proves vital in understanding Rose of Sharon's hopefulness; Red's friendship with Andy plays a similar role in *The Shawshank Redemption*.

Courage

Expanding our agency is necessary if we are to overcome limitations. We must either develop the necessary skills ourselves or acquire the ability to connect with those who have them. When hoping, we open ourselves to forces other than our own, and so we subject ourselves to change and reconstruction. In addition to persistence and resourcefulness, hoping thus requires the courage to change, grow, and take risks. To hope is to reach for an end which, though separated from our abilities by an often indeterminate gulf, is nevertheless attractive. The possibility of recovery realized by others lures the cancer patient to hope for the same. Similarly, the work promised by handbills distributed to the Okies in Steinbeck's novel fuels their migration westward. Pursuing these goals, especially in the face of indeterminacies, involves risks and so calls for courage. To more fully appreciate the role of courage, I first sketch its nature and then the kinds of risks which attend hoping. In the process, I will explore the dominant interrelations between courage, persistence, and resourcefulness.

Most generally, courage indicates willingness to face dangers and to take risks. It thus arises in contexts where we face trying tasks or pursue arduous goods. Soldiers are deemed courageous for risking their lives in battle, as are social reformers who jeopardize their well-being to secure goods such as justice. In cases like these, we risk something valuable, whether energy or life, for some other, usually higher, good; indeed, we need courage most when we face trials which may drain our

resources. Fear, of course, usually attends such situations, for we naturally tend to avoid what taxes our capacities and threatens our well-
being. At times, though, we must check fear and take risks if we are to
pursue certain goods. Tendencies to flee or avoid trying circumstances
must be met with determination to stay the course. The soldier likely
fears for his life when fighting in battle, but if he is to defeat the enemy,
he must resist temptation to succumb to fear. Similarly, Rosa Parks likely felt pangs of fear when she boldly refused to give up her seat to a
white person, yet she suppressed them to promote the higher good of
equal treatment, even in the face of arrest.

Hoping brings with it a host of risks. Andy's hope to escape prison
carries the danger that he will be caught, thereby losing the privileges
he has acquired, and so find himself in an even worse predicament. In
their quest for a better life in California, the Joads risk (and in fact lose
much of) their family cohesiveness as well as the remainder of their material resources. Cedric faces the possibility of personal failure, which
threatens to drain his life of meaning, while Martha risks irreparable
damage to her brain in undergoing ECT. While the risks we take when
hoping vary with the particular ends and means we choose, we can
identify the general *kinds* of risk that attend it. Most generally, hoping
requires us to face our limits and vulnerability, our dependence on
forces other than our own in securing goods we need or desire. Perhaps
the most important risks we take here concern our energy. When pursuing a hope, some energy must be dedicated to our chosen end; otherwise, we lack commitment to it and are easily distracted. This energy,
however, is wasted if our hope proves unrealizable. In such a case, not
only will the original problematic situation remain unresolved, but we
also will have lost the valuable resources expended in our attempts to
meet it. Sometimes such losses are recoverable; at other times they
devastate us. A cancer patient who selects one mode of therapy might
be too exhausted to explore different options should the chosen one
fail. Her cancer may have spread so that alternative treatments would
not work even if she had the stamina to undergo them.

The greater the degree of personal contribution involved in a particular hope, the higher the stakes. If realization of an end depends
largely on our own efforts, we have greater control over securing that

end than when others' contributions are also needed. Failure in such cases, however, brings with it increased risk of loss, especially loss of faith in ourselves. Judge Clarence Thomas emphasizes this lesson in talking with Cedric. When they meet during Cedric's last semester at Ballou Senior High School, the judge shares with Cedric the trials he has faced and warns him what is at stake in attending Brown University. He admonishes the young boy to avoid labels and to think about who he really is, noting that "if you're not sure about who you are, you could get eaten alive" (Suskind 120). Thomas underscores the seriousness of Cedric's upcoming venture into the Ivy League, warning him that "[s]ome of these kids will be ahead of you, for sure, but you just have to outwork them. That's the way you'll beat them. It was that way with me, too. There was no safety net. No choice. To fail means to drop all the way to the bottom" (Suskind 122). Once he leaves his home, with the support of his mother, family, and church, Cedric's success depends on his own efforts and his own faith in himself. Should he fail, Cedric can always return home, but he will do so demoralized, knowing that after years of trying to stand above the crowd, he had failed. Israel Atkins, the father of Cedric's friend Phillip, discourages his son from aiming too high, telling him that "hoping for too much in this world can be dangerous" (Suskind 68). Failed hopes lead to disappointment, frustration, anger, demoralization, or despair. None of these consequences is necessary, though, for strong habits of persistence and resourcefulness—as well as those of hopefulness—may sustain us. Nevertheless, hope's most serious risk is that we will be unable to pick ourselves up if it fails. Even hope's success can pose problems. Pursuing hopes usually takes us beyond our normal patterns of behavior, requiring reconstructions which separate us from our usual resources. We are thus vulnerable to the effects of change as well as to the loss of vital resources. I will discuss this scenario more fully below when considering Martha's courage.

A primary reason for our entire exploration of how to make hoping more practical is to avoid or learn to deal with risks such as these. Hoping *can* be dangerous, but there are ways of lessening its dangers so we can reap its benefits. The goal of the *intelligent* formulation and pursuit of hopes, fostered by careful attention to our habits, is to find realizable hopes. Yet risks cannot be avoided altogether. Whether in hoping or other activities, we need to attend to both immediate and distant dangers involved in facing problematic situations. Courage does not mean denying or ignoring possible risks, but rather acknowledging and assessing them. We must know what dangers are likely so that we can set aside energy to meet them. Denial leaves us unprepared to deal with them. The colloquialism "Hope for the best, but prepare for the worst" acknowledges the tensions between hope's promise and danger, and thereby provides valuable insight. Hoping, however, does not mean acting in defiance of risks; instead, it indicates careful consideration and preparation in meeting them.

Courage, then, is an *informed* risk taking. For instance, we do not judge people courageous if the negative effects of the risks they take are either too minimal or too severe. Making breakfast or going to get my mail may involve risks—I might cut myself on a knife or twist my ankle en route to the mailbox. Such acts usually do not call for courage, since these dangers are both unlikely and rather minimal. On the other hand, trying to run from a mugger who has a loaded gun to your head presents a risk so extreme that doing so is not courageous but foolish and rash. Consequently, goods for which we take risks must be valuable enough to warrant those risks. The ancient Greeks, for instance, distinguished the brave from the foolhardy soldier on the basis of the former's knowledge of what things should be feared. Death should not be feared, they argued, when the cause is noble and the alternative is enslavement or debasement.[18] One who runs from death in such cases is a coward. But risking death to accomplish something insignificant, like the momentary exhilaration that comes from jumping from a great height, signifies rashness. Since courage means overcoming fear and taking risks, the good for which we do this must be desirable—that is, evaluated as worthy of the necessary expenditures of energy, especially in light of competing goods.

Risk-taking is informed when it is based on an intelligent assessment of means and ends. As such, it requires careful consideration of actual conditions, abilities, and projected goods. We need to know both what problems we are likely to face and which are so severe they should be avoided. Certain ends provoke fear in us, and rightly so;

dangerous operations or procedures can result in agonizing pain or death. Those who have courage do not simply face threatening circumstances; they do so after assessing that such measures are necessary in order to secure some higher good. Chemotherapy is often painful and carries with it undesirable side effects; ECT can damage patients' memory and leave them confused. Yet when we have reason to believe that it will yield recovery, facing such trials is worth the effort.

Risk assessment should also attend to our means, especially our own abilities. Cedric would have been foolhardy aiming for the Ivy League if he lacked his special knack at mathematics. Given the educational and social hurdles he faced, he needed to know that he could persist in the face of trials. Bob DeMatteis defined the risks he was willing to take in light of his own personal abilities, defying conventional wisdom in the process. He first showed courage by overcoming his fear of medical technology to undergo exploratory surgery. Unfortunately, the resulting prognosis was grim. Nuland notes that Bob could have pursued further medical treatment. Many of us would choose such a route, especially since our society invests so much hope in the institution of medicine. Yet given his fear of that institution, coupled with his prognosis, Bob recognized that a more appropriate goal *for him* was to die with dignity; this required a courage all its own. Nuland recounts his final visit with Bob, just prior to the last Christmas party he would throw. Though ailing, Bob was determined to enjoy the party as though he was not ill. Nuland found that Bob had mustered a courage he never thought possible for him, noting that "in the short time left to him, Bob was able to see a form of hope that was his alone. It was the hope that he would be Bob DeMatteis to his last breath, and that he would be remembered for the way he had lived" (239). Bob did not simply accept the conventional wisdom that all the perils of medical treatment are worthwhile; rather he determined what risks he would take in light of his own abilities and ends. Though we frequently think undergoing treatment for a disease is courageous, doing so is foolish when we lack the resources to survive it or think the end it promises is not worth the price.

Intelligence functions in courage as it does in other contexts to assess means and ends in light of one another. Yet courage involves more than intelligent appraisal; it indicates the willingness and ability *to act* on that appraisal. When faced with the same grim situation as the soldier, the freedom fighter, or the cancer patient, some people retreat and simply accept their lot; to them, the courage to face those dangers appears to be a special power that only others possess. Viewed externally, courage often inspires awe and does have a seemingly mysterious quality. Red, for instance, is at first amazed that Andy could have jeopardized his rather comfortable status in prison by digging a tunnel out of his cell. Similarly, after noting all the hardships of their migratory trips, Steinbeck wonders in an early intercalary chapter where the Okies find the courage to leave all they know to pursue California's promises (Steinbeck 123). Faced with the same situation, many of us would quickly give up.

Courage then indicates the willingness and ability to summon energies to face and overcome risks. Those who are courageous are willing to meet obstacles and to play an active role in bringing about conditions necessary to realize desired ends. Such a willingness requires possession or continual development of the ability to so act. Appraisal of risks and willingness to act are not, of course, inherently separated, for every appraisal involves imaginatively matching our abilities, both actual and potential, with the trials current conditions pose. The greater our confidence in our abilities (whether individual or collective), the greater our likelihood to act. Though it can seem mysterious, the willingness to act is typically sparked by sheer willpower. Willpower, though, consists of those habits which channel and regulate our energy. Consequently, it is not mere confidence which propels us to act courageously, but *ability*. James likens courage to a kind of faith or trust in our abilities that makes us willing to act *as if*—that is, to take that step forward to see how we might contribute to realizing desired ends. We must be willing *and also able* to act, to commit to a course of action so that we face, meet, and overcome the challenges and risks which call for courage in the first place.

As it moves us to act, courage serves as a vital means to both persistence and resourcefulness.[19] Simply formulating a hope in the face of a problematic situation usually requires overcoming tendencies to fear or despair. When our action is interrupted, we typically feel disoriented and lost. If fear controls our response, we will likely be unable to focus on a particular good, or we will be hasty in our selection of it. Hope calls for the courage to face problems and to patiently and creatively survey our options. Once a particular end is selected, we also need courage to explore possible means, expand our agency, or simply persist in our commitment to that end. Though I will discuss more fully the interrelation between all habits of hope in the next chapter, here I will sketch the ways in which courage is both a means and an end for the other habits. Courage not only fuels steps whereby persistence and resourcefulness can be developed and expanded; it is itself aided by their structures.

Persistence requires courage in a variety of ways. Especially when we commit to unpopular causes which run counter to the status quo, persistence can be a lonely and trying affair. In such cases, we may be ostracized for persisting and so need courage to stay the course. This is Cedric's plight while he tries to survive Ballou Senior High School. His persistence is fostered by an armor to blunt the effects of what he calls "dreambusters," people who always tell him "you can't" or "you won't." The core of this armor is a simple code: "Don't give up, don't give in" (Suskind 129). Cedric tends to separate himself from others, recognizing the drag, direct or indirect, many of them will have on him. In the face of such a hostile environment, he nurtures his skills by turning to mathematics, where, as Suskind notes, "he can arrive at modest answers—small steps—that give him the sensation of motion" (18). These steps bolster his courage.

We especially need courage to persist when resources are drying up and trials are mounting. During the summer following his junior year of high school, Cedric is accepted to MIT's Minority Introduction to Engineering and Science, a program for promising students. Here he senses the possibility of companionship, a novel change on his solitary journey. Instead, Cedric learns that these other minority students are typically wealthier, not coming from the ghetto. Moreover, he experiences his first major setback, a dash of reality which tarnishes his hope, when he finds himself far behind the other students. He thus learns that determination alone will not enable him to succeed. Maintaining his hopes to escape the ghetto and to make it to MIT requires all the courage he can muster, especially as he returns to Ballou for his final year. Making matters worse, Cedric reaches out for assistance but finds none. He asks Andrew, one of the brighter students, if he will help him. Andrew politely refuses, explaining that "I really don't want to be tutoring people, okay Cedric? That's what counselors are for . . . I have to be looking up, not down, not beneath me" (Suskind 85). This refusal unsurprisingly demoralizes Cedric, undermining his confidence and reinforcing his tendency to avoid dealing with others—let alone reaching out to them. Suskind summarizes the impact of the summer by noting that prior to attending MIT's program, "it seemed like [Cedric] was infused with hopefulness, that he had a plan . . . But it's a lot harder to imagine all that now. He's not even sure, at this point, if he even belongs at some top college. For what? To have this summer replicated for four years?" (100)

In the process of dealing with such disappointment, Cedric learns that hoping frequently requires the courage to change in order to persist. Such a change may mean adapting by pursuing alternate means and ends, or it may mean changing oneself in order to better achieve that end. At first, Cedric salvages his hope by discovering Brown University, an Ivy League school that appears to be accepting of different kinds of people. He begins to realize that he must learn to deal with others and his differences from them. In the personal essay for his Brown application, he explicitly acknowledges that "[y]es, success depends on how hard one works. But individual advancement and continual progression depend on one's ability to deal with different people" (Suskind 107). These are profound words, the reality of which Cedric has yet to learn.

Ma Joad demonstrates the courage to persist when others have given up and *also* to change in order to persist. Late in Steinbeck's novel, the Joads have found a seemingly idyllic life in the government-operated Weedpatch camp. This camp has the sort of order lacking in other camps; there are clear rules that ensure proper and respectful treatment of all members of the camp. Moreover, the campers work together to ensure stability and so are free from the caprice of any external authority. Though this appears to be the sort of life for which the Joads had hoped, they cannot find enough work to feed the family. Ma notices that her young son, Winfield, is showing obvious signs of malnutrition. Though Pa and the others have all but given up hope of finding work, Ma urges the family to leave the camp and move elsewhere. Making and pursuing such a proposal requires courage, since the other family members prefer to stay. Yet Ma realizes that as good as things are at Weedpatch, this is not the life for which they hoped, for clearly they will starve if they remain. They must move north where there is greater promise of work. Such a change is, of course, all the more perilous, since they have no guarantee they will actually find work. Nevertheless, they must attempt this move to avoid starvation.

Ma scolds Pa for being too scared to even talk about the seriousness of their situation. When he suggests it might be time to take a stick to Ma for her insubordination, she defiantly tells him to get his stick (Steinbeck 352). She refuses to be threatened and refuses to give up. Capitulating to Pa's stick, or the stick of society for that matter, would mean running from trying circumstances. Unlike Pa, though, Ma is not afraid to face facts, and she certainly will not risk her family's well-being to placate him. In fact, she tells Tom that she *must* stir Pa's anger if they are to move forward.

Courage not only promotes persistence, it also serves as a means to expanding our resources. Once at Brown, Cedric realizes that his new environment demands a change in himself. His first semester is marked by frequent periods of conflict and isolation; yet he eventually acknowledges that he must let go his tendency to separate himself from others. Suskind notes that at Ballou, Cedric

> had to tie his identity to that notion of separateness; it was the only way he could stay on course and keep his sanity, really, as [other kids] hurled insults at him about racial betrayal or insufficient maleness and foolhardy optimism. Here, no one is really hurling anything. They're just all going about their business—everyone in their own little show—and he has to find some other way to feel special. Being alone doesn't seem to be working. (Suskind 293)

Cedric must summon the courage "to start unfolding in some fresh and frightening ways to keep moving forward" (294) unless he is to surrender his future to his past. He must also change his way of thinking if he is to succeed in academics. Prof. Larry Wakefield recognizes Cedric's passion about his own experience and life but also contends that he needs to balance it with a critical mind. Wakefield advises that "[i]f you're going to make it here, Cedric, you'll have to find some distance from yourself and all you've been through" (303). Brown thus challenges Cedric to move beyond his old habits; he must overcome his fear and tendency to isolate himself. Just as he had to summon plenty of courage to survive the dangers of Ballou, he must do the same—especially in adapting and expanding his own abilities—if he is to succeed and find acceptance at Brown.

A detailed look at Martha's battle with depression vividly illustrates how intricately habits of courage interweave with those of persistence and resourcefulness. Martha is a woman of considerable determination and self-confidence, a fact she makes clear throughout her book. At first, she compares her depression to her messy house; both her personal life and her material abode are marked by piles of unsorted materials, piles which keep growing. But her response to housekeeping and her growing depression is the same: face them with determination. Various comments testify to this, from her moral dictate, "you messed it up, you clean it up" (7), to her general attitude, "[s]omething is wrong and I will not allow it to get out of control" (59). Though embarrassed because she cannot heal herself, Martha musters courage to face the reality of her own situation: she is clinically depressed. She is not blind to the need to reach out for help and so enlists the professional assistance of a psychotherapist and a pharmacologist. She persists in tackling her depression head-on. She keeps active, continuing to see her patients and trying to live everyday life as usual. She is also resourceful, going on a spiritual retreat and trying medication after medication in the hopes of finding something that will work. Unfortunately, nothing stops her downward spin into depression. Martha must then summon the courage to cope with the growing frustration and isolation she faces.

Near the end of her rope, and thinking more and more about death, Martha finally turns to ECT as a possible means of salvation. Her doctors help her realize that she is suffering from a serious, even life-threatening, illness. She knows that ECT is an option, and she knows its dangers of confusion and memory loss. Yet she must still summon considerable courage to face this possibility. First, she must face the social stigma attached to the treatment. Second, accepting ECT means she cannot cure herself, and so she feels that she must let go of her self-reliance and give in. Martha finds this demoralizing, an assault on her autonomy. She explains, "I've never been good at letting go. I've always figured that if I held on hard enough and long enough, I would eventually prevail" (103). Yet she realizes that she must accept the limits of her own ability; she must turn to a treatment which she does not want (it will be a permanent part of her record) and which poses real dangers. Martha concedes that her real fear is not losing her memory, but losing "the last remnants of myself" (118). At risk is her very sense of self as it is funded by both memories and abilities. As she prepares to undergo her first treatment, Martha reflects that "[j]ust as I have lost so much of myself in the past years, now I lose more. I offer myself up to these strangers in exchange for the possibility of deliverance" (124).

Further trials await her following her treatment. Though the ECT successfully repositions her, pulling her out of the depths of her depression, she still needs courage to confront the reality of the effects of the procedure. She suffers some memory loss and confusion; furthermore, she must acknowledge that she will always have to take some form of antidepressant to keep herself in check. Yet her greatest challenge comes in accepting the changes that have affected her image of her very self. Martha explains that "[m]y criterion for healing has been to be able to pick up right where I left off, like midpage in a novel. I have waited and waited, but I'm still not back to that page." She soon realizes that she must face what others seem to be telling her: "that I'm never going to get back to that page. That I'm in an entirely new book now, most of it unwritten" (186). Her old self, defined so fully by feelings of omnipotence and an obsession with achievement, has been interrupted and replaced with a vulnerable self that must cope with limits and disorienting change.

Consequently, realizing her hope for recovery demands innumerable acts of courage. Martha needs courage to acknowledge that she was depressed, and to cope with the very trying crushing effects of depression on a daily basis. She also needs courage to face the fact that she needs help and to accept that she—a trained therapist whose primary occupation is helping to cure people of mental health problems—cannot do that very thing for herself. Determination is not enough. She has to seek others' help, even surrendering her very self in the process. Moreover, Martha needs courage to face ECT, both the treatment and its effects. She knows the procedure could have significant memory loss, thereby dramatically altering who she is. Yet she chooses it, not recklessly, but rather as a consequence of evaluating it, noting that if she stays on her present course, she will destroy herself as well. ECT at least holds the promise of release.

Martha's case richly illustrates the complexities which attend the life of hope. She does the right thing—keeps active and follows doctor's orders—and yet she still succumbs to depression. Her autobiographical account paints in detail a landscape few of us ever really see, firsthand or secondhand, and teaches a vital lesson to all who would hope. Doing the "right" things, especially as we first conceive them, does not guarantee hope's success. Additionally, even as hoping stretches us, it makes us vulnerable. Indeed, the life of hope sometimes requires letting go—of habits and preestablished goals—and surrendering a part of ourselves while we open up to the agency of others. For Martha, this is extremely difficult, because her habits of self-determination are so strong. She wants—indeed, expects—to be able to cure herself. But her own therapy requires acknowledging that as biological organisms, we sometimes face conditions (such as her illness) which lie beyond our control. Martha must courageously acknowledge her limits and surrender a part of herself if she is to keep hope alive.

Though courage can prove a vital resource to persistence and resourcefulness, it too draws on them as resources to ensure its success. Expansion of agency bolsters our confidence, thereby making us more willing and better able to face trying obstacles. Habits of persistence enable us to resist the impetuous demands of impatience, thereby avoiding unnecessary risks. They also foster our resolve and control, and so prevent us from capitulating to fear. During his first semester at Brown, Cedric takes most of his classes pass-fail, fearing that he will otherwise crumble under the pressure. He struggles considerably, yet by second semester, he feels secure enough to take more challenging courses for real grades. He gives himself space to adjust and adapt, and he grows stronger because of this. Consequently, persistence and resourcefulness can themselves contribute to courage.

We might be tempted to prioritize our habits of hope. Surely, without the courage to act, we would fail to develop or effectively employ habits. Yet we must also acknowledge that our resourcefulness fuels our confidence and courage; the more we are able to do, the more willing we are to try new, even arduous, tasks. Consequently, we should not give absolute priority to courage or to any of the other habits of hope. To do so would be to overlook the fact that our habits are usually in flux and capable of further development. Though every habit indicates that we have acquired an ability to structure our energy, that ability can be reinforced or consolidated through repetition of similar acts; it can also be developed into even more complex modes of acting. Ideally, habits of hope reinforce one another. Cedric's persistence and courage are inextricably interwoven with each other. Similarly, Martha's courage is tied to her resourcefulness and determination, each one growing off the development of the others. This is often, however, not the case. Red, for instance, is resourceful and even attentive. He has connections which enable him to get goods from the outside, and he is always alert to current conditions. Nevertheless, he lacks the courage to direct his abilities toward hoping. As we shall see, Andy's hoping inspires him to take that extra step, but Red still remains capable of fuller development of each of these habits, especially in concert with one another. Orchestrating habits of hope itself produces, as I will argue, a hopeful character.

To summarize, courage involves taking risks, but if it is to be a part of practical hoping, it must be an informed or intelligent risk taking. We must thus nurture attention to actual conditions—including our own abilities—in formulating hope's ends. Furthermore, we must be willing to act under the guidance of these ends, testing their desirability and realizability by attending to changing conditions and emerging consequences. Throughout this process, we draw on and expand habits of persistence and resourcefulness. Yet without the courage to act as if, our pursuit of hopes occurs simply in thought. Its promises, then, remain imaginary.

Habits of Hope and Particular Hopes

Courage, persistence, and resourcefulness provide the general framework of habits for hoping. They function as the primary means by which we pursue and realize our hopes. Frequently, as we have noted, supporting habits need to be acquired or developed. Before leaving the topic of habits of hope, we need to discuss more fully their interrelations and development. First, we have already discussed James's four practical maxims for developing flexible habits: we must decisively and persistently take advantage of every opportunity to develop our habits, keeping our faculty of effort alive every day so that we maintain control over our own abilities. Second, we should recognize that habits, especially habits of hope, are not developed de novo. Most of us have acquired some skills in being patient and seeking new means which expand our agency. As interacting organisms, we have a plethora of habits we constantly use in coping with and transforming our environments. We also often adapt them when they inhibit rather than foster smooth interaction, recognizing that habits can frustrate as well as reinforce one another. Moreover, our growth requires the ability to develop complex habits of integrating and reconstructing habits, as occurs in the project of the self. Acquisition of any one habit thus occurs in the context of other operative habits and so involves not only origination of new abilities but also further development or reconstruction of established ones.

Habits, then, are developed on the ground of other habits. Additionally, the social environments in which we live condition both their acquisition and growth. Especially since habits are functions of individuals interacting with environments, our abilities depend on the resources, direction, and support available in our environments. Other people play an especially important role in nurturing our habits. We noted above, for instance, that Rose of Sharon's ability to hope stems from her relationship with Ma.[20] As Aristotle argues, we develop habits, both as children and adults, by modeling the behavior of others. While we infuse our activities with a good deal of imaginative and personal adaptation, parents, teachers, friends, colleagues—even enemies—map out modes of activity which guide and condition our own. Though they ideally support our habits, other people can also, of course, impede them. Barbara Jennings does her best to bring Cedric up among the people of her church, protecting him from the influence of his father's ways, and Cedric himself must resist the damaging force of the violent and demoralizing behavior around him at Ballou. While growing up with good habits is the best way to acquire them, this is not always possible; education thus performs a vital role. In any case, readjustment of habits is needed as we face a changing environment.

The preceding points apply to habits in general. What is distinctive about habits of hope is that we cultivate and focus them on future goods which are arduous yet possible. Since they are defined in relation to these ends, their value as means depends at least to some degree on our ability to procure them. Clearly, our habits of hope gain or lose force as a consequence of our pursuit of particular hopes. For one thing, as habits utilized in hoping they are typically developed or expanded when we are engaged in the activity of hoping. We can, for instance, focus already established habits on our particular hopes. Suppose my ability to persist has largely been nurtured in order to retain past values, norms, and structures. When faced with a personally significant end, such as completing a book, I can transform this into a habit of hope by shifting my end-in-view from preservation to development. This is by no means an easy task; success in making the change itself depends largely on our other habits, such as the ability to intelligently adapt means to ends. Yet, especially when they promise what restores or promotes personal growth and integrity, hopes have enormous attractive power. As ends-in-view they provide a focal point in relation to which our energies can be directed. Motivated by hope's end, then, we can refocus our energies and channel them toward establishing future rather than past goods.

Though developed through particular acts, habits attain an independence from them. A habit's independence can be either good or bad, depending on its consequences. Once acquired, habits take on a life of their own such that, as Dewey notes, they are insistent and self-perpetuating.

Repetition, of course, can cement any habit, making it inflexible. In such cases, habits acquire a force we either do not or cannot resist. The more deeply and inflexibly entrenched they are, the more they lead rather than serve us. Nevertheless, intelligent formation and maintenance keeps habits flexible. Then their independence from particular acts does not frustrate our attempts but proves a source of sustenance and reconstruction. They either enable us to reconstruct other habits or are themselves fluid enough to be reconstructed. In either case, these habits sustain us and so enable us to survive, and perhaps transcend, the various trials and travails of life.

How, then, does the success or failure of particular hopes affect our habits of hope? Realization of hope's end, like that of any other end, leads to a consummation which both satisfies and produces smooth (or smoother) successful action. Of course, no consummation is final and no satisfaction absolute. Changing circumstances require employment of newly acquired abilities, as well as acquisition and development of others. Successful hoping involves transcending antecedent limitations by expanding one's own abilities through either their further development or their coordination with other agencies. Hope's consummation, then, not only marks a completion of previous activities; it also provides a basis for future growth and hoping. It thus signifies both restoration and renewal.

Even well-established habits of hope, however, can fail to secure a desired end. While habits of hope aim to make hoping more practical, they cannot eradicate the risk and indeterminacy involved in transcending original conditions. They provide anchors and resources, but these are not guarantees. Try as we might, realization is often contingent on forces other than our own, and so our limits can be stretched but not eliminated. Failure, whether partial or complete, arouses consciousness; indeed, consciousness functions primarily as the reconstruction of impeded interaction. We are then drawn to attend to conditions and consequences in light of which we determine whether to retain, reconstruct, or seek to eliminate particular habits. If we determine that our original end is faulty in the sense that it is unrealizable or undesirable, then we will typically seek to modify that end and, if necessary, our means. We might also recognize our own habits as too restricting and so seek to alter or replace them. In either case, intelligent assessment of means in relation to ends, and vice versa, provides the basis for their transformation.

Difficulty or failure prompts some people to give up their hopes and simply revert to old ways. Pursuits which fail sometimes convince us that we were wrong to hope in the first place. Such a response may be warranted, especially if we pursued foolish hopes which could not be realized by *any* individual or collective agency. At other times, when failure is due to the absence or inadequacy of supporting habits which can be developed, we are right to persist in hoping. In such cases we should not simply discard our hopes, but determine whether and how we can nurture or attain the proper means. When faced with failure, we can also, of course, modify the end, as when we change our hope for recovery to a hope that we can live our final days with dignity.

How individuals respond to the failure (and at times success) of particular hopes depends most on a mixture of considerations about the realizability and desirability of the end, along with an assessment of their abilities. More simply put, their response is conditioned by their other ends and habits. Hopes, of course, vary in importance, though typically the more that is at stake or has been invested, the greater its value to us. Facing possible death, a cancer patient likely pours himself into his hope for recovery. If a particular treatment fails, he may transform his hope or collapse in despair. Some people crumble while others find new reservoirs of energy when faced with vexing trials. Especially important to one's response to particular hopes is what in the previous chapter I called the "regnant habit" of the self. This habit weaves the different strands of the self together. If we lack or inadequately organize our habits (in conjunction with our ends), our desire and ability to respond with hope will be impaired. Yet, we *can* survive even the most dismal of failures. The extent to which we do so, however, depends on that final dimension of hope: hopefulness.

I have emphasized the development of habits of hope throughout this chapter. Most of us possess many of the needed habits, though in varying degrees. Hoping is not restricted to individual acts but can be an ongoing project. Its goal is the acquisition, further development, and coordination of our various habits in light of hope's ends. In the process, we grow and transcend antecedent limitations, expanding our abilities as we hope. Hope's transcendence, though, is always conditioned, both by the ends we pursue and the means we employ. Apart from consideration of the desirability and the realizability of the end, hoping proves foolhardy; ignorance of the relation between ends and means prevents the sort of intelligent appraisal of each which fosters practicality. Though hoping promises to deliver us from current conditions, we cannot leap into the future without the springboard of our past. Nevertheless, hoping *is* a form of leaping, as well as a form of growing and expanding. In the next chapter, we move from hope's first form of practicality to its second—that is, from its realizability to its capacity to sustain and nurture us. Hopefulness provides the focus for this discussion, but as we shall see, it is intimately interwoven with hope's other dimensions.

CHAPTER *Three*

Hopefulness

I N THE powerful final scene of *The Grapes of Wrath*, the Joads find shelter from rain and rising waters in a barn located on high ground. Upon entering, though, they discover the barn is already occupied by a young boy and his starving father. The boy explains that his pa has not had anything to eat for days and pleads with the family to help. Though Ma is the first to respond, reassuring the boy they will figure something out, Rose of Sharon proves the real agent of hope. By this point, her own particular hopes have crumbled. Connie has abandoned her, and her baby has been stillborn. The death of her child, around whom she formulated her hopes and dreams, presents a powerful blow to her future. Nevertheless, she calmly and deliberately nurses the dying man, a stranger. Steinbeck ends the book by noting that "[s]he looked up and across the barn, and her lips came together and smiled mysteriously" (Steinbeck 453).

How are we to understand Rose's action? What does her mysterious smile mean? Many interpretations have been offered, but I propose that it expresses a newfound hopefulness. With hopefulness comes a sense of calm and confidence, the kind expressed by a smile. Yet, can we really describe Rose of Sharon as hopeful? Not only has she flip-flopped between hope's exuberance and the mortification of fear throughout the book, but by the end she seems entirely bereft of her own hopes. Nevertheless, I will argue not only that Rose of Sharon is hopeful in the book's last scene, but also that she has been developing hopefulness throughout the story. She becomes hopeful by developing an openness to rewarding future possibilities. This is largely due to Ma's influence, so we can perhaps more accurately say she shares in Ma's hopefulness. We thus see a glimpse of the social nature of hopefulness; it does not live alone or in isolation from the nurturing agencies of others.

In *The Shawshank Redemption*, Red undergoes a transformation similar to Rose's. For most of the story, he considers himself an institutional man, one who is comfortable living within the strict boundaries of prison life. He fears life on the outside, sensing that he has no place there. Although he carefully observes life around him, he does so not to improve his situation but to avoid trouble. Unsurprisingly, while he expresses a sense of awe at Andy's hopefulness, he is repeatedly skeptical of it. In the film adaptation of King's novella, for instance, Red warns Andy that "[h]ope is a dangerous thing. Drive a man insane. It's got no place here [in prison]. Better get used to the idea" (Darabont 63). By the end of the story, though, Red has been released from prison and heads off to build a life with his friend Andy. The stirring last lines of the book express his newfound sense of hope:

> I find I am excited, so excited I can hardly hold the pencil in my trembling hand. I think it is the excitement that only a free man can feel, a free man starting a long journey whose conclusion is uncertain.
> I hope Andy is down there.
> I hope I can make it across the border.
> I hope to see my friend and to shake his hand.
> I hope the Pacific is as blue as it has been in my dreams.
> I *hope*. (King 107)

Though once critical of his friend's hopefulness, Red is now inspired by it. Just as Rose of Sharon draws on Ma's hopefulness, so too does Red on Andy's.

Both Rose of Sharon and Red change into what I argue are more hopeful people. Their transformations occur primarily through interacting with their more obviously hopeful counterparts, Ma and Andy. Steinbeck and King's stories thus illuminate hope's dynamic and developmental nature. My goal in this chapter is to examine more closely such development, particularly by focusing on the third and final dimension of the life of hope: hopefulness. In the process, I will make two central points. First, hopefulness is both dependent and independent of hope's other dimensions. The second point concerns hope's second form of practicality—that is, its capacity to nurture growth and creative transformation. Hopefulness is the primary and vital embodiment of this capacity, especially as it enables us to face adversity and dark times.

Rose of Sharon and Red each show signs of fundamental change in their orientation toward life's trials. Though both initially focus on their limitations, they later discover more fully their capacity to expand, grow, and creatively meet changing circumstances. In the process, they escape the trappings of despair. Martha and Cedric also struggle with despair and disappointment; the source of their rescue is their ability to nurture and coordinate their habits of hope, with the assistance of loved ones. Indeed, hopefulness grows out of and yet is more than our other habits of hope; it is itself a complex habit which synchronizes our abilities into a powerful source of support and creativity. As I argued in the introduction, to understand hope we must acknowledge its need for practical grounds and resources *as well as* its productive and creative capacity. The challenge in discussing the life of hope is recognizing the legitimacy of each dynamic; together they account for hope as conditioned transcendence.

In the next chapter, I will discuss more fully hope's meaning as conditioned transcendence. Presupposed by such a discussion is careful treatment of hopefulness, especially as it both relates to and differs from particular hopes and habits of hope. I will argue that hopefulness, understood as an orientation of energetic readiness, depends for its development upon, but also exhibits an independence from, the pursuit of particular hopes. As we should expect, given its embeddedness in the means-end continuum, it is thus both a means and an end in hoping.

The Nature of Hopefulness

In hopefulness we encounter perhaps the most elusive yet vibrant dynamic of hoping. Like happy people, the hopeful are inspiring and energizing to be around; they seem to possess an almost mysterious power, from the perspective of those who lack it, which enables them to rise above circumstances. By contrast, the hopeless have a dull, lifeless quality about them; their environment weighs heavily upon them, imprisoning them within its confines. Being hopeful means greeting adversity with confidence and resolve, if not eagerness, rather than shrinking away from or simply accepting it. Moreover, the examples of Red and Rose of Sharon suggest its infectious quality; their own hopefulness is sparked by Andy's and Ma's. But what is hopefulness, especially as it relates to hope's other dimensions?

We can provide both a simple and a complex answer. The simple answer is that hopefulness is an attitude of energetic openness and readiness to promising possibilities. Armed with this attitude, we face life's trials as opportunities to test our abilities and overcome our limitations. Yet this is too cheery a picture, overlooking the extent to which the hopeful must often grapple with dark forces. Hopefulness can smile with joy, but it can also grit its teeth in the face of life's messiest, most painful circumstances. The more complex account of hopefulness, then, recognizes its dynamic nature and sometimes checkered history, affected as it is by its complex interrelation with particular hopes and habits of hope. Both of these other dimensions affect hopefulness— particularly its development—but it sustains and nurtures them as well. Careful consideration of the interweaving of all of hope's dimensions is a primary goal of this chapter.

Sometimes we describe people as hopeful simply in light of the fact that they engage in hoping. While we may be hopeful on occasion, there is a deeper sense of hopefulness which indicates more than the ability to pursue particular hopes. Hopefulness is more properly a

distinctive *way* of hoping which some possess and others lack, albeit in
varying degrees. We can highlight the unique features of hopefulness
by contrasting it with particular hopes. When we pursue particular
hopes, our activity is aimed at an end generated in response to a problematic situation. That end provides a determinate point relative to
which hoping can be justified. Insofar as we determine the end (together with its means) to be both desirable and realizable, we have
grounds to justify the risk and expenditure of energy. Of course, this
end need not be singular or isolated; indeed, we have seen that formulating alternative hopes promotes adaptability. Yet pursuing a particular
hope remains defined by that end or cluster of ends.

Hopefulness, by contrast, lacks the focus on an end; it may en-
compass or embrace ends, but its nature and power are largely independent of them. Rather, hopefulness is an attitude or general
orientation toward the future which defines how we respond to life's
trials. As said above, it is an energetic openness to promising possibilities which enables us to think, act, and live within a rich horizon of
meaning. This horizon is dynamic, with a blend of determinacy and
indeterminacy. On the one hand, it has enough determinacy that we
sense there are concrete goods which we might pursue—specific ends
which are continuous with ourselves and so meaningful to us. Yet this
determinacy is coupled with adequate openness that we might truly
change and develop. Time is fluid and fertile for the hopeful, indicating room for growth and experimentation. Indeed, hopefulness opens
up an expansive horizon with lots of fresh air and plenty of room for
energies to spread. Consequently, it enables us to transcend the present even as we live in and through it. Hopefulness then involves a
complex sense of open time, imaginative space, and meaningful possibilities for action.

That hopefulness indicates an openness toward the future may
seem obvious and insignificant, until we reflect how easy it is to be
caught up in the past. Muley Graves in *The Grapes of Wrath*, for instance,
cannot break free from the past in order to hope. His anger at the
bankers who have taken over the farmland prevents him from going
with his family to California. Instead, he haunts his homeland like a
graveyard ghost.[1] Consequently, Muley remains stuck in a present

defined entirely by the past. Though circumstances have changed, Muley cannot escape the grip of previously established values and routines. More ghost than living being, he later also refuses the Joads's offer to travel with them to California.

The temporal orientation of Steinbeck's characters reveals much about their hopefulness. Muley is oriented to the past and repeatedly refuses to move forward. Tom, Casy, and Ma also show distinctive relations to time. At first, and largely a consequence of his time in prison, Tom focuses only on the present. He does not think; he does.[2] He focuses on immediacy, neither worrying nor planning, since such activities require attention to what lies beyond the scope of the present. Thus, in early scenes Tom's typical comment is "Let's eat" or "Let's do it." By contrast, Jim Casy is always thinking or talking about what he's thinking. While Tom is primarily an actor, Casy is primarily a thinker. From the start, though, Ma is more complicated than either Tom or Casy. She thinks and plans, but she also acts in a timely fashion. Yet, though she hopes for a better life in California, Ma also frequently worries about what the future holds.

As the story progresses, each of these three characters affects the others. Early on, Ma shares with Tom her worries about what lies ahead in California. She faces the future, yet in this situation she lacks knowledge of actual conditions. Ma thus speculates about numerous possibilities, including bad ones, and so worries. Tom tells her to take things one step at a time, as he learned to do in prison. His advice draws her in from the far reaches of the future. Shortly thereafter, when her son Al worries about what lies ahead, Ma shares Tom's lesson with him. She explains that "[u]p ahead they's a thousan' lives we might live, but when it comes, it'll on'y be one. If I go ahead on all of 'em, it's too much" (Steinbeck 125). We might conclude that Ma has shifted her orientation from the future to the present; indeed, she suggests as much by preaching the lesson that we have to take things a step at a time. This interpretation, however, overlooks the fact that she still maintains her various hopes for a better life in California. Thus, what changes is the *way* Ma approaches the future: taking things a step at a time ensures that fear and worry do not close her off from possibilities. It means she remains open to possibilities *which are meaningful and can be realized*.

Tom and Casy undergo similar transformations. Casy eventually complements his philosophical concern for the human family by acting to benefit the labor cause in California. Unfortunately, though, he is killed as a consequence of his action. Tom, on the other hand, changes from one who acts too quickly to one who acts thoughtfully. After killing Casy's murderer, Tom has to hide in a cave to avoid capture by the police. When Ma later visits him, he tells her he has "been thinkin' a hell of a lot" and has decided to continue Casy's crusade. In the process of sharing his plans with her, he surprises himself, noting "God, I'm talking like Casy. Comes of thinkin' about him so much" (Steinbeck 419). Having integrated Casy's ability to think on a broad scale with his own propensity to act, Tom leaves the family to help the labor movement.

What can we learn from these characters? Ma's transformation proves the most informative, for she deepens her orientation toward the future by integrating it with attention and concern for the present. By the end of the story, Tom and Casy are off the scene. Yet Ma remains as the family's formidable center. Her typical response to adversity is "We'll figger somepin out." When Pa is on the brink of despair, complaining that he is no good, Ma reprimands him by saying,

> Man, he lives in jerks—baby born an' a man dies, an' that's a jerk. . . . Woman, it's all one flow, like a stream, little eddies, little waterfalls, but the river, it goes right on. Woman looks at it like that. We ain't gonna die out. People is goin' on—changin' a little, maybe, but goin' right on. (Steinbeck 423)

Though she may here lack the ebullience we might expect from hopefulness, Ma has the calm confidence of hope and embodies the spirit that adversity can be overcome and turned to an advantage.

Ma, then, steers a course distinct from Muley, Tom, and Jim Casy. She is neither wedded to the past as Muley is, nor absorbed in the present like Tom. Her openness to the future is, unlike Casy's, tempered by her ability to act. She thus embodies what is distinctive about hopefulness. Hopefulness is an open orientation to the future, but not one that is blind to the present or paralyzed by multiple options. Similarly, it is not an openness to possibilities per se. Even one who despairs can acknowledge possibilities yet to be actualized. What defines his despair is that he thinks these are all either neutral or bad in light of what he wants; his horizon of meaning has been poisoned and transformed into a background of darkness. Thus, hopefulness is an openness to possibilities that are *meaningful* and *promising for us*. Complementing this openness is an energetic *readiness* to find, await, and pursue possibilities which suggest desired goods. Hopefulness, then, actively aims at future goods *and* embraces the growth required for pursuing them. Hopeful people are not simply those who pursue hopes. They are those who develop a complex habit which prepares them to hope in response to problems and opportunities.

Because of its focus on good possibilities, hopefulness is frequently confused with optimism. Though the two have commonalities, distinguishing them is important if we are to recognize the active ingredient in hopefulness. Each is an orientation toward future goods; what primarily differentiates them is the extent to which the victory of goodness over possible evils is guaranteed. Optimism faces the future confident that goodness will win the day. Our own past experience may foster this confidence; a more complicated faith in a preestablished harmony of the universe supports Leibnizian philosophical optimism. For the optimist, present evils may be trying, but they are either transitory or serve to promote some eventual higher good. The key to optimism is the belief that goodness *will* triumph, that things will work out for the best.

Hopefulness moves toward future goodness, but nevertheless lacks any guarantee of it. Cornel West summarizes its difference from optimism as follows: "Optimism adopts the role of the spectator who surveys the evidence in order to infer that things are going to get better. . . . Hope entails the stance of the participant who actively struggles against the evidence in order to change [our conditions]" (West xii). A hopeful person is uncertain that goodness will prevail but nevertheless commits to investing in its cause. Consequently, hopefulness is best identified not with optimism but with meliorism, described by Dewey as the position that "at least there is a sufficient basis of goodness in life and its conditions so that by thought and earnest effort we may constantly make better things" [sic]. Though it may appear virtually identical with optimism, Dewey argues that meliorism "attacks optimism on the ground that it encourages the fatalistic contentment with things as they are; what is needed is the frank recognition of evils, not for the sake of accepting them as final, but for the sake of arousing energy to remedy them" (MW 7:294).[3] So understood, hopefulness differs from optimism in having risk and *involvement* at its heart; goodness *may* win the day *if* we act on behalf of its cause.[4] A melioristic hopefulness acknowledges that good possibilities may *not* win the day, especially if we fail to support and realize them. It indicates, then, a propensity to participate, to play an active role in bringing about future goods. Optimism, by contrast, carries a spectator's assurance that things will work out. There is no requirement of personal investment, no genuine acting *as if*. Consequently, optimism may comfort us, as it does the philosophical Pangloss in Voltaire's *Candide*, but it does not prompt us to action. The difference can be summarized by noting that while the optimist views the world through rose-colored glasses, the hopeful person acts to make the world a rose-colored place.

Hopefulness is not simply a way of seeing; it is a way of acting and of being. It indicates the ability to keep hope alive by ensuring that our horizon of meanings remains vibrant and dynamic. Without hopefulness, this horizon risks becoming empty or dominated by possibilities of suffering. If we grow detached from it through the loss of energy or the failure of imagination, we become constrained, limited to past and present meanings rather than moved by possibilities of growth.

Pragmatically understood, hopefulness is rooted in habits, the seat of our activity and agency. Attentiveness and patience nurture openness, while resourcefulness fosters readiness. Courage enables us to remain open and ready, even when everything around us seems to fall into darkness. Hopefulness then grows out of habits of hope; indeed, it too functions as a habit of hope. Before discussing this point more fully, though, I wish to sharpen our account of hopefulness by contrasting it with despair and hopelessness. This will complete our preliminary sketch of hopefulness and prepare the ground for exploring its relation to the self and the other dimensions of hope.

Hopefulness and Despair

Just as its commitment to active involvement differentiates hopefulness from optimism, so too does it distinguish hopefulness from despair.

One who despairs is cut off from promising possibilities, disconnected from powers of growth and from the ideals which move us. Like hopefulness, despair is an orientation,[5] albeit one which traps and limits us. From its perspective, time either hardens into the deadening force of repetitive routine or simply ushers in ever greater evils. In such a case, the external world crowds around us, leaving us no room to move and no window of escape. Our horizon of meaning becomes poisoned, relegating us to live in a dark, cold, empty yet all-consuming space. Our abilities then remain frozen in the face of mounting difficulties so that we feel there is nothing we can do. When we are hopeless, hopes oppress rather than liberate us, for they indicate how far out of reach, if not impossible, all desires and goods are. Everything becomes bleak and weighs heavily upon us so that we are immobilized and unable to summon the energy to escape. Though others may be capable of pursuing hopes, this path is closed to us when we despair.

Despair arises in a number of different contexts and manifests itself with different degrees of severity. Of the individuals we have discussed, Red and Martha grapple with it the most. Careful consideration of the trials with which each must contend highlights the various dimensions of despair. Both Red and Martha's cases importantly show that despair is not a final or fatal condition; at the same time, they demonstrate the need not only to develop habits of hope, but also to actively coordinate them. Hopefulness can pierce through the gloom of despair, just as despair can darken its light.

Red's despair, like that of many of his fellow inmates, is largely defined by routine and restriction. Life in prison proves a rich breeding ground for despair. Red notes how sharply Andy's hopefulness contrasts with the general hopelessness of the other Shawshank inmates. In reflecting on his friend, Red recognizes with a sense of awe that Andy

> had something that most of the other prisoners, myself included, seemed to lack. Call it a sense of equanimity, or a feeling of inner peace, maybe even a constant and unwavering faith that someday the long nightmare would end. Call it what you want to call it, Andy Dufresne always seemed to have his act together.

There was none of that sullen desperation about him that seems to afflict most lifers after a while; you could never smell hopelessness on him. (King 56)

By contrast, most other prisoners—including Red himself—become institutionalized. This is not surprising since survival in prison requires learning and respecting the routines which define prison life. Routine becomes the primary form of stability in a world where the anger or caprice of guards and administrators can lead to increased misery, if not death.

The more a prisoner comes to define both his abilities and his well-being in light of prison life, the more he becomes institutionalized. Such a prisoner, Red explains, eventually fears the very freedom for which he once longed. Life on the outside constantly changes, but inside it stays relatively the same. Adaptation to a "free" life becomes increasingly daunting, especially for those serving lengthy sentences. As a consequence, many prisoners tend to cling to the familiarity of prison life. Thus, though they may persist in hoping for release, many also come to believe that even if they could win their freedom they would not know how to survive beyond prison walls. Red himself confesses that "I couldn't get along on the outside" (King 79). He explains that many prisoners who are released quickly commit crimes that land them back in jail. Why? Because they crave to be back inside, "[b]ack where [they understand] how things work" (King 83). They are thus truly prisoners of an institution, not knowing how to survive beyond it.

Consequently, when Andy shares his hope to escape Shawshank and flee to Mexico, Red unsurprisingly dismisses it as a pipe dream. Even if Andy could escape, he muses, survival on the outside would pose overwhelming challenges. Red acknowledges that he was initially inspired by Andy's hope, but "by that night in my cell I felt like a prisoner again. The whole idea seemed absurd, and that mental image of blue water and white beaches seemed more cruel than foolish—it dragged at my brain like a fishhook" (King 80). Red accepts his own institutionalization, explaining that "[w]hen you take away a man's freedom and teach him to live in a cell, he seems to lose his ability to think in dimensions" (King 83). Though Andy's hope at first energizes him, he later finds himself unable to sustain it and so slips back into the comforting but deadening familiarity of prison routine.

What does Red teach us about despair? First, one can despair and yet live a life with structure and habits. The institutionalized prisoner has a routine which defines his life; the problem, and the reason he despairs, is that the routine is so fixed and restricting that it precludes the pursuit of promising possibilities. Red notes the dull look in the eyes of prisoners, a look which reflects that there is no life or choice beyond the tight grip of routine. By contrast, he observes that "[Andy's] eyes never got that dull look. He never developed the walk that men get when the day is over and they are going back to their cells for another endless night—that flatfooted, hump-shouldered walk. Andy walked with his shoulders squared, and his step was always light, as if he were heading home" (King 73). One who despairs moves along, but not forward. Whether his life is typified by a whirl of change or monotonous repetition, salvific or extensional goods remain out of reach.

In dealing with her depression, Martha also grapples with despair. In her case, though, despair grows not from the roots of routine, but rather from their absence. Her depression debilitates her so that she is no longer able to perform many of the tasks she once did with ease. She increasingly longs for the comfort routine gives, yet she loses the sense of familiarity that comes with repetition and sinks deeper into the darkness of despair. Despite this difference, what is common to the despair Red and Martha experience is a sense of disconnection—from both the horizon of meaning and from their own empowering agency—which drains them of energy and vitality, dulling and restricting their activity in the world. Especially as her condition worsens, Martha becomes increasingly disconnected from others and her own abilities.

Although depression and despair are not the same thing, it is not surprising that they attend one another. To be depressed is quite literally to be pressed down by everything around us. This state naturally contributes to or derives from the shrinking of abilities and feelings of disconnection which typify despair. Psychologists themselves disagree about which is the cause and which the effect. There is likely no single formula that applies to all cases. Sometimes depression is a symptom of despair. Having lost the horizon of meaning and so a connection with promising possibilities, we become depressed and drained of energy. In Martha's case, though, depression seems to give rise to despair. As her autobiographical account begins, she is already suffering from depression (a condition with which her grandmother struggled throughout her life) even though she does not yet realize its severity. Part of her recovery comes from recognizing that depression is a serious illness rather than an attitude over which she has control. Despair, like hopefulness, is an orientation and so less an illness than a way of facing problems and responding to difficulties. Martha herself is generally hopeful, possessing habits of persistence, courage, and resourcefulness. Yet she also harbors the seeds of despair within herself. Though we typically do not fall into despair deliberately, our habits can make us susceptible to it. Once caught in its grip, it is very difficult to escape, for despair usually impairs the very abilities we need to fight it.

At first, Martha's depression manifests itself primarily in sleeplessness. Over time, this has the cumulative effect of leaving her feeling "slightly off." She finds herself unable to do simple house chores and increasingly reluctant to interact socially. Though she tries a variety of medicines, none brings lasting relief. Martha loses more and more control of her life and begins to feel the weight of depression and despair. While at a religious retreat, she gets a flat tire. Her immediate response is to complain that she cannot escape bad things even on a retreat. She reacts as though one bad apple spoils the whole bunch, reflecting that "I act like this one thing has the power to obliterate the goodness of this experience [at the retreat]. It's like diffusing a bit of black paint into a totally white space" (51). Consequently, her horizon shows obvious signs of being poisoned. Martha's depression spreads insidiously, affecting not only her sleep habits but also how she perceives, interprets, and responds to events. Gradually this wears on her so much that, especially during her sleepless nights, she finds that "time moves more slowly, and the fact that everyone else is at rest makes me feel so separate, so alone. I long to recover what comes so easily to everyone else" (61). She begins to feel increasingly disconnected from both her own agency—her own ability to live as she is used to living—and from others. Even worse, she feels that she is dragging her family and friends down with her. Her life becomes dominated by emptiness and numbness, until she gets to the point that she contends that "[a]ll escapes are illusory—distractions, sleep, drugs, doctors, answers, hope" (99). She considers this her own personal hell, defined by a debilitating sense of interminability.

Martha is not without habits which support her in seeking and undergoing proper treatment, yet she still brushes up against despair. The numbness and emptiness of her depression threaten to drain her life of all meaning. She finds herself weakened and disconnected to the point that she contemplates suicide as a possible release from it all. While I do not wish to suggest that Martha creates her own despair, she does harbor tendencies which bring her more firmly within its grip. In particular, her growing sense of disconnection and inability is exacerbated by the expectations she has of herself. As a trained therapist, she believes she should be able to heal herself. She overestimates her own abilities, or at least demands too much from herself. Martha slowly begins to recognize the debilitating effect this has on her. She assesses her situation as follows: "I think about how my anxiety often comes from the wish to be totally in control—even of things I can't possibly control. Who do I think I am? God?" (Manning 48). Even when Martha turns to her doctors, she still struggles in accepting her limits. Later, she explains that Dr. Kay Jamison, her psychotherapist, "tells me I have a very moralistic view of depression as a personal weakness and a condition under one's control. She counters with her belief that my depression is an illness. Her emphasis on the biological aspects of depression is surprising to me, coming from a fellow psychologist" (Manning 70). In addition to accepting the severity of her depression, Martha must also adjust her expectations and orientation toward a cure and recovery. Though depression poses enormous challenges, and ECT presents considerable risks that few of us would readily embrace, she has to learn to temper her self-reliance with the sort of humility which acknowledges and trusts the assistance of others. Without this, Martha would have little hope of recovery and would soon find herself consigned to a permanent hell of despair.

Both Martha and Red's encounters with despair show it to be a stultifying orientation infected with a horizon marked by disconnection and paralysis. When they feel hopeless, the horizon of meaning in which each lives is dull and limited, drained of promising possibilities. The primary condition of despair is not simply disconnection from specific goods or hopes; rather it is disconnection from the agencies which sustain, nurture, and enable us to pursue such hopes. Disconnection is most extreme, however, when it severs us from our horizon of meaning, for then all goods are drained of their power to attract and move us. Even if we could achieve them, their goodness would be insignificant to us.

Despair's disconnection can result from any number of causes. Sometimes it has its roots in our own behavior, and sometimes it is the direct result of external powers. Natural forces affecting the fragility of our bodies or environment can cut us off from habits, hope, and each other. Martha's depression demonstrates this when it leads to sleeplessness and contributes to her anxiety and increasing sense of despair. Victor E. Frankl provides a startling example of *deliberate* disconnection in recounting his own experience in a concentration camp.[6] He explains how the Nazis effectively stripped prisoners of everything signifying their past lives: families and friends were separated, clothing and all other possessions were taken, and all bodily hair was shorn away. Prisoners were thus left with virtually no trace of their lives or their selves. They had nothing but their own bare survival. Each prisoner was pitted against all the rest in the desperate quest to survive amidst squalid conditions and capricious guards who could show kindness one moment and unthinkable violence the next. Human connection of the sort that provides support and comradeship was thus all but extinguished in these camps. In the face of such deliberate human (albeit inhuman) isolation and cruelty, Frankl unsurprisingly saw many succumb to despair.

While systematic attacks by others can push us to despair, our own behavior can do the same, especially when we too readily assume that we have accurately ascertained what is and what is not possible. If we lack humility, we may overestimate the determinacy of either our problems or our powers (or both) and, upon failing to secure what we desire, assume we have exhausted all relevant possibilities. In a dark moment before she seriously considers ECT, Martha believes there is no end to her suffering. She wonders, "What wonderful thing could snap me out of this? I have sampled all the possibilities. . . . No good news or good times. Nothing. And all I can think of is the cruelty of it all. And the incapacitating dread that this time I won't come out of it. This time it will never end" (75). Red believes the combination of his circumstances and his own abilities renders hoping a dangerous waste of time; he thus actively avoids it.

Despair results from more than the mere observation of limitations; it is fueled by the sense that these limitations are fixed and permanent. Expenditure of any additional effort is thought to be useless against the irrevocable tyranny of present conditions. In cases like Martha and Red's, difficulties stand implacably before us, taking on an oppressive power that debilitates us. Sometimes, of course, conditions *are* obdurate and incapable of change. As noted in the first chapter, we often only discover their true determinacy by acting *as if*, testing their malleability as well as our own abilities to adapt. If we are already caught in the grip of despair, however, we will likely lack the confidence, energy, or motivation to attempt such activity. If we are not, we may repeatedly try, only to fail and then slip into despair. In either case, if we believe our own abilities incapable of growth and development to meet them, despair will likely take hold. We then find ourselves closed off from possibilities so that our horizon of meaning shrinks to the point of constricting and immobilizing us.

Thus, the hopeless are not simply those who do not hope; they are those for whom hoping becomes an impossibility. Truly these individuals are imprisoned in a drab world of limited opportunities. Without a horizon of meaning rich enough to breed promising possibilities, even the simplest of tasks becomes an onerous difficulty that is either unworthy of our efforts or altogether impossible to achieve. Of course, even when despairing, we might believe that promising goods are impossible for us and yet available to others. Martha's hopes crumble, for instance, as she repeatedly watches medicine after medicine fail to bring her lasting relief. Antidepressants or therapy may effectively curb others' depression, but not her own—and so despair gains a tighter grip on her own life. Similarly, a cancer patient may abandon hope of recovery for herself while still recognizing it as viable for others. As already noted, a good's possibility per se proves insufficient to fuel hope and avoid despair; what matters instead is whether that good is a *real* possibility for the one who hopes. Red finds himself shaking off Andy's hope, saying, "I just couldn't wear that invisible coat [of freedom and hope] the way Andy did" (King 80). Some goods *are in fact* possible for some but not others. Certain therapies may work effectively on one group of patients but fail to help another. In such cases, continued pursuit of that particular form of recovery becomes increasingly impractical. The consequence, though, need not be despair. Especially when fueled by hopefulness, we may also formulate and pursue new hopes or patiently conserve our energy until new possibilities arrive.

The belief or fact that promising goods are impossible for us only exacerbates the disconnection implicit in despair. In such a case, we are separated not only from promising goods but also from the companionship of our fellow human beings. We thus find little or no comfort in their company and become increasingly isolated and cut off from the rest of the world. Martha watches as she becomes a stranger amidst her own family and home; she attempts to avoid them to minimize the feeling of humiliation and helplessness. "I love them for caring, but I want to run from it. I have lost their language, their facility with words that convey feelings. I am in new territory and feel like a foreigner in theirs" (64). Especially if we recognize the importance of the connection of agency, this kind of disconnection only serves to further circumscribe the limitations of our agency. When we despair we are trapped in a constricted world and, like the institutional man, incapable of escaping from it. Our own limited abilities cannot secure desired goods; matters are only made worse when we cannot reach out to others for assistance. As I will argue in the next section, however, this sort of disconnection can and needs to be actively *avoided* and also *counteracted* through social means. We should deliberately reach out to those in despair, offering our support and resources to help them rediscover hope when we can. Even so, we must recognize that once someone drifts into the downward spiral of despair, it is often difficult to find, recognize, or accept assistance.[7] We thus should not underestimate the debilitating power of despair.

While despair signifies paralyzing disconnection, hopefulness indicates connectedness, especially the ability to connect with others when we pursue hopes, and so grounds for more complicated action. The hopeful person is not cut off from her own habits, from the support and assistance others can provide, or from her horizon of meaning. She orients herself to growth, to finding and nurturing conditions which will promote hopes. Rather than abandoning them when they appear beyond her reach, she awaits the emergence of means needed to realize her ends and actively seeks to expand her resources so that she can act when such means become available. She remains open to promising possibilities, both specifically and generally, recognizing that present disconnection can be overcome, especially with the aid of her own active contribution. She fights to keep alive her horizon of meaning. Hopefulness, then, signifies remaining energized *even when particular hopes fail.* The hopeful person does not translate the failure of one hope (even if it is especially dear) into the impossibility of most or all other hopes. Hopefulness then sustains us and enables us to persevere even through difficult times.[8]

Those who maintain connection are able to survive various trials and to resist the slide into despair, actively counteracting its forces. Martha meets her depression and fights her despair with considerable resistance, resourcefulness, and courage. After undergoing ECT, she recognizes the numerous ways her connection with others, fueled by her own efforts as well as those of loved ones, has kept her fighting and led to recovery. Indeed, she realizes how her refusal to give up has been evident all along, especially in reaching out to her doctors. Martha explains that "[g]oing in to see them week after week, awkward and mute and hopeless, was evidence of my fight against finality. Each time I entered their offices I gave silent testimony to the possibility of breaking out of hell" (150). Moreover, she acknowledges how much family, friends, and doctors buoyed her, explaining that "[t]he communication of hope, the administration of gentleness, and the sharing of some part of the self can make a long lonely journey, in all its circuitousness, almost bearable" (151). Even once she begins her recovery, Martha continues to struggle with feelings of disconnection, wanting to withdraw from those around her. She notes, however, that "the people closest to me make that very difficult. I am blessed with such kindness from my family, my friends, my doctors" (170).

The beneficence and love of others buoy Cedric as well. In particular, Barbara's love is manifest as she makes personal sacrifices when needed and encourages him to keep trying in the face of adversity. Her love plays a vital role in nurturing his feeling of connectedness, especially in the face of his own tendency to withdraw from others when the going gets tough. Cedric knows that she is always there to provide him a safety net or springboard whenever he needs it. This, together with the encouragement of his teachers at Ballou, helps him recover from the negative experience at MIT. The faith and love of others helps him avoid turning disappointment into despair.[9]

Similarly, both Andy and Ma demonstrate the power of hopefulness as they undergo their various trials. At one point, a new inmate, Tommy Williams, tells Andy that a former cellmate admitted committing a crime matching the murder of Andy's wife in exact detail. Energized by the prospect of a new trial, Andy pleads with the warden to look more fully into the matter, but his request is denied. He ends up losing control. As a consequence, the warden sentences him to twenty days in solitary confinement, an unusually long time. Not even his privileged status in the prison spares him this extreme punishment. After his time in confinement, Red notices that Andy has changed; he is more subdued and withdrawn. Yet he does not slip into despair. Shortly thereafter, Red says Andy was "wearing his freedom like an invisible coat" (King 73). This coat signifies Andy's refusal to let his immediate environment pull him down. Even after spending such a long time in solitary, he still maintains his capacity to face trials and to act, as Red notes, "as if he were heading home" (King 73). Consequently, Andy survives this dark night without losing his hopefulness.

Ma similarly holds onto her hopefulness as difficulties mount. As noted in the last chapter, Ma refuses to share Pa's defeatist attitude when they cannot find work. Indeed, she repeatedly responds to the numerous trials the family faces with strength and willingness to find a new alternative, drawing variously on her habits of persistence, courage, and resourcefulness. Ma is able to coordinate these habits of hope so that they sustain her even in the face of adversity. Together, her habits constitute her hopefulness as a steadfast and sustaining orientation. First, she has courage to face risks, such as confronting Pa to motivate him to work. She also persists, refusing to give into fear or to allow others to do the same, recognizing that keeping active protects us from such. We see then that her hopefulness consists in and is supported by the coordination of her various habits of hope.

What do Martha, Cedric, Ma, and Andy share which makes them hopeful in contrast to the apparent hopelessness of Red and Muley? Most importantly, none is a prisoner of routine. They have habits—especially habits of hope—which enable them to face the future and to actively pursue hopes. Of course, they each find their hoping challenged; none escapes serious trials and momentary setbacks. Yet, because they are hopeful, they *remain* open to and are able to actively pursue promising possibilities. Martha slips deeply into despair, yet she still maintains the sort of connection with others which buoys her and keeps her in the game. While circumstances can tax our abilities to the breaking point, we can nevertheless arm ourselves with habits which keep alive our agency, our connection to others, and our attachment to promising possibilities. Though some may choose paths of self-destruction and despair, most of us do not. This does not make us immune to despair's force, however. While we do not deliberately throw ourselves into its debilitating whirlpool, we must recognize that some of our habits make us more susceptible to it. We thus must foster productive habits which will enable us to resist it and, when we slip, fight it off. Our greatest security against hopelessness comes from actively promoting habits of hope and nurturing hopefulness.

Doing so, of course, is no small feat. Cedric and Martha face numerous challenges to their hopefulness. Red and Rose of Sharon develop hopefulness, but not without considerable struggle. Of course, their development occurs in relation to the more hopeful characters of Andy and Ma whose abilities prove instrumental in supporting and nurturing them; we thus must not overlook their contribution to Red and Rose's hopefulness. Since we acquire hopefulness and so embody it in varying degrees, a fuller understanding of its nature can be gleaned from further consideration of its different stages and possibilities of development.

Developing Hopefulness

While hopefulness is an orientation of openness, *acting* in a hopeful manner is not necessarily the same as *being* a hopeful person. The difference is primarily the degree to which hopefulness has been developed as a habit. Of course, its development depends, as it does with all habits, upon acting in a particular way; we become hopeful by doing things in a hopeful manner. Yet we can act in a hopeful manner without having habituated hopefulness, especially when interacting with hopeful people. Our own hopefulness is then inspired and modeled after that of others. Moreover, we can be hopeful with respect to some activities but not others. This is not to identify hopefulness with a particular end but rather with a particular set of abilities we have. For instance, I may face financial problems eagerly, especially if I have a knack for solving them, and yet shy away from car difficulties to the point of fearing and loathing them. Thus in the face of a particular problem or set of problems, I may be hopeful, and yet not be so in relation to others. The deeper more abiding sense of hopefulness which can define our character and not just certain specific activities is the more important one for our discussion, for it concerns hope's second form of practicality—that is, its ability to sustain and nurture us. Acting hopeful on occasion may be enough to pull us through trying times, but hopefulness is transitory and fleeting until it is developed into an enduring habit. As a habit, it requires development of supporting abilities which enable us to *be* hopeful.

My claim is that we acquire the *habit* of hopefulness by developing and coordinating our habits of hope. Hopeful people are those whose persistence and resourcefulness match their courage, thereby generating and sustaining an enduring ability to *be* hopeful. Hopefulness becomes more sustaining when our habits mutually reinforce one another, keeping us energized and preventing us from slipping into despair. Of course, our particular habits may exhibit varying degrees of development. We may, for instance, have better developed habits of persistence than resourcefulness. This does not mean that we cannot be hopeful, but rather that our hopefulness has a limited scope and can be developed more fully. The more fully it is developed, the more enduring is our ability to face trials without losing hope or sinking into despair. To the extent that habits of hope are susceptible to development, so too is hopefulness. It thus varies in stability and strength with the coordination of these habits, so that we can with good justification describe some people as more hopeful than others. The more hopeful are those whose *habit of hopefulness* is more deeply rooted, forming a more stable part of their characters such that it is less likely to wax and wane with changing circumstances.

What evidence is there that hopefulness involves habits of hope? The relevance of persistence is particularly prominent when we focus on hopefulness as an openness to promising possibilities. To persist requires the ability to sustain one's commitment to an end. As I argued in the previous chapter, patience—understood as awaiting conditions appropriate for the realization of that end—forms a central part of it. This in turn is bolstered by attentiveness to actual conditions and their possibilities; proper humility is also needed. Hopefulness bears the mark of each of these features, for being hopeful requires that we do not judge events to be more settled than they are, for good or ill. Rather, we persist by remaining open and attentive, recognizing that acting rashly or giving up too quickly opens the door to despair.

Hopefulness is moreover an attentive *readiness* and so also requires resourcefulness. We must be able to act on or in light of emerging conditions if we are to contribute to the realization of a chosen end. One who hopes does so poorly if she overlooks or misses an opportunity to move toward her desired good. Moreover, resourcefulness indicates the growth of connectedness and so the expansion of our agency so that we can act when necessary. As a readiness, then, hopefulness draws from the abilities fostered by resourcefulness. Courage, of course, also functions to initiate and support both persistence and resourcefulness. Hopefulness bears the mark of courage in enabling us to approach often daunting situations with this open attentive readiness, rather than the aversion typical of fear or the malaise of despair.

The varying degrees to which we possess habits of hope affect the strength and stability of our hopefulness. We may, for instance, have well-developed habits of persistence and yet not be very resourceful. In such a case, although we might successfully formulate and await the arrival of conditions needed to realize our hopes, we will likely fail to properly implement them when they arise. Consequently, possession of one habit of hope does not guarantee possession of them all. If hopefulness is to be developed as an enduring habit, however, our habits of hope need to be coordinated and developed in sync with one another. Otherwise, hopefulness will be easily undermined by life's trials.

Being hopeful requires sensitivity to the delicate coordination of our habits of hope which keep us properly oriented to meaningful horizons. Consider, for instance, how confidence and pride differently affect Cedric and Martha's hopefulness. Martha is resourceful in finding means of recovery and courageous enough to embrace the risks they pose; moreover, she possesses most of the habits of persistence articulated in the previous chapter. In particular, she thoughtfully attends to the reality of her situation—eventually acknowledging that she is clinically depressed—and also considers the various possible means of dealing with it. Moreover, she intently keeps active, always seeking some means of curbing the debilitating effects of her depression. Nevertheless, Martha watches her energies dry up and her hopes begin to crumble. As I noted in the previous section, her tendency to expect too much of herself impedes her ability to open herself as the situation demands; she thus has difficulty letting go her desire to control things. What she needs is a fuller sense of humility. This means being willing to acknowledge the limits of her own agency and to put her trust in forces other than her own. Without these, her persistence actually threatens to foreclose the openness necessary for hoping. Martha does in fact develop this needed humility, but doing so proves one of her major challenges in facing depression and freeing herself from despair.

Cedric also struggles with a certain sort of pride. Though he has faith in his academic capacities throughout his story, his confidence in his ability to get along with others—so vital in not just succeeding in school but in living a meaningful life—wavers. At Ballou, Cedric tends to subordinate social relations to his hope of getting into the Ivy League. Though he has some friends, he generally isolates himself. Once at Brown, he is challenged by the fact that few of his colleagues grew up in an environment like his. Compounding matters, he must live with a roommate with whom he does not get along. When things get tough, he typically withdraws, due to a mixture of his desire to find academic success and his insecurity about his interpersonal skills. Cedric is additionally unsure how much pride or confidence he *should* have in any of his own abilities. His classmates at Ballou resent him for his confidence, thinking him arrogant. Moreover, he is warned at church not to believe too much in himself, for pride is a sin. Yet before his second semester at Brown, Cedric recognizes he has accomplished so much and that losing his pride—his confidence or belief in himself—during that difficult first semester did him no good. He comes to realize that the key "has always been pride. Over years, it had quietly knitted itself into his core" (Suskind 275). This revelation fills him with strength and purpose, fueling a more hopeful orientation to his second, ultimately more successful, semester.

Consequently, Martha has too much confidence in her own abilities, while Cedric has too little. In their struggle to be more hopeful, they face opposing challenges centered around pride, confidence, and humility. Martha and Cedric must find the balance proper to their situation and abilities or else they will be unable to keep hope alive. We must thus remember the significance of contextuality and so be sensitive to the conditions which define our own process of hoping. While habits of hope are generally necessary to make hoping practical, how we utilize and coordinate them cannot be summarized in a pithy principle or maxim. Instead, we must acquire the sort of practical knowledge which enables us to face concrete problems and generate specific solutions.

Consequently, we learn to coordinate habits of hope through our own individual experience. The social dynamics of the life of hope, of course, also play a significant role. Interaction with others can variously sustain and nurture (as well as impede) our habits. As noted above, we maintain our agency and expand our resourcefulness through connection with others. Similarly, social relations can promote courage. Though generally courageous, Martha draws extra strength and comfort from the reliable support of family and friends; without this, she probably would not have been able to let go and acquire the needed humility. Similarly, Barbara's unwavering love for Cedric adds fuel to his determination. She resists being overbearing and gives him his own space so that his hope is not reduced to her own. This bolsters his confidence in himself and so fosters the courage needed to match his own persistence and growing resourcefulness.

In developing hopefulness, though, we must also recognize that we acquire and learn to coordinate habits of hope by modeling the behavior of others—directly and indirectly. Red and Rose of Sharon each develop hopefulness by modeling or imitating that of others. Through their respective stories, we see them grow into more hopeful individuals. At first, Rose's participation in the life of hope is minimal and precarious at best. She and her husband Connie formulate ends which neither knows how to secure. By the story's conclusion, all of these ends have vanished as though they were mere dreams. Under Ma's tutelage, however, Rose of Sharon has grown, particularly in her capacity to function within the family. When Ma assigns her tasks to prevent her from fretting, Rose keeps active and so avoids the paralyzing effect of fear. But Ma's assignments also foster in her daughter habits of helping others. In the process, Rose begins to acquire Ma's habits and so possesses at least the basis for hopefulness. As I argued above, Ma's persistence, resourcefulness, and courage provide the backbone of her hopefulness. To the extent that she shares in these, Rose has the ingredients necessary to develop more fully a hopefulness akin to Ma's.

In the book's last scene, Rose shows significant signs of hopefulness. A starving man lies in the corner of the barn. Ever resourceful, Ma looks around to see what might be done to help. At first she looks to Pa and Uncle John "standing helplessly gazing at the sick man." Earlier in the book, it was the women who looked to the men for security and direction. The men, however, have proven less resourceful than the women, especially Ma. Pa has even lost his standing as the central authority of the family, having surrendered it to Ma. Ma thus looks beyond the men to Rose of Sharon. Rose's breasts are full with milk intended for her now dead infant. "Ma's eyes passed Rose of Sharon's eyes, and then came back to them. And the two women looked deep into each other. The girl's breath came short and gasping" (Steinbeck 453). What passes between the Joad women? My argument is that Rose shows signs of the exhilaration which hopefulness engenders. She comes to see herself as someone who is *able:* able to help, able to foster growth, able to nurture. Though previously she depended on others for guidance and support, here she provides for another. Consequently, even though her own particular hopes have withered away, she is still able to participate in the life of hope—now acting as an agent of hope for others.

Ma's hopefulness provides the spark which ignites the same in Rose. Why does this happen? Rose shares an intimate personal relationship with Ma. As a consequence of the trust, respect, and familial closeness she has with Ma, she fashions her own character after Ma's. Tender moments illustrate the tight bond between the two women. After Connie leaves her, Rose complains to Ma that all her hopes are slipping away. Ma gives her a pair of gold earrings, one of the few things she has saved from the past. These earrings symbolize a connection between mother and daughter and the past, thereby reinforcing the bond of one generation to another. While none of Rose's individual acts seem particularly hopeful, collectively they reveal a general pattern of habituation and growing connectedness developed in the mother-daughter relation. Consequently, though her own hopes are crushed, she manages to build a basis for hopefulness in her relationship with Ma.

Red's development similarly occurs in the context of an intimate personal relationship. For the bulk of the story, Red and Andy contrast sharply with one another, especially with respect to hope. Shortly after Andy's extensive time in solitary confinement, the Red Sox win the 1967 World Series. Red explains that "a kind of ebullience engulfed the whole prison. There was a goofy sort of feeling that if the Dead Sox could come to life, then maybe *anybody* could do it" (King 73). Red and Andy share in the general euphoria. Afterward, Red and the other prisoners slip back into their usual despondency, but Andy does not. Though now more somber and also more patient as a consequence of his recent punishment, he is still able to sustain the cheer from the Sox's win. While Andy's hope to escape fuels his own persistence and resourcefulness, Red concedes that he could not have lived with the hope of escape, for the very thought of it "would have tormented me endlessly" (King 84).

Nevertheless, by the end of the story, Red professes his hopefulness in the lines quoted at the beginning of this chapter. Moreover, he explains that his tale about Andy is really a tale about himself.

It's *all* about me, every damned word of it. Andy was the part of me they could never lock up, the part of me that will rejoice when the gates finally open for me and I walk out in my cheap suit with my twenty dollars of mad-money in my pocket. That part of me will rejoice no matter how old and broken and scared the rest of me is. I guess it's just that Andy had more of that part than me, and used it better. (King 100)

Why is Andy's story *really* about Red, and what accounts for his new ability to hope? In answering, we should first look at what basis Red has for developing hopefulness. He shows resourcefulness—he is the guy who gets you things in prison—but he lacks persistence. He waits and endures, but he does not await. Red's activity is defined by the limited horizon of meaning circumscribed by the routine habits which enable him to survive prison life. Nevertheless, by the story's end, we see the effect Andy's example has on him. Before his escape, Andy describes to Red the location of a rock in a Maine hayfield and tells him to look for it should he ever get out of Shawshank. After his release, Red finds himself looking for the rock, spending weekends roaming the countryside in search of it. He calls his little expeditions "[a] fool's errand," but adds that "so is chipping at a blank concrete wall for twenty-seven years" as Andy did (King 104). When he finds the rock, Red discovers underneath it the following message left by Andy: "Remember that hope is a good thing, Red, maybe the best of things, and no good thing ever dies" (King 106).

In his quest for the rock, Red shows signs of persistence. Consequently, he begins to complement his resourcefulness with a newfound ability and willingness to await. His journey is not complete, however, until he violates parole in search of Andy. Once afraid of hope, he is now inspired by it. Andy's example gives him the courage not simply to break parole, but to actually hope. Indeed, Red's ability to hope is perhaps the most significant development in the story. By the end, his horizon of meaning is as expansive and rich as the open sea. His habits are oriented toward promising possibilities; they are habits of hope. Red now shows a propensity to hope, both in pursuing particular hopes and in being hopeful, willing and able to participate in the life of hope.

Why, though, does Andy's hopefulness inspire Red? The answer, I believe, lies in the concrete friendship he has with Red. Throughout the story we learn of Red's respect for Andy, whether arising from his ability to survive gang rape, his patience in carving rock sculptures, or his resourcefulness in regenerating the prison library. But Red not only respects Andy, he also shares a warm friendship with him, as evidenced by the small but significant favors the two do for one another. Red gives Andy free cigarettes and posters. Andy gives Red rock sculptures as gifts and also shares his hopes with him. Moreover, though Red first considers Andy's hope to escape a mere pipe dream, after Andy actually acts on and realizes it, that dream becomes something determinate that inspires Red. He sees that hope not only sustained Andy through twenty-seven years of prison life—a significant feat in its own right—but it also propelled him out of prison. Contributing to Red's change, then, is the realization that hope was efficacious for his friend, that realizing his good was a *real* possibility. Interacting and being closely connected with a successful hoper proves the vital ingredient in developing his own hopefulness.

Andy serves as both symbol and a prompt in Red's life. He symbolizes the hopefulness which Red was unwilling to let grow; he also prompts development of Red's own hopefulness by making him feel ashamed of not letting it grow. We see this when Red is tempted, after his release from prison, to commit a crime so he can return to the institutional life he knows so well. Yet he is ultimately unable to succumb to that temptation, for, as he explains, "I kept thinking of [Andy], spending all those years chipping patiently away at the cement with his rockhammer so he could be free. I thought of that and it made me ashamed and I'd drop the idea again" (King 103). Rather than slipping back into the comfort of routine, Red finds in the example of Andy the strength to live on the outside and, in the end, the courage to join his friend in Mexico, where they together pursue a free life nurtured by hope.

Hopefulness and the Self: Living Hopefully

Both Red and Rose of Sharon show the significance of close personal relationships in igniting and nurturing the development of hopefulness.

Red's transformation is the more striking, since he was originally skeptical of hoping. Nevertheless, he learns to embrace its value, turning himself from despair and hopelessness to the promise of growth in a new life. Though Red and Rose of Sharon learn to participate in the life of hope, we should recognize that their efforts must be developed more fully or they will wither away. Their continued hopefulness depends on the extent to which it is nurtured, through both individual actions and the active support of loved ones, to the point that it becomes a deeply ingrained part of their character. In order for hopefulness to become a *characteristic* way of being, we must develop it into the complex habit of coordinating habits of hope, which keeps alive our capacity to hope. This habit must become deeply entrenched so that it molds and directs the integration of ideals and habits; it then defines our character and typifies our way of acting and being. Hopeful people, understood in this light, are those who develop and exercise their abilities under the guidance of hoping.

In the first chapter I explained the pragmatic view of the self as an activity, a process of integrating our various dimensions. Conditioned by abilities developed through past activities, the self is a structured way of integrating habits and ideals, resolving conflicts, and bringing means and ends together. Though rooted in antecedent accomplishments, it can transcend them as well, particularly if it involves flexible habits. When conflicts arise between habits, ideals, or both, consciousness and intelligence function to assess and resolve them through creative and selective integration. Habits that are fixed and routine impair integrating activity so that it results in the repetition of past behavior. But intelligently formed habits make possible new modes of integration.

The particular manner of integrating is governed by a regnant habit. This habit interweaves what we *want* to become with what we *have* become. It functions like the conductor of a symphony orchestra. Under its guidance, habits and ideals are integrated so they can work in concert, though of course such integration may take many forms. At one extreme, integration is guided by a regnant habit which preserves already established structures, minimizing or eliminating ideals which require change. Routine habits dominate in such an individual. At the

other extreme, integration may prioritize novelty, creating an individual who always chases after new ideals, thereby undermining the estab-
lishment of deeply rooted or complex habits. In between lie various
modes of integration which privilege neither ideals nor habits, but intelligently evaluate and modify means and ends in light of one another.
In these cases, habits that conflict are then subordinated or transformed in light of particular purposes; similarly, ends are modified or
discarded when their attainment either taxes or disrupts the organism
too much.

Hopefulness as a regnant habit falls into this middle range. It orients the self toward growth, understood as expansion and transformation rooted in continuity. Consequently, neither ideals nor habits are
given absolute priority over one another. While ideals provide opportunities to expand and transform established abilities, they drain
our energy when disconnected from those abilities. Similarly, though
habits provide structures which allow us to act in the first place, they
become rigid and fixed without the infusion of novelty and redirection
made possible by ideals. Hopefulness aims to match ideals with sustaining abilities and resources. Even when ends lie beyond the reach of
present abilities, we must be able to move toward them, actively seeking their integration by stretching our abilities. Both Cedric and
Martha learn this as they pursue their hopes and embrace sometimes
frightening means. Moreover, hopefulness sustains us by nurturing the
growth of agency through connection. Such connection means maintaining our abilities without unduly taxing them, even while we also
expand and keep them flexible. Hopefulness, then, is a manifestation of
intelligence. It indicates the ability to remain open to hopes by preventing habits from becoming too rigid and ideals from becoming too
lofty or unrealizable.

In such a case, difficulties that arise when pursuing hopes do not
derail or impede the ongoing activities of the self. Ends are adapted or
habits transformed to better facilitate their pursuit. Though his experience at MIT makes Cedric question his desire to get into the Ivy
League, he is able to bounce back. Instead of giving up his hope altogether, he recognizes that a school like Brown (still Ivy League) might
better suit his needs. Similarly, Andy's courage enables him to endure

the hell of solitary confinement without loss of hope. Even when particular hopes prove unrealizable after attempts at modification, however, a hopeful self's integration need not be frustrated or undone, for hopefulness has two significant effects on us. First, it keeps alive our ability to hope by energizing us. This occurs through coordination of persistence, which conserves ability, and resourcefulness, which expands it. Together, these provide structure for our energies. As a regnant habit, hopefulness functions to integrate habits of hope so they work together in fueling and sustaining hope. Should one habit be underdeveloped or in need of alteration, the appropriate changes are then made. A hopeful self establishes a continuity of habits, thereby ensuring concerted action and making possible more complex activities. Such a self has abilities that continue to grow and energies that find new outlets. Ideals indicate possibilities for expanding and transforming habits rather than a curse of what we could be but are not. We are then able to live in a rich and expansive horizon of meaning. Consequently, hopefulness sustains us by ensuring that our energies spread and that we will not be trapped in routine or stalled by fixation on a single ideal.

Flowing from this first effect, the second effect of hopefulness is preventing frustrations or failures from draining our energy. This, of course, enables us to resist falling into despair, as Ma knew, or helps us combat it, as Martha discovered. The failure of particular hopes typically means the loss of energy and carries with it the possibility of demoralization. Sometimes, of course, failed hopes result from poor formulation. We can and do at times pursue hopes whose disconnection from actual conditions robs us of our energy and cuts us off from our resources. Nuland learned this through his brother Harvey's painful quest for recovery through treatment. In addition, however, we must recognize that not even careful attention and effort in formulating and pursuing particular hopes guarantees the desired success. As an underlying disposition, however, hopefulness provides a reserve of energy—or the vital resource of connection with others—which enables us to withstand the demise of particular hopes. In such a case, their failure does not also indicate the failure of hoping. Should it become apparent that a chosen end is unrealizable, it is foolish to waste energy persisting in its pursuit. Yet, remaining hopeful is not foolish, especially when we have complex habits that provide sustenance and help prevent the slip into debilitating despair.

By contrast, one who despairs lacks the complex coordination of habits of hope and so is unable to rebound from the failure of particular hopes. A despairing self is characterized by disconnection and paralysis rather than by growth and connection. In this case, integration is stymied. Despair means that the self aims at but is incapable of integrating new ideals with past integrations. When past habits have been routine and so resist transformation, connection through integrating movements of the self is not possible. Ability to adapt to changing circumstances is thereby limited, as we saw in Red's acknowledgement that he could not function in the world beyond his prison bars.

Kierkegaard calls despair the sickness unto death, for in despair we long for death (at least the death of this particular self) and yet cannot die. He explains that "despair is veritably a self-consuming, but an impotent self-consuming that cannot do what it wants to do" (Kierkegaard 18). The self that now is—that is, the integration that is possible on the basis of the past—is inadequate to realize attractive ideals. The self then lives in the painful conflict between ideals which represent what it could become and the limiting abilities which prevent it from realizing that ideal. In such a case, we are trapped in the present and restricted by fixed habits to such an extent that the self is intolerable. This self cannot become anything better, and yet it is inescapable. One in despair is caught between the imperious claim of an ideal and recalcitrant or ineffective habits, without any means of changing either. Consequently, one despairs over being incapable of consuming this self, of being rid of it with all its limitations. Despair, then, is the inability to escape or die, the curse of being condemned to an intolerable present that stretches out indefinitely.

Unless we have the ability to transform habits or adapt our ends, their disconnection from one another becomes entrenched, often resulting in paralysis. We are then imprisoned not merely by limited abilities but also by the tyranny of ideals that appear to be very desirable but forever out of reach. Though comfortable in the routine of prison life, the institutionalized man nevertheless remains ever aware of how restrictive it is and how disconnected he is from the ends others value; indeed, he himself would value and pursue those ends *if only* he could. He thus suffers a double disconnection: one between his own abilities and ideals, and one between himself and others.

When our selves are defined by despair, we lack the very kind of connectedness, both personal and social, which hopefulness establishes. We are uprooted and cut off from sustaining and nurturing resources. We are truly alone and limited in our being. If a way out is to be found, connection must be reestablished and nurtured. Though this chapter has focused primarily on the development of hopefulness in individuals, we have nevertheless seen much evidence of its social nature. Habits, by their nature, implicate the environment, and this is true of habits of hope as well. Both Red and Rose of Sharon develop hopefulness through close interpersonal relationships. Both are inspired by the courage of their more hopeful counterparts. We may expand on this social dynamic by noting that hopefulness can characterize not only individual selves but also communities.

Though the move from individual to community is not without difficulties, we can here note the following similarities. Communities have habits, though these are more appropriately called customs or social mores. Such communal habits not only embody shared values and ideals but also shared abilities. They structure behavior that is as automatic as that governed by the habits of individuals. We can thus consider such things as the resourcefulness of a community. Our own American society possesses an ever-growing technology that enables us to connect more readily and effectively with societies. Air travel, the telephone, and the Internet are among the most obvious such technologies. They increase our access to a greater variety of means and make more complicated modes of coordinated action possible, thereby fostering our resourcefulness. Similarly, we can identify elements of persistence we possess in pursuing and developing social structures that are more conducive to a broader spectrum of people. The American commitment to fostering democratic forms of government and to overcoming the blights of racism provide examples of our persistence. Finally, we can consider our society's courage in tackling serious problems and mounting ambitious reforms, such as the protection of basic civic liberties.

I do not wish to suggest that ours is a predominantly hopeful society. Fear hovers in many corners of our lives, especially given its prominence in consumer advertising, political campaigning, and the entertainment industry. We face a barrage of violent images and the day-to-day risks involved in a technologically complex society. Nevertheless, we can also find individual, familial, and communal models (including those discussed above) in light of which we can develop the hopefulness of individual communities and perhaps of our society as a whole. Becoming a more hopeful society means assessing our resources, especially the extent to which they debilitate as well as promote meaningful action, and seeking to expand them where appropriate. It also means considering how best to match material resources with human abilities, promoting greater justice and thereby increasing the likelihood of concerted efforts. A hopeful society can profit from advanced technology, but not without such basic habits as trust and courage. Careful attention to development of such abilities should be the task of not merely preachers in their pulpits, but people at all levels of society. For just as Rose and Red of Sharon were nurtured by their more hopeful counterparts, so too can we be nurtured by the widespread growth of hopefulness. By finding greater connection and support, we can both profit from and contribute to a hopeful society. Such an attitude is itself a key element in the growth of hopefulness.

Before leaving the topic of hopefulness and the self, I want to emphasize the profound effect it can have on the development of the self. In particular, pursuing hopes generally and fostering hopefulness specifically can promote both desired and unforeseen forms of growth. We have already noted how hope changed Rose and Red. It has similar effects on Cedric and Martha. In Cedric's case, his hope in the unseen, his quest for a place where he can exercise his abilities and also feel at home, proves to be a key ingredient in his development and maturation. Indeed, in recognition of this fact, Suskind titles the last chapter of the book "Meeting the Man." Cedric summarizes his own growth best:

> I always imagined the unseen as a place, a place I couldn't yet see, up ahead, where I'd be welcomed and accepted, just for

who I am. And I still feel like it is a place, an imagined place, really, either here or somewhere else, that I'll get to someday. But first, you know, now I realize that there's work I need to do, too. I need to know—to really know—who I am, and accept who I am, deal with some of my own issues. That's got to come first, before I can expect other people to accept me. The good thing, though, is that it seems like I'm just now coming into focus to myself—you know, beginning to see myself more clearly. (Suskind 330)

At this point, Cedric really has grown, learning to confront problems with others rather than withdrawing from them, and enjoying "[f]ull membership in the Brown community, won fair and square" (357).

Now increasingly confident in his own academic *and* social abilities, Cedric is able to face challenges without fear or awkwardness. Meeting his father used to leave him feeling anxious and out of sorts, but not now. As Suskind notes, "nothing seems to knock him reeling like that anymore" (356). Cedric has begun to know who he is and is strong enough to carry himself. But he is also strong and wise enough to see how he can aid others. Upon returning home from his first year at Brown, he recognizes how selflessly Barbara has invested herself in his life. She has sacrificed so much, both energy and money, and now risks losing her apartment because she has run up so much debt. Not wanting to distract Cedric from his own endeavors, she has failed to mention her problem. Now, however, she faces eviction and can no longer hide it. Cedric bursts out at her: "This is *really* the sin of pride . . . Too proud to tell [me] you got a problem" (347). Barbara, he recognizes, must learn to tend to her own problems and seek what makes her happy. Moreover, she must learn to receive as well as to give. He tells her, "You can't be the only one doing the caring. I'm strong enough to do some now, too" (361). Cedric is now himself an agent of hope, able to sustain himself and others as well. Pursuit of his hopes for success and acceptance, complexly interwoven as they are, helps Cedric mature, forcing him to match his persistence with increased resourcefulness and self-confidence. Hoping stretches his abilities so that he learns just how much he can do.

By contrast, Martha's hopes bring her face to face with her limits. She discovers that sheer willpower by itself cannot solve every problem. She must reach out for help and let go so fully that she risks losing her very self. Early in her book, she notes how Annie, a cancer patient in therapy with her, comes to grips with the fragility of her own life. Martha observes that "[s]he struggled with so many of the things people must tackle when they go through something like this: changes in her body and in her self-confidence and image, disruptions in work and family, the loss of innocence that comes from seeing the fragility of your own young life, long before you thought it was time" (20). In many ways, Martha must learn the same lesson; she must accept her own fragility without losing hope. Bolstered by resourcefulness as well as the love and nurturing of family and friends, she is able to recover from both depression and despair. But in the process, she also grows. She learns to let others help and so relaxes and opens herself more fully to the world around her. She also comes to accept the contingency of events without feeling that she must control them before they control her. She acquires a greater sense of humility and adaptability. In the end, she has developed a more sophisticated self, one better able to interact in the world.

Martha learns that we cannot always succeed by effort alone; sometimes we have to accept our vulnerability and surrender a part of ourselves, especially that part which demands to be in control. In this way, we acknowledge limits without letting them limit us. Martha comes through her ordeal stronger, recognizing that the world may be fraught with contingency and the possibility of great suffering, which need not destroy us. She notes near her story's end that we cannot avoid the undercurrents of life. Yet, "[t]he tide will come and go. The sun will be warm again and the salt on your skin will remind you of what you have done. And you will rest your tired body on the shore, falling into that delicious sleep that comes from knowing you are alright" (194–195). Martha survives her ordeal with a strong sense of hope, grounded in a more realistic understanding of her own abilities in the face of adversity. She learns to see beauty and find peace even in the midst of a dangerous contingent world. Participating in the life of hope—developing hopefulness—thus not only provides Cedric and

Martha a safety net but also promotes personal growth in perhaps unexpected ways.[10]

The Interweaving of Hope's Three Dimensions

In the introduction I sketched the interweaving of hope's three dimensions in order to underscore its twin senses of practicality. I noted that
particular hopes, habits of hope, and hopefulness can be conceptually
distinguished, but their interrelation constitutes the life of hope. We
are now in a position to reconsider each dimension, especially in its dependence and independence from the others.

Particular hopes are defined in light of a specific end or group of
ends. Since hopes lie at or beyond the reach of our agency, we must
evaluate them in light of their desirability and realizability if we are to
justify our commitment to them. Pursuit of particular hopes requires
various means, though we can identify three central habits of hope that
are needed. Habits of persistence enable us to patiently await further
means that will make possible realization of our chosen end. Resourcefulness, in turn, expands our agency through connection, enabling us
to reach those ends through the growth of abilities. Important to both
of these habits is the courage to face risks in the process. We can, of
course, pursue particular hopes even when some of these habits are underdeveloped or absent. This is often the case, since means such as
these are frequently acquired in the very process of pursuing particular
ends. The adversities faced in hoping provide excellent opportunities
for growth and development. Moreover, successful pursuit of particular
hopes brings satisfaction and so reinforces the habits that contributed
to its realization.

Hopes, of course, can fail, and for a variety of reasons. For instance, we may carelessly commit to particular ends that are either undesirable or unrealizable. Given actual conditions, including individual
abilities and desires, some hopes simply suit us better than others. We
may also lack the ability to maintain commitment to a particular hope,
especially if we are impatient, have limited resources, or simply fail to
have the courage needed to pursue it. In such cases, hoping is impractical in the sense of wasting our energies and tempting us to despair.

Even when pursued intelligently, though, hopes are still susceptible to failure; we cannot control the conditions of our environment and so must sometimes give up our pursuit of a desired end. Hoping in these cases, though, can be underwritten by hopefulness, understood as a disposition of ready attentiveness to promising possibilities. The more fully it is developed, the more fully it proves a vital resource which fosters particular hopes and enables us to withstand the trials and travails that beset their pursuit. Just as hoping generally indicates our transcendence of antecedent conditions, hopefulness signifies our ability to transcend particular failures without losing our capacity to hope.

Hopefulness without habits of hope, though, is a mere passing attitude and not a sustaining disposition. We may act in a hopeful manner, especially by modeling the behavior of hopeful individuals, but to *be* hopeful we need to develop and coordinate habits of hope. When their development is promoted by the pursuit of hopes, hopefulness itself is indirectly fostered by particular hopes. We should not underestimate their efficacy upon it. Success with particular hopes employs, expands, and solidifies habits of hope, and we enjoy the satisfaction of achievement as well as the growth and reinforcement of those habits which made our success possible. Indeed, the effects of hoping and developing hopefulness often spread. Whether that success belongs to us or those we care about, it can have a ripple effect, just as the Red Sox's triumph inspired Shawshank's prisoners. The realization of ends proves all the more powerful when fully utilized—that is, when treated as a potential contributor (and so means) to further ends. The glow of success should be enjoyed, but it should also be employed.

While the failure of hopes can undermine hopefulness, it need not do so. If our habits are underdeveloped and we lack support from other people, failure is likely to drain our energy. We can avoid such consequences both by acting with others who are hopeful and by pursuing the development of our own hopefulness. Those whose hopefulness is strong can endure failure and remain energized. Though setbacks or the taste of despair debilitates some, as James notes, it "wakes others fully up" and taps into their reserves of power. James recounts the story of a French colliery explosion in which many died. Twenty days after the explosion, rescuers discovered a group of fourteen survivors rallied together by one man who "disciplined them and cheered them, and brought them out alive." Five days later a single man, all of whose companions were dead, was found alive, having survived because he "had been able to sleep away most of the time" (MS 243). Though each passing day made less likely their hope for rescue, these survivors did not give up but rather found ways to keep hope—and themselves—alive.

Indeed, the true practicality of hopefulness consists in orienting us to growth and helping us resist disconnection and destruction. It aims at continuity and not discontinuity, even though it enables us to transcend current limitations. Consequently, its transcendence is conditioned by our own abilities as well as those of others, and by the constraints and resources of our environment. Hopefulness keeps our energy flowing, helping us overcome obstacles and avoid potential threats; it keeps us going. We should not forget, however, that it indicates not only the ability to resist despair, but also the capacity to embrace and move toward the future's promising possibilities. Living hopefully means being *ready* to hope, living within a rich expanding horizon. Consequently, even when pursuing a particular hope proves impractical, remaining hopeful is still desirable since it sustains us and keeps us aimed at growth.

What can we do, then, to foster hopefulness and avoid despair? Since its fundamental nature is that of habits, our most important move is to develop and coordinate our habits of hope whenever possible. One of the primary lessons of a pragmatic theory of hope is that we bear great responsibility for hope; it is neither something mysterious nor something mundane. Though hopes lie beyond the reach of our immediate grasp, there is much we can and should do to reach out for them. If we are to promote the life of hope, we must ensure that it is practical in both of the ways we have discussed. This means intelligently formulating the ends for which we hope and their means, judging them in light of their desirability and realizability. It entails that we must actively foster adaptability, funded by the imaginative exploration of possibilities, and basic connection with others. We should also nurture the development of hopefulness in ourselves and others.

While I have discussed at length the means of fostering hopefulness, what are we to do when we find ourselves or others slipping into despair? Although the best response is to rely on the support provided by our habits of hope, many people lack one or more of them. How can we respond when habits fail and we find ourselves staring straight into the darkness of an abyss? How can hope empower us in the face of suffering? To reply that we must depend on our own abilities is simplistic, for as despair takes hold, our agency tends to diminish. Reaching out to others and at least maintaining basic connection with them is vital, yet this too can prove very difficult. When we are caught in the grip of despair, hope lies in the hands of others—of those who can still hope. Frankl, whose own experience in a concentration camp forced these questions on him as urgent issues of survival, observes that "any attempt to restore a man's inner strength in the camp had first to succeed in showing him some future goal" (Frankl 97). Reminding someone in despair of a meaningful end, and so a reason why he should continue to struggle, can help revitalize and reinvest him in his horizon of meaning. Frankl's own life-preserving "why" was to rewrite the manuscript which the Nazis confiscated from him when he arrived at the camp. Yet, getting those who despair to acknowledge and invest in goals can be incredibly difficult, for their horizon of meaning has typically been poisoned or drained. Without the fertile soil of a horizon in which an end can actually possess goodness, holding out possible ends proves futile. The deeper the despair, the more sterile the horizon of meaning, and so the less likely any end will be considered desirable by those who despair.

Pragmatically, we can respond in one of two ways. First, in recognition of the interweaving of our habits and activities, we can try to inspire by example, drawing on the powers of human connection, as strained as they may be. As Red demonstrates, seeing loved ones living hopefully jars some people out of despair. But in other cases, it only serves to alienate those who suffer, as happened with Martha. In such a case, though, there is always the second response: to acknowledge the suffering of those in despair and to commit to *being there* with them. Accepting suffering, whether our own or that of others, proves vital in overcoming it. Martha's experience teaches her the value of this lesson. In the last chapter, we noted how she benefited most from having her husband simply be there with her rather than trying to find some way of solving her problem. She shares the benefits of her experience when a patient who has had breast cancer explains that she cannot even show her husband the scars from her surgery. Martha explains that "[i]n acknowledging the torment of her isolation, I understand what I have to do with her for the rest of this hour. I have to sit with her, with her blouse open, and her awful wounds, both visceral and psychic. I have to sit with her in her pain" (Manning 172). To ignore suffering and loss is to blot out the significance of things once valued. If pushed to an extreme, this drains our horizon of meaning so fully that we lose contact with all value, all goods, all meaning in life. Then all we are left with is the pain and emptiness of our suffering. By acknowledging the reality of suffering, we recognize (and so reconfirm) the value of what we have lost, whether it be health, agency, or a loved one. We thus kindle the flames of meaning in our lives, even as the winds of affliction threaten to blow them out.

Furthermore, we can (indeed, Frankl argues, *must*) find meaning even in the face of suffering. We do this not only by vigilantly wiping out its causes, but also by curbing its debilitating effects, summoning our best resources to protect what we value and hold dear. For instance, we can actively maintain our dignity when circumstances take over our lives, even if only by summoning the courage to endure suffering, to resist sinking into the depths of inhuman behavior as our situation becomes grim. Sadly, Frankl notes, "On the average, only those prisoners could keep alive who, after years of trekking from camp to camp, had lost all scruples in their fight for existence; they were prepared to use every means, honest and otherwise, even brutal force, theft, betrayal of their friends, in order to save themselves" (Frankl 23–24). Frankl's own story of survival, however, shows how courage and a refusal to let go his connection to his horizon of meaning enabled him to withstand the horrors of a concentration camp. He recounts a speech in which he told his comrades that "[t]hey must not lose hope but should keep their courage in the certainty that the hopelessness of our struggle did not detract from its dignity and meaning" (104). He encouraged them to seize their suffering as an opportunity to give life meaning, summoning, for example, the fortitude and courage to face the darkest of hours. Frankl's goal was not to ignore or sugarcoat his comrades' suffering, but to draw them back to a life invested with meaning and value by showing them that goods could still be achieved and virtues still employed.

Frankl's message is an important one, especially if we interpret it to mean that even in the most hopeless situation we can still actively maintain our habits of hope and hopefulness. Doing so keeps us active-ly invested in and connected to our horizons of meaning and so pro-vides a powerful defense against the deadening effects of helplessness and apathy which attend despair. To acknowledge and overcome suf-fering requires considerable courage, and courage of course helps pro-mote hope. But for those who lack the energy or motivation to find meaning, we can simply be with them. Job's comforters sat with him for seven days and seven nights, simply being with him without saying a thing. Martha's husband did the same with her repeatedly, and she did it with her patient. In being with another, quietly and unobtrusively of-fering them human contact, we keep alive the embers of human con-tact and connection.

Sometimes the power of hopefulness draws us on to great achieve-ments. But sometimes it functions best by enabling us to navigate the dark terrain of despair. The life of hope is fragile. We have our respon-sibility to develop habits of hope, especially in their coordination as hopefulness. It is this which enables us to persist and overcome despair as well as to help others, whether by promoting development of their hopefulness or by simply being there with them. Nevertheless, if our pragmatic theory of hope is itself to be practical, it must acknowledge that there are limits to what we can do in the face of despair. Hopefulness has its independence and is a powerful force when devel-oped, but it is not impregnable. Sometimes it fails; sometimes not even being there pulls others out of despair. Disconnection can be so severe that even our most valiant efforts fail. A pragmatic theory of hope ac-knowledges that we are conditioned and limited by the environment in which we live. Much happens without our consent and beyond our control, forcing us to face circumstances which restrict and at times devastate us. Yet our theory also recognizes that as interactive organ-isms, we also have powers by means of which we can face and at times overcome or transform the constraints of current situations. These pow-ers develop through our interaction with the environment, whether it is favorable or combative. We must embrace the contingency of events (as Martha learns to do), accepting our finitude and limitations, but we

must also match them with our best efforts and the practical knowledge of knowing when and how to adapt. Hope gains its resilience to
and independence from its environment as it develops more fully.
That, of course, is why we must actively foster hope in all its dimensions.

The development of hopefulness marks the crowning achievement
in the life of hope. We do not become hopeful apart from hoping.
Pursuing particular hopes provides occasion for developing those
habits of hope without which hopefulness itself cannot be made a
habit. But once developed, hopefulness can survive the success or failure of particular hopes. Moreover, habits of hope are reinforced
through it, since it involves their coordination into a new complex
habit. Consequently, the more we develop habits of hope, the more
successful we are in pursuing particular hopes and the more likely we
are to have the raw materials out of which hopefulness is built.

We can summarize by returning to our original discussion of the
means-end continuum. Each dimension of the life of hope can be
viewed as both an end and a means. Particular hopes provide the ends
for which we hope. Such ends are ends-in-view and so are also means
in guiding the selection and organization of materials which serve as
means to their realization. Included among these means are habits of
hope; without them, our commitment to the end (or end-in-view) falters. Habits of hope we do not possess but need can themselves be ends
developed through the process of hoping. Pursuit of particular hopes,
then, can function as a means to acquiring habits of hope. Hopefulness
is, in turn, an end generally realized through the development of habits
of hope. Moreover, especially in the degree to which it develops as the
coordination of habits of hope, hopefulness can itself become a habit
of hope. When it is, it both energizes and sustains us in pursuing particular hopes. It can become the dominant habit of the self, in which
case it functions as a further means to the life of hope; it then provides
the basis for a hopeful person and, in turn, for a hopeful community.
Hoping then provides the opportunity for the development (or, more
often, the further development) of each of its dimensions. Hope influences its own realization by generating, drawing on, and manifesting
itself in the form of hopefulness.

CHAPTER *Four*

Hoping against Hope

IN OUR exploration of a pragmatic theory of hope, we have uncovered the life of hope as the rich interweaving of three dimensions: particular hopes, habits of hope, and hopefulness. Though each has its own element of independence from the others, none functions in complete isolation. Habits of hope provide a hinge between the other two, especially insofar as they nurture both the pursuit of particular hopes and the development of hopefulness. Yet hopefulness itself is a habit of hope, one which has special significance in enabling us to keep hope alive even when particular hopes fail.

The interweaving of these dimensions allows us to account for the two senses of hope's practicality articulated in the introduction. The first sense concerns the grounds and realizability of particular hopes. To make hoping practical, special care must be given to both the formulation and pursuit of hoped-for ends. In the grips of a problematic situation, we should not hasten to focus our energy and attention on the most common or readily available end; rather we should assess its desirability and realizability. Both of these features are contextual, depending on the end's relation to the rich fabric of our own lives (including abilities and ideals) as well as that of the community in which we act. Neither desirability nor realizability should be evaluated independently of one another, especially since ends are often determined undesirable in light of the time, energy, and potential changes required for their realization. Assessment of actual conditions should include consideration of the original problematic situation as well as our abilities and those of others with whom we interact. Viable ends must promise some resolution of that situation, but they must not overwhelm us or drain our resources. Consequently, we must intelligently evaluate ends in light of our means.

Hoping is not a simple matter of detached calculation, though; rather, it is a complex activity of deliberating about and pursuing a particular end, richly funded by imaginative exploration of possibilities. Acting *as if* plays a significant role, especially in determining whether our own efforts can support and contribute to ongoing commitment to hoping. Chief among our means are our habits. Of course, the frustration of one or some of these abilities is typically the source of the problematic situation, since hoping usually arises when interaction has been interrupted. Hoping is nonetheless an active response to such a situation whereby we assess, test, and seek to overcome limitations and perhaps transform ourselves in order to resolve the original problem. This is the seat of its danger and risk. Attractive though it might be, an end may drain our energies and tax our abilities even further. We thus must pay special attention to those habits which enable us to maintain our commitment to hoping and, when possible, to grow.

As we have noted, hoping itself can contribute to the formation or transformation of needed abilities. It provides us an opportunity, indeed a lure, for further growth. When hoping, we often expand our habits by further developing them and connecting them with others' habits. In the process conditions and abilities will change, so we must repeatedly reevaluate our chosen ends. As we seek to realize them, ends should function as ends-in-view, guiding our activities and efforts. We should remain open to scrutinizing and revising them, or else we risk being stifled rather than guided.

Practical grounds nevertheless do not guarantee that hoping will be successful. Failure at times is unavoidable, especially since hopes arise in contexts where our control is limited. Consequently, intelligent acting should be the hallmark of practical hoping. Since hoping sustains, energizes, and keeps us open to growth, we here encounter hope's second form of practicality. The growth it makes possible indicates our capacity to develop and expand our abilities, especially by connecting them with those of others, so that we can secure or produce more comprehensive ends. Pursuit of particular hopes often nurtures expansion of our habits of hope and also the development of hopefulness. We can be hopeful, of course, in varying degrees, but the more deeply we root hopefulness in our character, the better we are able to grow and resist the temptation to despair. Despair, by contrast, indicates stagnation or paralysis, often the result of routine habits incapable of modification to meet changing circumstances. Problems then become prisons whose bars are our own rigid limitations. Developing hopefulness as the regnant habit of the self increases our ability to respond creatively to problems (modifying our habits when needed) and to survive the failure of particular hopes. Hoping, then, is practical in promoting better, richer lives aimed at more comprehensive ends.

Consequently, hoping is a conditioned transcendence. It is *conditioned* because it is rooted in our habits (and the environment which they implicate), but it is also a form of *transcendence* since the very activity of hoping both requires and enables us to go beyond antecedent limitations of agency. When hoping, we can transcend antecedent conditions and expand our abilities, but only by understanding and establishing that transcendence in continuity with its roots. Transcendence occurs, yet—especially if it is to be productive—it must be both compatible with antecedent conditions and sufficiently different from them to signify a consummating change. Hope's transcendence does not simply provide us freedom from the past but also the power of improving, of stretching ourselves to do and become more. Hoping needs to be practical by being rooted in actual conditions and abilities. Otherwise, it does not deliver us to a future with enhanced meaning and enriched possibilities, but deceives us with false promises and dreams that vanish as we move toward them.

Some will object, however, that a pragmatic account falls short of explaining genuine hoping. They will contend that our presentation has emphasized too fully hope's proximity and continuity with other activities, especially by rooting it in ordinary habits. We have thus made hoping too mundane or commonplace. Worse, we have robbed it of its true power by not recognizing that its transcendence can be un-restricted—if only we acknowledge its proper ground. Better are those traditional theological accounts which recognize hope's grounding in something absolute and unconditioned and which therefore ensure that hope can transcend any situation. Typically, this ground is identi-fied with as a divine being which, to fulfill its proper function of mak-ing possible what transcends human ability, must be understood as possessing a nature that is radically different from our own. Apart from such a god, according to this objection, hope remains pedestrian and forever limited. We cannot, then, offer hope to the cancer patient who longs for recovery when none is available. Equally bereft of hope on a pragmatic account is the prisoner of war who lacks resources in the face of daily torture. Human hope—rooted in habits and action—may suffice in some cases, but not in these.

The Apostle Paul presents precisely this sort of position in Romans 4:18. He explains to his Roman friends the central role of faith, rather than law, in establishing a living relationship with God. Paul recounts the story of Abraham, whom God promised to make father of a great nation, before there was divine law. Human wisdom, of course, gave Abraham no grounds for believing God's promise, for he himself was old, as was his wife, Sarah. Yet Abraham had faith in God's word. Paul writes:

> *Hoping against hope,* [Abraham] believed that he would become "the father of many nations," according to what was said, "So numerous shall your descendants be." He did not weaken in faith when he considered his own body . . . or when he consid-ered the barrenness of Sarah's womb. No distrust made him waver concerning the promise of God, but he grew strong in his faith and gave glory to God, being fully convinced that God was able to do what he had promised. Therefore his faith "was reckoned to him as righteousness." (Rom. 4:18–22)

In this passage, Paul makes clear that Abraham's hope had more than a human basis. If he relied simply on human abilities, grounded as they are in the conditions of our lives, Abraham would have determined his hope foolish to pursue. Faith in God, understood as *unwavering* belief in the word and power of a deity, grounds this hope which would otherwise be impossible. *Hoping against hope,* then, means hoping even when there is no human or conditioned basis for hope.

Paul's passage expresses a common view of hope. Just as Abraham hoped in the absence of human grounds, many of us long to believe that hoping has the power to deliver what we want regardless of finite conditions. The Melians defiantly rejected the Athenians' demand that they surrender, justifying their position by appeal to such a hope. When dealing with Harvey's illness, even Nuland fell prey to thinking of hope as a mysterious power that would enable his brother to overcome actual conditions. Rather than acknowledging the real limits of his situation, Nuland offered Harvey the false comfort of attempting what he otherwise determined to be impossible, since he believed "telling [Harvey] the absolute truth would 'take away his only hope'" (Nuland 226). In these cases, hoping is thought to transcend all practical considerations and to deliver what we truly want or need. Only an unconditioned ground can make this form of hoping possible.

The proponents of this view of hope, or some variant of it, are numerous. I will sketch a few of the more prominent examples. My goal is not to provide detailed accounts of these alternatives to our theory, but rather to highlight how the unconditioned functions in them. In the final section of this chapter, I will develop a pragmatic response.

Hope and the Unconditioned

Aquinas, whose theory we have already discussed at some length, treats hope as a theological virtue and so roots it in our living relationship with God. Aquinas structures his analysis around hope's final and efficient causes. The proper end or object of hope, he argues, is eternal happiness, and its attainment is impossible apart from a proper relationship with God. Our ultimate welfare is tied up with hope, for "hope makes us adhere to God, as the source whence we derive perfect goodness, i.e., in so far as, by hope, we trust to the Divine assistance for obtaining happiness" (II-II.17.6). Since it makes our actions good and helps us attain "due rule" in our behavior, hope is a virtue. Moreover, since it depends on God's assistance, so that we can expect eternal happiness, "God is the principal object of hope, considered as a virtue" (II-II.17.5). Consequently, hope is a theological virtue, along with faith and charity. While eternal happiness, as its end, proves impossible on purely human grounds, our relationship with God makes it possible.

Immanuel Kant also weds the hope for happiness with the existence of God, albeit in a manner consistent with his transcendental philosophy. Hope concerns the possibility of the *summum bonum*. The highest good delivers the reward of happiness proportionate to our *worthiness* to be happy; we establish such worthiness by perfecting virtue—that is, by following the moral law. To keep morality free of heteronomy, Kant separates moral from empirical matters. Moreover, he argues that morality cannot have happiness as its object without introducing heteronomy. Kant explains that "morals has to do only with the rational conditions (*conditio sine qua non*) of happiness and not with means of achieving it."[1] The highest good, nevertheless, requires happiness combined with virtue. Though from a strictly human or moral perspective attaining this is impossible, Kant postulates the immortality of the soul and the existence of God to ensure that the highest good required by the moral life is indeed possible. The hope for happiness, attained in due proportion to virtue, is then a hope for something which does not lie within the power of a finite will. While we are responsible for our own virtue, we lack the power to ensure its proper reward of happiness. Apart from God, we cannot conceive of a cause capable of bringing about happiness in proportion to our attained virtue. Thus we must postulate His existence to preserve the promise of the moral life and the hope that arises from it.

Kant does argue, however, that postulating God does not absolve us of our own responsibility. We must perfect our virtue by seeking to act on purely moral grounds; otherwise we will never become worthy of the reward of happiness. Kant insists that "man is not entitled on this account to be idle in this business and to let Providence rule. . . . Rather must man proceed as though everything depended upon him; only on this condition dare he hope that higher wisdom will grant the completion of his well-intentioned endeavors."[2] Consequently, though realization of our ultimate hope depends on God, it also requires our own efforts and contributions. What is possible to us and lies within our own power (and indeed, *only* our own power) is duty—that is, following the moral law. What lies beyond that power is guaranteeing that our efforts will not be in vain. Kant thus captures the sense in which hoping is active and aims to contribute to the realization of some higher good; on his account, however, something more than human activity is needed to ensure the possibility of the highest good. That something more is God.

Kierkegaard also establishes a place for God in his account of hope. Kierkegaard does not focus primarily on hope but rather on despair, from whose grip hope delivers us. He articulates three different forms of despair, each of which involves a misrelation in the self, particularly in its relation to God.[3] Kierkegaard argues, for instance, that "only that person's life was wasted who . . . never became aware and in the deepest sense never gained the impression that there is a God and that 'he,' he himself, his self, exists before this God—an infinite benefaction that is never gained except through despair" (Kierkegaard 26–27). Despair results from failing to acknowledge our relation to that transcendent power which established us. Kierkegaard contends that we usually do not become aware of this relation until we have been brought to an extreme situation in which, "humanly speaking," there is no possibility. In the face of the impossible, we must decide whether we will believe in God and recognize that "with God everything is possible" (38). Such a belief, of course, means abandoning our reliance on finite human conditions and ends. Human abilities may seem powerful, capable of bringing us the goods we desire, yet they ultimately remain limited. Failure to recognize their limits leads to what Kierkegaard calls "despair of the eternal," which he describes as "an unwillingness to be comforted by and healed by the eternal, an overestimation of the things of this world to the extent that the eternal can be no consolation" (70). One lost in such despair focuses on and so is imprisoned by the limited conditions of the finite world. By contrast, one who truly believes is one who hopes; he acknowledges that with God everything is possible and so "leaves it entirely to God how he is to be helped" (38).

Consequently, without the ability to relate ourselves to God, Kierkegaard argues, we remain in despair. Proper relation of the self to itself requires relating to God, for though the self is a relation that relates itself to itself, it is a relation established by God. Whether things go poorly or even well, one who is unable to relate to God suffers a misrelation of the self and so despairs. The believer, though, has the "infallible antidote for despair—possibility—because for God everything is possible at every moment" (Kierkegaard 39–40). What is humanly impossible is nonetheless possible to God, but apart from bringing the self before God, we remain constrained by human limitations. Breaking out of despair requires coming before God and recognizing our "infinite benefaction."

Kierkegaard's position gives classic expression to the view of faith as a power that counteracts and leaps beyond reason. As such, it proves a natural ally of hope in the unconditioned. Its value and force lie not in establishing connection with habits and action, but rather in going beyond them and rejecting the limited ability they provide. Only such a faith, embracing the unconditioned in active defiance of "reasonable" conditions, can make meaningful the impossible; its absence leaves us tethered to the mundane possibilities which populate our daily life but really isolate us from the full life made possible by God. For Kierkegaard, faith sharply contrasts with reason and is shorn from the conditions of human life, which are too finite, limited, and—ultimately—limiting. Indeed, he celebrates Abraham's faith for its embrace of the impossible. He explains that "[b]y faith Abraham received the promise that in his seed all the generations of the earth would be blessed. Time passed, the possibility was there, Abraham had faith; time passed, it became unreasonable, Abraham had faith."[4] In facing the impossible, faith proves its conviction and commitment. Consequently, on this view, faith and hope are distinctive in enabling us to transcend not only our antecedent conditions but also our human condition.

This treatment of faith and of hope of course directly opposes the pragmatic theory developed here. Its faith depends on a force of conviction and choice severed from the conditions which make them meaningful and establish continuity with our other activities. Its hope lives by embracing the impossible freely and without a concern for context. By contrast, of course, our pragmatic view articulates a faith that is an integral element of intelligent activity manifested in acting *as if*. While it must acknowledge actual conditions, pragmatic faith does not thereby restrict us to them, for it aims to discover or create the very conditions which make possible new abilities. Similarly, pragmatic faith does not actively embrace the impossible, for such a move defies intelligence and renders our creativity random, disconnected, and dangerous. We then become beneficiaries of accidental rather than directed goods, and so lack the means of actively securing them again. Our creativity needs to be connected and fueled by our efforts, even as it stretches them. I return to these points in the next section.

Marcel's treatment of hope sounds a note similar to Kierkegaard's. In his complex characterization of the many dimensions of hope, he describes an "invincible hope" which arises "from the ruins of all human and limited hopes" (Marcel 47). He calls this hope an absolute hope, describing it as "inseparable from a faith which is likewise absolute, transcending all laying down of conditions, and for this very reason every kind of representation whatever it might be" (Marcel 46). When we surrender ourselves to absolute hope, we attain an absolute confidence and transcend all possible disappointments.[5] Since it sets no limits, there are no conditions relative to which absolute hope can fall short. While setting down conditions may provide guidance in realizing hope, Marcel argues that it also prepares the ground for despair, for if these conditions are not met, hope is lost and despair ensues.

In a passage reminiscent of Kierkegaard, Marcel further identifies the source of this hope as the absolute Thou, "the infinite Being to whom [one who hopes] is conscious of owing everything that it has and upon whom it cannot impose any condition whatsoever without scandal" (Marcel 47). Moreover, he argues that hope is best characterized not as a covetous desiring, but rather as a dynamic relationship captured by the phrase "I hope in thee for us" (Marcel 60). This relationship involves a communion—akin to love—between oneself and another.[6] This other, the "thou," can be another finite thou, but *absolute* hope requires an absolute Thou. The absolute Thou guarantees, Marcel argues, the union which holds the I and thou together, yet it is not something external to a preexisting union. Rather, he argues, the absolute Thou is "the very cement which binds the whole into one" (Marcel 60–61). Without an absolute Thou, we are left with only finite thous and so with a conditioned hope that is bedeviled by the specter of despair.

The Pragmatic Response

If hope is to be absolute such that we can embrace the impossible and hope against hope, it needs an unconditioned ground. What is conditioned is limited and so cannot be relied upon all the time. Habits are acquired and thus peculiar to specific individuals or communities; moreover, their efficacy waxes and wanes over time. Human agency can grow, but it cannot transcend all limitations. Not even intelligent habits provide the sort of stability and guarantee needed for an absolute hope. If hope is conditioned, it contains within itself the seeds of despair; if these conditions are not or cannot be met, we risk despondency. Consequently, pragmatism affords no absolute hope.

From a pragmatic perspective, however, hoping against hope depends not on an unconditioned ground, but rather on hopefulness. Though particular hopes may fail, hopefulness, when properly developed, functions as an enduring habit which energizes and sustains us. It enables us to forge new hopes on better grounds. Those who are hopeful remain steadfast in their openness to the future, ever ready to turn a spark which promises something more into a flame that burns brightly, warming and guiding us. As hoping indicates our constant commitment and investment in further possibilities, growing within a rich horizon of meaning, hopefulness promotes our ability to do so. Like optimists, the hopeful view the future as bright and filled with goodness; unlike optimists, however, they recognize that their hopefulness is itself a formative contributor to that future.

Nevertheless, hopefulness does not make possible what is impossible relative to finite temporal conditions. Hopefulness is a *conditioned* form of transcendence, not one which enables us to escape the world or transform it without limit. In hoping, we seek to respond to and overcome some original problematic situation. The end which proposes a resolution to the problem represents our liberation from it, but we can only realize that end *by building means to it.* When we are able to transform habits whose operation was frustrated, we transcend our antecedent limits and so alter the matrix of habits and ideals whose integration is the activity of the self. Hopefulness represents a form of transcendence by enabling us to maintain hope apart from the trials of particular hopes. It is nevertheless conditioned by particular hopes and their habits, since it develops through their pursuit and coordination. While it enables us to survive the demise of particular hopes, hopefulness does not enjoy complete independence from them. Hoping is a forward-moving activity that leaps beyond our limitations not by escaping them, but rather by modifying them.

To insist that everything is or should be possible through hoping, then, is to overreach the bounds of hope's practicality. It means drifting from hoping into wishful thinking, for we then lack means in virtue of which we can build connections to our ends. From a pragmatic perspective, hoping is practical in both of the senses we have examined *precisely because* it is conditioned. Abraham's hope, if interpreted as the human embrace of the impossible, serves not as the paradigm of hoping, but rather as the very sort of activity which drains hope of practicality. To demand from hope the power to not only encounter but also to embrace the impossible is to sever it from our action and our horizons of meaning. While such a demand may express our desire to be more than we currently are, it debilitates us by turning us from the very conditions which make possible and meaningful our transcendent activity. Rather than a flight from natural conditions, hoping is a *transformation* and *enhancement* of them.

One could object that Abraham exemplifies the very best of our human capacities, defying the conditions around him through the force of his faith. Indeed, it could be argued that while his hope is not practically grounded in his own abilities, it is nevertheless incredibly productive in promoting the kind of growth and strength which can only come from the unlimited power of the Lord. Any other form of hope is by comparison a mundane counterpart of planning and not a genuine hope.

Certainly, Abraham's hoping embodies habits we can praise. He shows patience and also a trust in external forces. Yet from a pragmatic perspective, hoping requires much more than this. It requires active participation and engagement; indeed, hoping is an active readiness. We are not passive recipients of hope's gifts but rather contributors to its achievements, funding its creativity with our efforts even as that same creativity transforms us. To designate adherence to the impossible as the hallmark of hoping is to be bewitched by the specter of despair, to find it lurking everywhere, and to overlook our resources in meeting it. Hope's power is not primarily one of avoidance, but one of enhancement and growth. This pragmatic position is not naively optimistic; rather, it acknowledges the power of our capacities and their continuity with the environment. Our environment may smite us, but we also live vibrantly in its bosom by means of resources it makes possible. Though we can admire Abraham's patience, we should recognize that his faith in the impossible leads him to do what is deeply problematic: namely, attempt to kill his son. Abraham does not even question the Lord's command, but simply acts in obedience. Since his faith is measured by its demonstration of fealty, it is shorn from the checks of intelligence. Tethering hope to the impossible and severing it from intelligence, then, may encourage us to act in a manner that is blind and defies the directives of rationality and morality.

In response to theories which contend that hope must be tied to the unconditioned, we can argue four central points. The first we have already discussed. The demand that hope provide a guarantee that will make the impossible possible is simply too high a demand—and one that drains hoping of its meaning. Second, an unconditioned ground is unnecessary and, moreover, undesirable, especially insofar as it fosters neglect of actual conditions and breeds resistance to adapting ends. While the traditional position does emphasize hope's transcendence, it does so by severing it from other human abilities and activities. Third, not all hopes should be pursued; some are poorly formed and destructively pursued. Finally, though they do not provide an absolute ground, habits and human abilities are not thereby unduly frail and unreliable; they still possess incredible power to transform ourselves and the environment.

From a pragmatic perspective, the appeal to something unconditioned or absolute is generally both unnecessary and undesirable; this is no less true of hoping. Both Dewey and James, for instance, argue at length against the need for an unconditioned ground of knowledge or truth as well as an absolute, transcendent standard of value.[7] Their standard argument is the contextualist one that truths and values are conditioned by the features of their relevant contexts. Truths have a bearing and ends are valued not absolutely but rather in relation to their particular uses, especially in response to problematic situations. Truth and value, then, are understood functionally as rooted and tested in particular contexts. This is not to deny that there are pervasive beliefs and shared goods which transcend limited contexts; indeed there are, but these do not transcend all contexts or require an unconditioned ground to justify them. Rather, their ability to function in guiding our activity, especially to desired ends, provides their warrant. Moreover, our ability to break out of limits is a function of human creativity that springs from the embeddedness of human life and activity. It is rooted in the continuity of individual and environmental powers that is embodied in habits.[8]

Important to contextualist arguments like these is the pragmatist's allegiance to the empirical method. This method places emphasis on making clear the conditions relative to which beliefs and values can be tested. Dewey argues:

> The adoption of an empirical method is no guarantee that all things relevant to any particular conclusion will actually be found, or that when found they will be correctly shown and communicated. But empirical method points out when and where and how things of a designated description have been arrived at. It places before others a map of the road that has been traveled; they may accordingly, if they will, re-travel the road to inspect the landscape for themselves. (LW 1:34)

Careful assessment of actual conditions plays a significant role in determining what can and needs to be done. Apart from it, we act blindly, either following past patterns without concern for their continued efficacy or happening upon goods and evils without knowing (or taking measure to know) how we can further secure or avoid them. We then act without the guidance of purpose and choice, which function as principles of selection in directing our activities. Finite contextual conditions, then, provide touchstones relative to which we can test the efficacy or value of ideas and gauge our progress in realizing desired ends. Apart from such conditions, a problematic situation cannot be defined and a proposed end lacks relevance in virtue of which it can function as a resolution. Ends then become free-floating and arbitrary, imposing demands upon us which cannot be evaluated. This independence does not give them greater worth, but either drains them of their value or suppresses their relations to an actual context in which they are valued and valuable.

Suggesting that hoping requires an unconditioned ground which ensures that even what appears impossible is really possible provides us no actual conditions relative to which we can guide or judge our action. The assurance that our hopes will be realized, thus, does not provide us any indication as to *how* this will occur.[9] Hoping then becomes random and passive rather than an activity in which we vitally participate with intelligence and creativity. Moreover, to the extent that it makes unnecessary the search for and assessment of the finite conditions which can function as means to our ends, the appeal to an absolute or unconditioned ground curtails intelligent action and habit formation. Consequently, absolute hoping has an inescapably blind element in it. The danger in not attending to concrete conditions is that we then typically defer to already established habits rather than intelligently assess and transform them in light of current problems. Of course, we also may smuggle in, perhaps unknowingly, contextual conditions, finite though they may be.[10] We better direct our activity, though, when we deliberately attend to specific contexts with specifiable conditions, for these provide us materials with and upon which we can act, thereby giving us greater ability to regulate our interaction with the environment.

Additionally, to the extent that it sanctions neglecting actual conditions, grounding the activity of hoping in the unconditioned often leads to an impairing fixation on specific ends. They then function as terminations rather than means. Consider the cancer patient who has exhausted numerous possible treatments, only to find herself no better.

If she believes that the unconditioned guarantees her hope for recovery, she will not seek any alternate forms of hope, such as facing death with dignity and living the remainder of her days in a manner continuous with life before the onset of the cancer, as Bob DeMatteis did. Pursuing a hope is risky since it involves focusing and expending energy on one end rather than another. Precious alternatives can be lost in the process. Fixation on a single end (or one kind of end) when there are no means through which it can be realized heightens hope's risk and potential tragedy, for it leads to overlooking viable alternatives. In such a case, "faith" indicates not the willingness to act *as if*, but rather immovable devotion to a belief despite actual conditions. Consequently, it ceases to function as an active instrument of interaction. Instead, it signifies our capacity to rigidly defy and become indifferent to our environment. As noted above, though our environment can crush us, it also harbors the materials by means of which we can transform and enhance natural conditions. This is the power of hope to enrich the world rather than to escape it. By contrast, hope that is fueled by a faith ambivalent to actual conditions lacks the ability and commitment to test the beliefs on which it is based, and so reveals itself as stubborn adherence to desired ends and dogma.

Abandoning a particular hope does not in itself necessitate abandoning hope. The impossibility or failure of one hope need not lead to despair, for we can pursue other, better, ends. Nor is there something powerful in implacably embracing the impossible as the proper sign of genuine hoping. Particular hopes may be limited, but it is rarely, if ever, the case that *every* alternative is impossible. While persistence and courage in the face of great odds are powerful virtues, they are even more powerful when coupled with resourcefulness, whether our own or that of others. Moreover, even when we have no particular hope in sight, hopefulness can sustain us as we patiently await new possibilities in which to invest ourselves. Consequently, though a pragmatic account of hope fails to offer the sort of guarantee that absolute hope purportedly provides, the objection that conditioned modes of hoping invariably or typically lead to despair is ill-founded.

We should also recognize that some hopes simply should not be pursued. Though our investment in them indicates their value to us, the desirability of ends should be assessed and reassessed in light of changing circumstances. The more severed they are from our means, the more they approximate wishes and heighten the risk of wasting energy. Martha's hope to beat depression on her own proved unsuccessful and only compounded her troubles. Our adherence to ends which increasingly threaten to deplete our resources and undermine supporting habits is foolish and destructive. Indeed, it is ignorance or defiance of real conditions, and *not* the pursuit of hopes in light of them, which leads to detachment and so to despair.

Finally, a pragmatic theory of hope recognizes that though habits are limited in scope and susceptible to both liberating and inhibiting forms of change, they nevertheless provide our primary structures of guidance and support. Habits can fail, but they rarely, if ever, all collapse at once. We should not rest complacently in our habits, simply accepting the structures they provide. Though rooted in habits, practical hoping should not be restricted by them, for hoping is practical precisely in developing and transforming habits. Cedric learns to be sensitive to those habits which hold him back, especially in interacting with his fellow students; Red eventually does the same in shaking off his tendency to wait rather than await. We should strive to form more intelligent habits which are flexible enough to enable us to meet changing circumstances and also foster development of more complicated coordinated activities. While a faith that faces the impossible may demonstrate conviction and commitment, it does not reveal our power to adapt and grow—to make possible a conditioned form of transcendence which transforms both individual and environment. Flexibility, and not fixity, is the key to good habits; through it we can maximize our habits' capacity to aid our quest for more comprehensive goods. Participating in the life of hope is itself one way of doing this.

Flexible habits provide the basis for a faith in meliorism. Such a faith means acting *as if* our contribution can improve conditions— intelligently assessing means and ends, testing the success of our ends-in-view as guides by acting on them, and adapting ends when necessary—to see if this is actually the case. In the process, of course, coordinating our habits with those of others increases the scope of our abilities and the security of our accomplishments; otherwise, progress is more likely restricted and fleeting. We may in fact seek to connect our actions with greater powers than our own. Pragmatists are averse not to the idea of divinity per se, but rather to positions which demand that we understand divinity as an absolute or unconditioned being. Such a being is so radically distinct from us that we lack the ability to make it continuous with ourselves and our activities. Our relation to divinity, so understood, is typically grounded in the sort of blind unwavering faith that allows no room for reason or intelligence. Though believing in such an unlimited deity may humble us, it does not stir our imagination. As we have noted, appeals to the unconditioned undermine our attention to conditions and so leave us blind. We then either smuggle in conditions (but without careful attention to context, thereby increasing the risk of error) or simply act randomly.

Pragmatists embrace either a finite temporal god or a god that is more an ideal than a being with an antecedent existence; neither option ignores the influence of contextual conditions or the role of intelligence. James opts for the first alternative. He argues against the typically philosophical accounts which treat God as something absolute and thereby radically different from us. He rejects such an unconditioned being, for it lacks an environment or context. James explains, "I can hardly conceive of anything more different from the absolute than the God, say, of David or of Isaiah. *That* God is an essentially finite being *in* the cosmos, not with the cosmos in him, and indeed he has a very local habitation there, and very one-sided local and personal attachments" (PU 111). In contrast to the position which places God outside of time and history—presumably to ensure that He can know in advance whether good will prevail over evil—James's God is a finite being, more an ally in the cause of goodness than its guarantor. Without abandoning his pragmatic commitment to contextuality, James professes that "there is a God, but that he is finite, either in power or in knowledge, or in both at once. These, I need hardly tell you, are the terms in which common men have usually carried on their active commerce with God" (PU 311). Such a deity has more power than we do, but He still needs and benefits from our assistance in securing the place of goodness in this world. We are thus allies with God in the cause of improving the world.

Dewey favors treating God as an ideal (or collection of ideals) inviting us to action. He argues that the problem with belief in God as a supernatural being, disconnected from and yet efficacious in the world, is that it does not improve (and often impedes) our ability to deal with natural conditions. Reliance on the supernatural comes at the price of attention to actual conditions. Consequently, Dewey contends that we should reconsider how we understand God. Rather than thinking of Him as a being with a complete antecedent existence, he suggests we think of God as "the unity of all ideal ends arousing us to desire and actions" (LW 9:29).[11] This is not to deny God "reality," for, as Dewey notes, the power of ideal ends is "vouched for by their undeniable power in action" (LW 9:30). God is thus conceived as the unity of ideals around which we focus our efforts and to which we give our loyalties.

Dewey rightly notes that ideals need not be hypostatized to have power. He argues that we have traditionally vouchsafed our ideals by locating them in God's nature, where they are free from the caprices of existence. The problem with such an approach is that securing these ideals in this world then becomes not a matter of natural action aided by intelligence, but one of supernatural intervention. Reliance on supernatural control indicates an attitude of externality and a lack of faith in human intelligence. Dewey argues that "appeal for supernatural intervention in improvement of social matters is also the expression of a deep-seated *laissez-faireism;* it is the acknowledgment of the desperate situation into which we are driven by the idea of the irrelevance and futility of human intervention in social events and interests" (LW 9:52). Yet, appeal to the supernatural impedes progress in human achievement, for "[t]he needed understanding [of actual conditions] will not develop unless we strive for it. The assumption that only supernatural agencies can give control is a sure method of retarding this effort" (LW 9:51).

Kierkegaard, of course, argues against such views of God precisely because they shun the assistance which the eternal can provide. When we despair of the eternal, he argues, we prefer reliance one our own abilities. Dewey's point, though, is that since reliance on the eternal or supernatural draws our attention away from actual conditions, it does not help us achieve greater security in the world. Rather than diverting our attention to the supernatural, we better promote the cause of goodness by attending to concrete natural conditions. The eternal *can be* understood as the ideal, yet what is significant about it as an ideal is not its exemption from current conditions but its fruitfulness in helping us improve them. Importantly, this conception of the divine separates neither God from us nor us from our human powers. Dewey argues that "this idea of God, or of the divine, is also connected with all the natural forces and conditions—including man and human association—that promote the growth of the ideal and that further its realization" (LW 9:34). A conception of God as representing those ideals which we seek to realize does not preclude or limit our intelligence and imaginative creativity but *actively employs* them.

Moreover, this conception of God is compatible with a natural piety which acknowledges that we are cooperating parts of a larger whole, for it recognizes our place and interaction in nature and the relevance of natural conditions to securing goods. We can then embrace Kierkegaard's general point that we despair when we fall out of relation with our ground, but we should pragmatically understand that ground to be the habits which make possible our interaction with natural and social environments. This becomes especially clear by the fact that our abilities are limited and frequently stagnated when our habits are not or cannot be coordinated with others. Similarly, when we persist in routines which do not foster productive interaction, we become increasingly isolated from our environment and from our ideals. Consequently, despair results from disconnection, and hope is fostered by restoring and expanding connection.

Though neither articulates clearly the nature of the deity in which they believe, Cedric and Martha are both people of religious faith. Through hoping, their faith is both challenged and deepened. While I do not wish to pretend to truly understand the details of their faith or to impose my own interpretation upon them, I do think it appropriate to note how these two very powerful hopers develop a faith that is compatible with pragmatism. One of the securities Barbara ensures for Cedric is the love, support, and community of Scripture Church, a congregation of mostly black Pentecostals. When delivering the salutatory address at his high school graduation, Cedric explains that whenever faced with the chiding remarks of his peers, "I said to myself, 'THERE IS NOTHING ME AND MY GOD CAN'T HANDLE'" (Suskind 137, capital letters in original). The faith he learns from his church downplays human reason and abilities,[12] and Cedric largely shares this belief. Yet, as often happens with young college students, he begins to question his faith while at Brown. As he faces adversity in his new environment, Barbara tells him that his difficulties are trials from God, which he needs to meet with prayer and devotion. Gradually, though, Cedric begins to suspect that more is needed, especially to realize his hopes. He wonders, "if God created everyone . . . what ultimately differentiates the winners from the rest? Take the kids who made it to Brown. Some are people of faith, most are not. But . . . very few of them arrived by putting their trust in God and praying everything would work out. Took a lot more than that" (Suskind 274). After his first year, he returns to Ballou and talks with Mr. Taylor, whose advice to Cedric was always sprinkled with messages of religious inspiration. Cedric reminds Mr. Taylor that he once misquoted scripture, tying hope to an unseen place. He tells his former teacher (in a passage we have already noted) that he still believes in that place, but now realizes "that there's work I need to do, too. I need to know—to really know—who I am, and accept who I am, deal with some of my own issues. That's got to come first, before I can expect other people to accept me" (Suskind 330). Cedric thus recognizes that he needs to play an active role in pursuing his hopes, in realizing his "hope in the unseen." Later, he talks with Bishop Long, explaining, "I still believe in God, that Jesus is my personal savior, and my friend, and my guide, but I just don't feel as tied to the church so much anymore. I like coming and all, but, at the same time, I feel like I'm ready to venture out" (Suskind 358). Cedric does not abandon his faith, but he does modify it to allow room for his own contribution. (His position is akin to Kant's in that he comes to realize how very much human effort is required to realize the goods we hold dear.) He no longer separates faith from reason and human ability, but comes to see them as integrated.

Martha's religious faith also changes as a consequence of her experience hoping. Though raised in a Catholic home and educated in

Catholic schools, Martha is, as her tale begins, estranged from her faith. She still attends church and listens to the sermons, yet God seems to play little role in her personal life. She feels disconnected not only from Him but also from nature. At one point, as allergies only add to her suffering, she bitterly notes, "I know it's beautiful and everything, but to be perfectly honest, I hate nature. And with my itchy face, swollen nose, bloodshot eyes, and wheezing lungs, I'm pretty sure the feelings are mutual" (89). Thus, she feels disconnected not only in her daily life but also in her spiritual life. As she begins to recover, though, she renews her faith, largely by tapping into nature's passing but vital beauties as well as its reassuring patterns. When she discovers tulips left anonymously in her mailbox, she finds herself entranced by their beauty, transitory though it may be. She explains that "[t]hey are breathtaking—a fiery re-orange opening to reveal the most incredible golden stars in their centers. Each time I catch sight of them, I am enthralled. I lose my focus, my balance . . . . for a moment I let myself believe in God again" (167). Moreover, she eventually comes to find solace in nature's recurring patterns. Upon viewing a beautiful sunset, Martha explains that "[o]nce more, I acknowledge the possibility of God. In my own narcissistic and grandiose way, I image that God is trying to tell me that nature is bigger than I am, that beauty will eventually win out over shit. That the sun will come up and go down despite every lousy fucked-up thing that happens on this earth. . . . It always leaves and it always returns" (174). Tapping into natural patterns is precisely what she needs, especially since she lost touch with the comfort of patterns during her depression. Personal rituals seemed to fade away, and natural patterns tended to oppress rather than console. Yet now Martha finds herself open to the world again, reestablishing contact, letting the divine back into her life, albeit in predominantly natural manifestations.

Both Martha and Cedric demonstrate the power of habits of hope and also different ways of synthesizing faith with their own limitations and abilities. Cedric's faith, like pragmatic faith, is integrated with intelligent adaptive activity. Martha's renewed faith bears the marks of natural piety. Having weathered her depression via the remaining forces of her hopefulness, she reawakens to a sense of divinity manifested in our natural environment. Neither she nor Cedric invokes the unlimited power of an unconditioned god, yet each blends religious faith with his or her habits of hope. Neither builds faith on the platform of an unconquerable force or clings to hope as a means of escaping the world. Similarly, neither lives a life of hope in ignorance or defiance of the natural web of life. Each finds meaningful connections in and through human and natural contexts. Both Martha and Cedric build hope on practical grounds and enjoy the growth of abilities made possible by hoping.

Hope does have limits, yet we can continually strive to transcend or transform them. Hoping aims at the realization of arduous ends which not only strain but also foster the expansion of our abilities. At times, we find ourselves unable to overcome obstacles, either through directed action or through patient attentive awaiting. In such cases, we should intelligently determine whether it is best to modify our ends or persist in pursuing them. We have seen that adaptation of ends is especially profitable, for it keeps our energies flowing and so prevents the slide into despair. Nevertheless, we should recognize that when cut off from the grounds needed to realize a hope, our own efforts are not the only ones that bear on the situation. Our habits operate in the larger context of communities, which interweave values and abilities to form a rich shared life. We can and should generally seek to coordinate our activities with others who share similar values and ends. Doing so, of course, not only grows out of the fertile seat of already existing ones, but also prompts the development of new ones. As we have seen, hoping lives in concrete relationships, especially in the habits and ideals we share with family and friends. Consequently, we can foster hopefulness in ourselves and others.

In celebration of this point, I end this chapter with the quiet but powerful final scene of the film adaptation of *The Shawshank Redemption*. Red has broken parole and traveled to Mexico to find his friend. Though most of the movie is set in the cold dark confines of prison life, the last segment shows Red walking along a white beach, approaching Andy, who works on a boat. As the two friends reunite, the camera shifts to frame the scene against the backdrop of the deep blue ocean and a bright clear sky. This final image dramatically combines an exhilarating sense of liberation with the rich meaningfulness of close

personal friendships.[13] Both ocean and sky represent the infinite expanse of possibilities, the *more* toward which hopefulness orients us.
Tethering this expanse, providing a point relative to which it can be accessible and meaningful, is the concrete connection between two
human beings. The film's closing sequence visually embodies the
power of hope in its conditioned, transcendent nature. This is the heart
of hope: born in the intimacy of concrete relationships, it opens up
broad new horizons that stretch beyond the limits of our current capacities.

Conclusion

Celebrating Hope

Red and Andy, Rose of Sharon and Ma, Cedric and Barbara, Martha and her family all possess and are supported by individual and social habits which make possible rich lives of hope. Especially in the case of the first three groups, we see reciprocity develop between those in close relationships, which allows hope to spread from one individual to the next. Red is warmed by the flames of Andy's fire, Rose assumes her mother's role as agent of hope, and Cedric realizes his hopes aided by his mother's faith and determination. In the process, Red and Rose in particular grow into the life of hope under the strength and guidance of Andy and Ma. Moreover, as a consequence of their pursuit of hope, Rose of Sharon and Cedric become agents of hope who are able to support others and nurture the life of hope beyond themselves. Indeed, we see novice become guide, as Cedric pushes Barbara to invest in hopes for herself rather than simply for him. Hope thus spreads by means of an infectious social quality that invigorates the life of hope. Far from being a mysterious force disconnected from our abilities, hope is integrated into the fabric of our lives, developed through our activities and nurtured through our interpersonal relationships.

We have examined how hope reinforces its own habits, as well as how the hopeful nurture those with whom they interact. We have also noted both the dynamics which promote its growth and the growth which it in turn promotes. We develop habits, and so virtues, under the example of those who already possess them. Not only children, but also people of all ages model the behavior of others, drawing inspiration from living example and precedent. The life of hope, then, is shot through with social influences at every level. We learn to formulate ideals in tandem with others. We pursue particular hopes, sometimes succeeding and sometimes failing, in the company of those we love. And as we develop habits of hope and the hopefulness which helps us weather our trials, we reach out to others, inspiring *them*, sharing our own hopes with them, and contributing our abilities as best we can to foster the growth of agency.

We should expect hope's reciprocity as a natural flowering of the life of hope. Helping others and nurturing hope is expressive of hopefulness itself. It is an extension of the hopeful self to reach out to others, promoting the connection of agency and the enrichment of horizons of meaning. Hope's reciprocity grows out of the very social nature of hope; we thus frequently see it live in family relations, in intimacy, in love. And so hope spreads. This spreading should not surprise us; like love, it is freely given, fostered, and nurtured. St. Paul rightly groups hope with faith and love. We have already noted how hope is interwoven with faith, albeit of a pragmatic rather than insistent or blind sort. But hope is also interwoven with love. It has a dynamic, expansive, infectious quality which grows from the concern and investment of others, and which in turn fosters the same. We become cohorts, companions in our journeys of hope. Those we love provide invaluable support for us when we face the difficult situations that generate hopes. Hopefulness itself, the jewel of the life of hope, radiates its own warmth, possessing an expansive and social dimension which, though it can characterize the self, does not belong solely to one individual person.

Consequently, whether our participation in the life of hope is rooted in the deep intimacies of love or simply the shared pursuit of ideals common to more general communal relations, the life of hope lives beyond mere individuals in vibrant communities. A community, of course, is more than a generic social relationship. It is one in which individuals share ideals and habits and so play an integral role in affecting the needs, goals, and abilities of one another. Sometimes communities are developed when antecedently distinct individuals deliberately come together to form new unions. This happens when we create special groups or societies to address specific human needs. Far more often, however, we find ourselves already thinking, acting, and living in communities comprised of family, friends, and neighbors. We develop our values and habits as we grow up in these contexts. If we find these too restrictive or inadequately expressive of who we are or want to be, we can establish new associations, new families, and new communities in which to act and live in ways that better foster development of a hoped-for self. Hope can play an integral role in the genesis or reconstruction of communities. For instance, by transmitting wisdom, dreams, and skills from one generation to the next, our schools mark a complex means by which we promote our hopes. Hospitals, though often grim to visit because of their halls filled with tragedy and loss, are bastions of hope, for we have marked them out, both physically and morally, as places of healing, recovery, and restoration. Communities of hope also exist in private organizations, in benefactor relationships such as those Cedric enjoys. We thus can, and do, become a people unified in hope, not only in some abstract ideal but also in the concrete habits that make a community.

We have many communities of hope, formed deliberately or otherwise. If we are to be active agents of hope, responsibly cultivating the conditions which foster it, we must attend to the habits which define ourselves and our communities. We must intelligently assess the ways they nurture hope and do our best to keep them directed at hope. The primary thesis of this book has been that we are invested in the life of hope, directly or indirectly, by means of our habits. These provide the conditioned basis for hope's special transcendence. By hoping, we develop, consolidate, and transform our basic abilities, widening our horizons in the process to direct ourselves toward growth. We need to recognize the threads of hope that weave through our very being and to continue to weave them into our practices and communities. In that

way we make hope an integral part of our legacy. One message a pragmatic theory of hope gives special emphasis to is our responsibility for
the life of hope. Recall the contrast between optimism and meliorism
articulated in chapter 3. The optimist has a spectator's assurance that
things will work out for the best. The meliorist, by contrast, knows that
the fate of goodness depends in part on our own contribution. The
vital ingredient is our own ongoing active participation. The life of
hope has a special power to draw us on beyond ourselves, yet in its
essence it is not something that transcends human abilities and capabil-
ities. Some think hope an intangible force, but while it can have intangible effects, it is not itself intangible. The heart of the life of hope
consists in habits, and though they are products of interaction rather
than the sole possession of isolated individuals, our habits are those
abilities which lie within our control. Hope's most "elusive" power—
the creative and sustaining power of hopefulness—is itself born of the
complex coordination of habits. Hoping beyond hope, if it is to have
pragmatic meaning, must have some connection with the modes of
agency we form by interacting with our environments. Hope is not a
mysterious force imbued with supernatural power which allows us to
transcend any and every condition, but rather a creative ability whereby we overcome limitations and transform ourselves and our environment. This is not to say that hope's progress is not marked by surprises.
Such surprises are likely as we discover and develop new abilities and
possibilities as we hope. Hope's transcendence is affected by the indeterminacies of interaction and life itself, indicating events that grow
into confluence because of what we and other forces do. This is the
pragmatic meliorist faith. The life of hope requires that we nurture it.

A pragmatic theory of hope does not guarantee that every hope
will be realized, nor that developing habits of hope will insulate us
from the specter of despair. Traditional theories claim to give us hope
in every set of circumstances by grounding hope in the inexhaustible
resource of the unconditioned. A pragmatic account also provides for
the possibility of hope in every situation, but relies on our powers of
intelligence and adaptability to find its proper manifestation. We can
find hope even in the worst of times, though we may not be able to
find a particular desired hope. Our pursuit of hopes does not take

place in a spiritual vacuum, but storing our treasures in the unconditioned puts them out of our reach and so disconnects us from the life
of hope. A far more vibrant picture is the meliorist one in which we
are members of the family of God, contributors whose actions matter
and play an important, if not decisive, role in the fruition of goodness
and meaning. There is much that we can individually and collectively
do to build up the life of hope, so that hope is a companion in our
darkest hours. Martha's case is a glowing example of this. She is armed
with formidable abilities. She turns to those who can help her, and
she learns to let them do so. She keeps hope alive where she can, and
she lets her family's love protect her with the warmth of human companionship, even as she slips into the frigid darkness of depression.
There is so much we can do, for ourselves and for others, to promote
hope; indeed, there is so much we already do. And so we should sal-
vage the good name of hope and actively promote its life at every
turn.

How do we do so? The obvious starting point is to take stock of
the habits we already have, asking which structures of our own behavior reinforce and make pursuit of hope possible and fruitful. But we also
need to attend to the negative forces that either compete for or drain
our energies. Fear, in particular, is a potent enemy of the life of hope,
one whose effects we far too often ignore or underestimate.

Fear can play a productive, indeed life-saving, function by alerting
us to dangers to which we must quickly respond. As security specialist
Gavin De Becker observes in his book, *The Gift of Fear,* however, we
often confuse this sort of fear with worry. De Becker describes worry
as the "fear we manufacture."[1] While authentic fear responds to a real
threat in our present environment, worry builds up potential threats in
the indefinite future. Worry, whether fostered in our own imaginative
flights of fancy or in the media marketplace, carries an artificial urgen-
cy that tends to distract us, encouraging us to funnel our energies into
warding off every potential evil, whether near or remote. The media,
especially advertisers and the news agencies, know all too well how
the scent of fear stops us cold and makes us focus on fear. Television
commercials advertising the topic of news programs are infamous for
using fear or worry as a hook. They announce an ominous situation

that is spreading, posing a potential threat to each viewer, and then suggest that if you watch the program, you will receive the needed information to avoid dreadful consequences. De Becker is especially critical of local media, arguing that "[l]ocal news rarely provides new or relevant information about safety, but its urgent delivery mimics importance and this gets our attention" (358). Fear is legitimate in our immediate environment, yet the news usually either reports events that have already happened (and so are not authentic objects of fear) or suggests that similar threats lurk around every corner and plague all of us. We are far better off, De Becker argues, attending to our immediate environment than to the stories served up on the local news, for otherwise we buy into paranoia—literally and figuratively. Fear, as De Becker argues, "has a rightful place in our lives, but it isn't the marketplace" (358).

The danger in the media's embrace of fear and worry is that we waste precious energy and also poison our horizons of meaning. Worrying tends to attach itself to the indeterminate, spreading to and infecting every potential situation. Each possible good is then sabotaged by innumerable "what-ifs" of the kind which paralyze rather than prompt action. This moves in quite the opposite direction from hoping, which, like planning, always keeps an eye on real conditions. Of course, hoping requires that we consider the pregnancy of current situations, yet it does so aimed at securing goods we desire. Staying active and building continuity, then, are the key, and both of these require focusing on determinacies rather than getting lost amid indeterminacies.

We must be attentive to and cautious about fear, but of course we should not make it the primary focus of our attention, especially if we want to nurture the life of hope. In his interview with Cornel West, Bill Bradley rightly remarks that "[w]e need to begin to share the good news as well as draw back from the bad news and to recognize that the bad news is not as pervasive as it seems." He adds that "[a]t the same time, [we must] not run away from real problems" (West 47). This is a call to look squarely at reality, acknowledging the actuality of evil and of good, but also perceptively seeing possibilities pregnant in the present. Similarly, rather than becoming prisoners of fear and worry, we need to *celebrate* hope, rejoicing in its images and various manifestations while also nurturing its habits. Even though the news media tend to emphasize fear, there are also outlets which focus on stories of hope. Televisions newsmagazines often include a segment that charts the victory of courage in helping individuals overcome contemporary forms of adversity. The *Reader's Digest* and supplemental magazines to Sunday newspapers do the same. These prove potentially valuable resources in spreading hope. In order to truly celebrate hope, however, we need to ensure that these images are practical, presented with enough detail so we can see the workings of habits. They must give adequate attention to the actual problems and challenges faced as well as the sometimes imperceptible development of powers of response. Otherwise, our images may stir our emotions, but they will not inspire the activity of hoping.

Furthermore, we should recognize the role external forces play. As we have noted, other people can play a powerful part in promoting or hindering our hopes. Moreover, the contingency of events can also affect the outcomes of hoping. Hopes sometimes come to fruition because of changes in events not entirely of our own making. The life of hope does not lie fully within our control. Yet as I have argued throughout this book, there is much we can do to actively participate in and strengthen hope. We can nurture habits of hope in ourselves and in others. Even when we are at the limits of our agency, facing events we cannot control, we need to be attentive to those ways of acting that enable us to keep hope alive. As we celebrate images of hope, we should appreciate the full range of hope. We should not locate it solely in the domain of tragedy and luck, for hopes are extensional as well as salvific, though they may be both at the same time. We must not restrict our images of hope or our appreciation of its power to cases where "hope beyond hope" is the paradigm. Hope has power here, but that power is the force of hopefulness, a force which grows out of seemingly more mundane habits of hope.

We celebrate and promote hope by telling stories of hope, whether real or fictional. Doing so carries the benefits discussed in chapter 2. Imaginative explorations prompted by the stories we hear, see, and read open new worlds to us. But just as important are the stories we tell of shared histories, detailing the struggles and triumphs which bring together families and communities. Indeed, personal stories of hope carry added meaning to us, for they define the events which have shaped our identities and our horizons of meaning. They establish links of continuity between generations, giving ancestors a distinct identity and awakening a sense of heritage which runs through us from past to present and future.

Many of the interviews in West's book *Restoring Hope* articulate this point. For instance, in addressing the grounds of hope for contemporary African Americans, Charlayne Hunter-Gault explains that "it's our history that has always been our source of hope" (West 65). She notes that intergenerational values and historical knowledge provide us a suit of armor to wear in the face of continued struggles. Rather than reinforcing the impression that nothing can be done to change things, the personal stories of hope which shape the contours of black history in America prove a source of hope, for they provide reminders that others, linked to us by blood or history, have struggled and survived. The personal link—the power of personal connection—is significant here, for it indicates not simply that certain acts have been possible before, but also that they have informed, shaped, and sustained those with whom we share a history. They indicate real possibilities whose realization has made us what we are. Hunter-Gault argues that if we share our history with young people, then "that suit of armor and the knowledge base, historical knowledge [alive, we should add, in our sinews by means of habits] will give them the strength to challenge and not back down" (West 68). Consequently, histories of hope not only perform the general function of funding the imagination by broadening our sense of possibilities, but especially where there is some personal connection, also give us greater confidence and so courage to act. Insofar as we are continuous with these hopers, we can say, "We have done this before; we can do it again."

West describes African Americans as a people of hope (West 45), a people who have successfully retained and lived on hope as they have weathered vicious forms of oppression ranging from slavery to a prejudice that robs them of opportunities and challenges their dignity. West's book is a call to remind the different generations of blacks in

America how much their history is a history of hope, to remind them that hope is fragile and needs to be tended and renewed. He argues that restoring hope includes reminding ourselves of our stories of hope, of the habits of courage, persistence, and resourcefulness, which buoyed our ancestors and which can do the same for present and future generations. His book is itself an expression of this hope. While his primary focus is the role of hope in the history of African Americans, West's message should be heard by all Americans—indeed, by all people. We are successors to generations who invested their lives in the hope for a better life. If we are to carry on this legacy, we must actively tend to hope, recognizing how its power enriches the meaning of our lives. We all have stories of hope (as well as of despair) which color and sometimes direct our actions as they did those of our ancestors. From the Renaissance hope to better understand the natural world to the twentieth-century hope to overcome debilitating disease and misfortune, our history bears the imprint of hope. Hope leaves more than footprints in the sand—it creates legacies, buildings, families, communities, institutions, histories. We bear responsibility for continuing the legacy of hope; it requires our active commitment and our creativity.

Celebrating images of hope proves a powerful source of inspiration, but of course hope lives in the habits, communities, and institutions that we inherit and continually re-create. We must acknowledge the variety of agencies of hope that range from individuals like Martin Luther King, Jr., and Martha Manning to the communities of hope formed on the forces of medicine, technology, and education. Hope requires time to develop and come to fruition; consequently, it often does not take the spotlight. Nevertheless, we should actively ensure that it does not live entirely behind the scenes but rather in the open sunshine, breathing the clean air. We should celebrate hope as a revitalizing force in our lives, but also recognize how that revitalization requires work, care, and intelligence.

In addition to sharing images of hope, then, we should also celebrate those existing structures (whether complex institutions or common practices) which form the basis of various communities of hope. In the remainder of the chapter, I will highlight three such bases:

technology, education, and volunteerism. While much more attention needs to be given to each of these, I want to sketch here the contours of each—as well as the prominent problems that attend them—in order to demonstrate just how fully the forces of hope permeate our lives. Our first example consists of the various communities of hope grounded in technological advances. Technologies promote communities of hope when they are a means to enlarging our agency and so bring ends closer to us, thereby multiplying the meaningful and satisfying goods that are really possible to us. Moreover, like habits, they increase the efficiency with which we perform tasks and so free our time and energy for the pursuit of other activities. Consequently, technologies make new things possible. The last century has witnessed incredible development of powerful tools of hope and has rendered old things more efficient. We have discovered or created new treatments, vaccines, and antibodies that significantly fight disease and alleviate suffering. From bone marrow transplants to open heart surgery, from penicillin to pain-relieving aspirins and multivitamins, we now have at our fingertips innumerable ways of realizing our hopes for basic health and physical well-being. We also possesses an ever-growing technology that enables us to connect more readily and effectively with one another. New modes of communication help us establish homes that are physically distant but emotionally close. Air travel, the telephone, and the Internet are among the most obvious such technologies. These increase our access to a greater variety of means and make more complicated modes of coordinated action possible, thereby fostering our resourcefulness. They thus signify and promote the growth of means, making more accessible a more diverse range of ends. It is with a sense of awe that we should recognize how fully technological developments have increased our control of our environments and secured greater goods.

While they represent instruments of hope, however, we must ensure that these means do not become tools which overwhelm or suffocate us. Technologies can take on a life of their own, to the point that they become ends to which we are enslaved rather than means to our liberation. This is especially true as they become more sophisticated, such that fewer people understand how they operate and what their real effects are. We noted in chapter 2 Nuland and Steinbeck's criticisms of the abuses of technologies; both insist we ensure that mechanical means be matched by humane technologies. Otherwise, the means of production become instruments of oppression and segregation, and medical technology becomes the focus rather than the actual pain and suffering of the patient. Psychologist Erich Fromm similarly cautions us about the uses and abuses of technologies. In particular, he warns of the effects of dehumanization that occur if we allow ourselves to be enslaved, whether by machines or by bureaucracies. We then become passive, manipulated servants rather than purposive agents of creativity. Fromm argues that the first principle of our modern technological society is "the maxim that something ought to be done because it is technically possible."[2] Consequently, we tend to pursue every technological development, regardless of its effects. In the process, ends are insulated from intelligent assessment. Moreover, Fromm warns against the dehumanization that results from the efficiency of technology. Mass production (and consumption) of goods obliterates individuality, both in the process of production and in the imaginative formation and pursuit of ends. This dulls our creativity and responsiveness, decreasing our participation and so our actual investment. Moreover, as technology makes possible the move to larger systems which govern agency and decisions, our own abilities are pigeonholed and entrenched without proper room for growth and adaptability. Once technology becomes an end in itself and is severed from our individual needs and abilities, it limits our activities, promoting as Fromm argues the tendency to have more and use more at the expense of *being* or *becoming* more.

Technologies are sophisticated means; they can entrench and limit us or they can be supple agents of growth and adaptability. As with all habits, which of these they are depends on how fully we have formed them with intelligence. When we craft technologies, we need to focus on them as ends; otherwise, we are unable to coordinate means for their construction. Yet while any means can also function as an end, no end should be a final end or an end in itself that is incapable of intelligent assessment and transformation. The key to preventing this lies in our ongoing active involvement in their development; we must remain attentive to their effects and to their place within the broader contexts of life. Sensitivity to context proves vital in ensuring that technologies play their proper role and support rather than undermine communities of hope. As Fromm argues, we must promote the humanization of our technologies by ensuring that we remain active, responsible participants in their development and employment. We must ensure that they are aimed at and promote the growth of agency typical of hope. Otherwise, our technological blessings become curses.

Among our other communities of hope are those rooted in education. In chapter 2, we examined how education generally promotes resourcefulness. Schools, in particular, have always been the primary training ground for the young, arenas where we help them develop skills which will enable them to function successfully as well as to pursue and embody our broader hopes for humanity. Schools not only assist students in developing basic communication skills, like reading and writing; they also help the young habituate social skills and virtues, interacting with a broader array of people than they typically do in the context of family and friends. The net effect of this is to teach them to understand differences, thereby funding the imagination in its quest for new modes of response and reconstruction. An equally important effect is teaching the young (and old) how to request, be assisted by, and assist the agency of others.

Our schools are not, of course, without serious problems; as communities of hope, many of them are challenged. Sadly, while some successfully nurture the young, providing them with innumerable skills and resources, others are mere weigh stations which do little more than postpone their entry into lives of limited opportunities. Jonathan Kozol's book *Savage Inequalities* presents a bracing look into the plight of schools in poor regions and in the inner cities.[3] These institutions are typically overcrowded and underfunded, surrounded by housing projects, and beset by the plight of drugs. Not only do they suffer limited finances for books and basic equipment, but teachers are also in short supply. Failure rather than hope defines the atmosphere of many of these schools, sometimes setting in as early as the fourth grade (57). Dropout rates are also high. Even those who stay in school must struggle to learn, often fighting the sort of crab-bucket syndrome Cedric faced.

Moreover, we are increasingly witnessing that no community is isolated or freed from the effects of society at large. Violence has spread to even suburban and small-town schools at an alarming rate. While bullies, harassment, and the occasional fight have always been common, guns have now invaded schools, bringing with them unprecedented fear to all. The randomness of brutal attacks and killing sprees makes our children feel unsafe. Without this basic safety, it is that much more difficult for them to stretch to encounter what is different; it is equally difficult for them to trust external forces to support and advance their goods. Consequently, our schools run the risk of inadvertently constricting skills and hopes *rather than promoting them.* It is thus especially important that we focus on educating hopes— both in the sense of fostering skills of hoping and emphasizing those hopes that generally educate and help us grow. Fear must be fought here as it is elsewhere. Though violence is a fact of life, that does not mean it should be an essential ingredient in education. The young need to learn to deal with loss and fear, but not on a widespread and immediate basis.

None of these points is novel, but they do acknowledge that if our schools are to remain communities of hope, we must act deliberately and decisively. Proper financial and humane funding is vital if schools are to promote resourcefulness. Security guards, metal detectors, and similar responses represent a step toward controlling violence, but they also institutionalize it, making it an integral part of life. The same can be said of the gated neighborhoods which have become all too common, especially in larger cities. While gates (and fences) may promote a feeling of greater security, they can also undermine it. They are ever present, defining (even if only subtly) some of our habits and so conditioning the contours of our lives. Time must be spent with and memory must be attuned to lock and key. Consequently, a more aggressive and direct approach is needed, or we will all too quickly come to accept these problems as integral dynamics of our lives. Part of the solution requires understanding the embeddedness of all communities. Though our schools need to be safe havens, they cannot be such when violence dominates the surrounding streets and neighborhoods. Dangers must be faced, but we must not live in fear or let it define our lives. We must be sensitive, then, to how we respond to these problems, determining whether our efforts are guided most by what fosters hope or fear. In fighting fear and its effects, we should recognize how a pragmatic hope that attends to hope's conditions is itself practical. Education promotes the development of its supporting habits, and so it needs to be an educated hope. But a pragmatic hope is also *educating* in providing us a resource for facing complicated problems whose solutions are not obvious or within our immediate reach. A pragmatic hope is thus itself a source of hope and also a resource in overcoming fear.

Finally, we possess rich communities of hope manifested in volunteer programs and community outreach. These demonstrate the moving force of the human spirit as it builds continuity and agency, shares needs and problems, and promotes ideals of growth, love, and community—often beyond the constraints of common history, class, or economic bracket. A recent *New York Times* article notes the rise in the number of nonprofit citizen-based organizations—not only in this country but worldwide—over the past thirty years.[4] Many of these organizations are formed by private individuals whose primary goal is social progress. As such, they indicate a commitment to and confidence in our ability as freely organized individuals to influence causes and realize ends without recourse to larger forces, such as the government, on which we must sometimes await indefinitely for resources and support.

On the one hand, volunteer service is an obvious manifestation of meliorist faith. Robert Coles quotes Dorothy Day, founder of the Catholic Workers movement (a volunteer organization working with the poor), saying, "There is a call to us, a call of service—that we join with others to try to make things better in this world" (xxiii).[5] Coles charts the different kinds of service we can render as well as the various motivations, unexpected effects, and satisfactions encountered in the world of volunteerism. Volunteer groups can be rooted in the coordinated efforts of a church or simply in a community itself defined by those who freely wish to serve.[6] Regardless of its roots, volunteerism signifies active involvement in ends whose realization does not solely or immediately affect ourselves. It thus represents the growth of agency and the expansion of horizons of meaning in light of new and diverse ends and means. The potential consequence is that agency is extended on behalf of both servee and server. Such active involvement typically generates a "can-do" spirit of the sort which builds confidence and courage.[7] Volunteering also promotes greater understanding of how ends foreign to ourselves can be living, with the power to move others. Moreover, we see how others develop and utilize habits in contexts quite different from our own. Persistence, resourcefulness, courage—even hopefulness—can wear different forms as they operate in the face of diverse modes of adversity. Close interaction with others, then, not only discloses new means but also empowers the imagination by introducing new goods that can enrich our horizons of meaning.

Of course, one of the challenges of any volunteer work is to ensure that the ends being realized are truly desired and needed. Hopes must be living, embraced by those who enjoy them, and not imposed externally by those who serve or help. The key is to help and inspire. Yet we must do so by attending to real conditions, especially insofar as they are needed to assess not only the realizability but also the *desirability* of ends. When we intelligently approach volunteerism, our activity signifies the ongoing investment in the life of hope beyond our own particular hopes. It shows the contagious power of hopefulness to nurture hope in every corner.

One common thread that links these communities of hope is their ability to promote resourcefulness and the growth of agency. Similarly, inequalities within communities that restrict access to resources diminish their contribution to the life of hope. We should not think of communities of hope in isolation from one another, for they can obviously supplement one another in fruitful ways. Technological communities without educative connections tend to become the domain of a select few, leaving the bulk of society ignorant of the mechanisms of technology. This need not be the case if we actively link education and technology. Communities of hope grounded in education and volunteerism similarly reinforce one another. My own college has a long-standing tradition of service to the local community, which is currently being supplemented by classes in most of the major disciplines that include a service-learning component. Students in designated courses are required to engage in some form of service work that is integrated with normal class material. My experience with such classes has been rewarding and educative, demonstrating the need in formal education for outlets that actively engage students' practical knowledge, expanding it and fostering the sensitivity required for its application to real, concrete situations. In this way, education and volunteerism come together to strengthen one another and promote the life of hope.

Our discussion of these communities of hope is admittedly general and in need of a more detailed treatment. It does, however, indicate the extent to which we possess institutions and practices that form the basis of more full-bodied communities of hope, beset with problems though they may be. Hope thus lives actually and potentially in both the broader arena of social interactions as well as in the narrower contexts of our personal lives. My primary goal in this book has been to articulate the basic virtues and structures of hope, especially its twin senses of practicality as they are rooted in particular hopes, habits of hope, and hopefulness. The interweaving of these three dimensions renders hope a conditioned transcendence whereby we actively transform ourselves even as we hope. Celebrating hope requires emphasizing both the manner in which hoping is conditioned and the extent to which it is a creative transcendence. Consequently, we should be attentive to reality but realize that it does not limit what we can do. We should acknowledge our limits, come to grips with disappointment, and struggle with despair; we must also recognize that hope's success is not always what we intend it to be. While the power of hopefulness is sometimes best seen in the darkness, there must be balance. We should not only recognize the darker side of life, we should also celebrate the light of hope.

Vital to celebrating hope is recognizing its role in promoting growth and the expansion of agency. We celebrate hope by telling stories and painting images that detail the contours of the life of hope; we also do so by developing individual and social habits that nurture hopefulness. We should realize that we do not act in a vacuum, however, since we have numerous structures already in place on which we can

build stronger, richer habits of hope. Our task is to tend to our abilities
and resources so that they become the fertile soil in which the life of
hope can grow. In the process, we must acknowledge actual conditions
and impediments that bear on hoping; otherwise, we undermine its
practicality in both senses discussed throughout this book. As characters such as Martha, Cedric, Andy, and Ma so vividly illustrate, our active engagement in the life of hope is needed to secure its means,
enrich its horizons, and extend its boundaries. The seeds of an enhanced celebratory life of hope lie within and about us, awaiting our
efforts to nurture them.

Notes

Introduction: Hope and Practicality

1. Sophocles, *Antigone* in *Three Tragedies*, trans. David Greene, 2d ed. (Chicago: University of Chicago Press, 1991), line 660.

2. See, for instance, Sherwin B. Nuland, *How We Die* (New York: Alfred A. Knopf, 1994), especially 246. Hereafter referred to as Nuland.

3. Thucydides, *On Justice, Power, and Human Nature: Selections from* The History of the Peloponnesian War, trans. Paul Woodruff (Indianapolis: Hackett Publishing Co., 1993), 123. Hereafter referred to as Thucydides.

4. *The New Oxford Annotated Bible with the Apocryphal/Deuterocanonical Books*, ed. Bruce M. Metzger and Roland E. Murphy, new revised standard version (New York: Oxford University Press, 1994). All biblical selections are taken from this version.

5. See, for instance, Kaye Herth, "Fostering Hope in Terminally Ill People," *Journal of Advanced Nursing* 15 (1990): 1250–1259. Herth lists (1251) various studies that show hope's instrumentality as a coping response for the critically or chronically ill. In a similar vein, a study by University of Kansas psychologist C. R. Snyder reveals that hope is a better predictor of the grades of college freshmen than standard measures of intellectual ability, such as SAT scores ("The Will and the Ways: Development and Validation of an Individual Differences Measure of Hope," *Journal of Personality and Social Psychology* 60, no. 4 [1991]: 579; cited in Daniel Goleman, *Emotional Intelligence* [New York: Bantam Books, 1995], 86–87).

6. St. Thomas Aquinas, *Summa Theologica*, trans. Fathers of the English Dominican Province, Benziger Brothers, Inc., 1947, EWTN Online, Hypertext ed. by New Advent staff, Hypertext Version Copyright 1995, 1996, New Advent, Inc., June 25, 1997, II–II.17.1. Hereafter referred to as Aquinas. References will be to Parts, Questions, and Articles. Consequently, II–II.17.1. refers to the second part of the second part, question 17, article 1.

7. Immanuel Kant, *Critique of Pure Reason*, trans. Norman Kemp Smith (New York: St Martin's Press, 1965), A805/B333.

8. Søren Kierkegaard, *A Sickness unto Death: A Christian Psychological Exposition for Upbuilding and Awakening*, trans. Howard V. and Edna H. Hong (Princeton: Princeton University Press, 1980). Hereafter referred to as Kierkegaard.

9. Ernest Bloch, *The Principle of Hope*, trans. Neville Plaice, Stephen Plaice, and Paul Knight, 3 vols. (Cambridge: MIT Press, 1995).

10. Gabriel Marcel, *Homo Viator: Introduction to a Metaphysic of Hope*, trans. Emma Craufurd (Chicago: Henry Regnery Co., 1951), especially 29–67. Hereafter referred to as Marcel.

11. Joseph J. Godfrey, *The Philosophy of Human Hope* (Dordrecht: Martinus Nijhoff Publishers, 1987). Hereafter referred to as Godfrey. See especially page 3 for definitions of ultimate hope and fundamental hope. These two "hopes" share much in common with what I call particular hopes and hopefulness. Indeed, Godfrey's account shares much with my own. The central differences are those one would expect to arise from working in a Continental, rather than American pragmatic, tradition.

12. Cornel West, *Restoring Hope: Conversations on the Future of Black America*, ed. Kelvin Shawn Sealey (New York: Random House, 1999). Hereafter referred to as West.

13. My primary goal in this discussion is to develop a *pragmatic* theory of hope; it is not to develop a Deweyan theory of hope. While there are indeed differences between Peirce, James, and Dewey, there is also a common shared vision, especially that of the human being as an interactive biological organism powered by habits that can be transformed through thought or intelligence. It is this upon which I wish to draw. I use primarily Dewey's language to develop this view, though it can be found in Peirce and James to varying degrees. But I also borrow insights from Peirce concerning continuity and the self, as well as from James on faith and the will to believe.

14. Though *contextualism* is not a term frequently used to describe pragmatic theories, the emphasis on context is obvious in numerous places. See, for instance, John Dewey's "Context and Thought" (LW 6:3–21). More generally, Dewey's contextualism is presented in the language of instrumentalism. See in particular the introductory chapter on philosophic method in *Experience and Nature* (LW 1:10–41) and chapter 8 of *The Quest for Certainty* (LW 4:156–177). James's contextualism is most apparent in *Essays in Radical Empiricism*, especially chapter 1, "Does 'Consciousness' Exist?" (ERE). For a detailed exposition of Jamesian contextualism, see Charlene Haddock Seigfried's *Chaos and Context* (Athens: Ohio University Press, 1978).

Though not usually identified as pragmatists, Justus Buchler and Stephen David Ross develop similar themes under different names. See in particular Buchler's *Metaphysics of Natural Complexes* (Albany: State University of New York Press, 1990) and Ross's *Perspective in Whitehead's Metaphysics* (Albany: State University of New York Press, 1983).

I have discussed contextualism as a form of systematic philosophy in my master's thesis, "The Contextualist Alternative to Rorty" (Colorado State University, 1990). See in particular chapter 3.

15. Dewey articulates these points in various contexts. See in particular his "Theory of Valuation" (LW 13:189–251, especially 226–236). See also Michael Eldridge, *Transforming Experience: Dewey's Cultural Instrumentalism* (Nashville: Vanderbilt University Press, 1998), especially chap. 2.

16. Hopefulness can be generated through inspiration or example in some situations; its development nevertheless requires the reinforcement of habits of hope. I will discuss this point more fully in chapter 3.

Chapter One: The Practicality of Particular Hopes

1. The following two points apply to nonhuman organisms as well; plants and animals are also conditioned and energetic. What distinguishes the human from the nonhuman is primarily the degree of complexity with which interaction may occur. For a fuller discussion of the relation between the human and the nonhuman, see chapter 7, "Nature, Life, and Body-Mind," of John Dewey's *Experience and Nature* (LW 1:191– 225).

2. Elsewhere, Dewey differentiates between adjustment, accommodation, and adaptation. *Adjustment* typifies any change which results from the interplay of human being and its environment. *Accommodation* means the organism changes itself to better interact with the environment, while *adaptation* means it alters the environment to meet its needs and ends (MW 6:360, 364).

3. C. S. Peirce, *Reasoning and the Logic of Things,* ed. Kenneth L. Ketner (Cambridge: Harvard University Press, 1992), 189. Hereafter referred to as Peirce.

4. As a music teacher of mine used to say, "Practice doesn't necessarily make perfect; sometimes it simply makes permanent."

5. Thomas M. Alexander has explored the centrality of imagination in classical American pragmatism in a variety of articles. See for instance "Pragmatic Imagination," *Transactions of the Charles S. Peirce Society* 26 (1990): 325–348. For an extensive discussion of the structures of imagination, see Mark

Johnson's *Moral Imagination: Implications of Cognitive Science for Ethics* (Chicago: University of Chicago Press, 1993). Hereafter referred to as Johnson. My own discussion is indebted to the insights of both of these thinkers.

6. Thomas M. Alexander, "John Dewey and the Moral Imagination: Beyond Putnam and Rorty toward a Postmodern Ethics," *Transactions of the Charles S. Peirce Society* 29 (1993): 371.

7. *Little Voice*, Mark Herman, Director, Miramax Films, 1998.

8. The April 1999 tragedy in Littleton, Colorado, where two high school boys stormed their school and killed twelve fellow students as well as a teacher before turning their guns on themselves, seems to support this point. The two boys were avid players of video games. Badgered and treated as outcasts by many students, their plan was to strike back. When they went on their shooting rampage, they targeted the more popular students. Their action, motivated by personal insecurities and anger, was also fueled by their imaginative explorations in the violent arena of video games.

9. The difference between imagination and intelligence is largely tentative and functional. Imagination is a dynamic of intelligent activity, momentarily liberated from present demands to act, and so able to explore possibilities never before realized. It creatively explores and combines possibilities. As such it potentially enriches the horizon of meaningful activity, indicating not avenues already traveled, but fresh paths to try.

10. Martha Manning, *Undercurrents: A Therapist's Reckoning with Her Own Depression* (San Francisco: HarperSanFrancisco, 1994). Hereafter referred to as Manning.

11. For a more in-depth discussion of the self in process, see Dewey's *Ethics* (LW 7:285–310). Johnson provides a similar account in chapters 6 and 7 of *Moral Imagination*, giving special attention to the narrative structure of the self.

12. An exception occurs, as we shall see, in those who despair. Striving no longer holds any meaning for them, for a variety of possible reasons. I will discuss this more fully in chapter 3.

13. Ron Suskind, *A Hope in the Unseen: An American Odyssey from the Inner City to the Ivy League* (New York: Broadway Books, 1998). Hereafter referred to as Suskind.

14. See, for instance, *Nichomachean Ethics*, 8:2.

15. For James's discussion of living options, see "The Will to Believe" (WB 13–33) and "The Energies of Men" (MS 229–264).

16. In the following chapters I will discuss several examples (including Cedric and his mother) that underscore how vitally powerful such social contagion is.

17. Dewey makes a similar point in different language. He explains that a *purpose* is a *wish* about whose conditions and consequences we have obtained *knowledge*. A purpose is thus a wish made more determinate; not only have we formulated an end, but we have also designated and assessed the means to it. In such a case, we have a specific purpose—that is, the end of a plan. See MW 14:161.

Aristotle presents a similar account with a decisive difference (*Nichomachean Ethics*, 3:4–7). He differentiates *wishes* from *intentions* (or deliberations) by noting that, among other things, the former concern ends and the latter means. Aristotle's account differs from the pragmatist's primary in its denial that we can deliberate about ends. This conclusion follows, in part, from his view that some ends need to be final and the subsequent denial of the means-end continuum.

From a pragmatic perspective, the important point is that we recognize the continuity between wishing, hoping, and planning. Since its means are neither so indeterminate as in wishing nor so determinate as in planning, hope's ends and correlative means lie in between.

18. And beyond. These limitations isolate Cedric from his colleagues. He is both embarrassed by his shortcomings and also required to devote extra time to rectifying them. This leaves him uncertain he will ever fit in.

19. Some will argue that prayer marks an opportunity to affect the outcome. From a pragmatic standpoint, this poses numerous problems by presupposing the agency of a supernatural being. (I address the general problems associated with this in chapter 4.) Apart from the fact that tests of the efficacy of prayer in cases such as this are enormously difficult to perform, there is the additional problem of accounting for the efficacy of a present prayer on an event that has already occurred.

20. See "The Dilemma of Determinism" (WB 114–140, especially 117ff). Pragmatists tend to subscribe to indeterminism, understood as the doctrine that, since change or process is at the heart of reality, determinacy is never absolute. Process always has an element of indeterminacy about it, and the choices or selections we make contribute to the determination of that process. The pragmatist's "indeterminism" plays an important role in understanding hopes as conditioned possibilities.

21. The same can be said of human (as opposed to technological) progress. In the face of entrenched racism, many considered Martin Luther King, Jr.'s dream for equality to be just that, a dream. Southern sensibilities, many charged, were simply too deep to change. King had the strength of vision not only to see his dream as a real possibility, but also to inspire others to do the

same. Though his dream has enjoyed only partial realization, it vividly demonstrates how efficacious individual views of possibility can be in changing reality (even when counteracted by the powerful forces of custom and conventional wisdom).

22. In fact, James identifies faith with "the same moral quality which we call courage in practical affairs" (WB 76). I will say more about the relation of courage to faith and hope in the next chapter.

Chapter Two: Hope's Habits

1. Stephen King, *Rita Hayworth and Shawshank Redemption*, in *Different Seasons* (New York: Signet, 1982), 15–107; hereafter referred to as King. King's novella was made into a movie, given the shortened name *The Shawshank Redemption*, based on a screenplay written by Frank Darabont (published in *The Shawshank Redemption: The Shooting Script* [New York: Newmarket Press, 1996]; hereafter referred to as Darabont). Though retaining the spirit of King's story, the movie differs from the book in a number of cases, some of which provide even clearer illustrations of my points. I will thus draw examples from both sources; citations will make clear the source.

2. John Steinbeck, *The Grapes of Wrath: Text and Criticism*, ed. Peter Lisca with Kevin Hearle (New York: Penguin Books, 1997). Hereafter referred to as Steinbeck.

3. Hoping not only has means which realize its end, but is itself a means to the development of those means. This is an obvious consequence of its being an activity embedded in the means-end continuum. I will discuss hope's ability to sustain us more fully in the next chapter when considering hopefulness. I shall then argue that hopefulness is the primary sustaining habit in the life of hope.

4. Grampa provides another illustration of this point. At first excited about the prospect of a new life in California, he refuses to go once the time arrives. The family slips cough syrup in his coffee to sedate him and takes him along anyway. Grampa dies within one day. Noting that Grampa really died the minute the family took him off family land, Casy explains, "He was jus' stayin' with the lan'. He couldn' leave it" (Steinbeck 147).

5. For example, the author writes to the church at Ephesus, "I know your works—your love, faith, service, and patient endurance" (Rev. 2:19).

6. The relevance of attentiveness to both patience and resourcefulness shows the artificiality of separating these habits. Indeed, patience itself functions as a means or habit of resourcefulness. These habits need not be distinct, but

often interweave with one another, thereby reinforcing one another and, when properly coordinated, constituting new, more complex habits.

7. Though I here focus on our interconnectedness with each other, Steinbeck's story also emphasizes the significance of our interconnectedness with nature. See, for example, John J. Conder, "Steinbeck and Nature's Self: *The Grapes of Wrath*," reprinted in Steinbeck 625–642.

8. James, for instance, identifies faith in its most general form as "the greeting of our whole nature to a kind of world conceived as well adapted to that nature" (SPP 111), or again as belief that "[t]he inmost nature of the reality is congenial to *powers* which you possess" (WB 73).

9. Of course, education should not be rooted primarily in another's authority. When it is, its primary means tend to be the mere routinization of habits rather than their intelligent development. As Dewey argues, education is most productive when it aims to foster the student's exploration of individual capacities as well as pregnancies in natural and social conditions. See, for instance, MW 9:107–117, "Aims in Education," especially 114–115.

10. Nuland argues eloquently that "[a] promise we can keep and a hope we can give is the certainty that no man or woman will be left to die alone. . . . Unless we are aware that we are dying and so far as possible know the conditions of our death, we cannot share any sort of final consummation with those who love us. . . . For it is the promise of spiritual companionship near the end that gives us hope, much more than does the mere offsetting of the fear of being physically without anyone" (243).

11. For MacIntyre's discussion of the narrative structure of our character and practices, see *After Virtue: A Study in Moral Theory*, 2d ed. (Notre Dame: University of Notre Dame Press, 1984). Nussbaum emphasizes our moral sensitivity to contingency in *The Fragility of Goodness: Luck and Ethics in Greek Tragedy and Philosophy* (Cambridge: Cambridge University Press, 1986). Rorty also discusses contingency and its effect upon our efforts to develop solidarity through stories in *Contingency, Irony, and Solidarity* (Cambridge: Cambridge University Press, 1989). Mark Johnson provides a summary of these positions in developing his own in *Moral Imagination*, especially chapters 7 and 8. Finally, psychologist Robert Coles discusses the role of imagination in our moral development in *The Call of Stories: Teaching and the Moral Imagination* (Boston: Houghton Mifflin, 1989) and *The Moral Life of Children* (Boston: Houghton Mifflin, 1991).

12. *The Call of Stories: Teaching and the Moral Imagination* (Boston: Houghton Mifflin, 1989). Hereafter referred to as Coles. Phil's story is recounted in chapter 2.

13. Because of its affinities with such works, my book and theory belong to what is now called the tradition of virtue-ethics. For more on the specific strengths of a pragmatic ethics of virtue, see Johnson's *Moral Imagination* and Thomas M. Alexander's "John Dewey and the Moral Imagination: Beyond Putnam and Rorty toward a Postmodern Ethics," *Transactions of the Charles S. Peirce Society* 29 (1993): 367–400.

14. See, for instance, MW 9:4–13, "Education as a Necessity of Life."

15. Indeed, the title of Suskind's book comes from Mr. Taylor's misquote of Hebrews 11:1: "Faith is the substance of things hoped for, the evidence of things not seen" as "The substance of faith is a hope in the unseen."

16. This calls to mind one of the important, but easily overlooked, lessons of the Book of Job. When Job suffers his various miseries, three friends come to comfort him. For seven days and seven nights they say nothing, but rather sit with Job. After that, they provide various explanations of his situation, but to my mind they demonstrate one of the most significant responses to suffering: being there with those who suffer. Recall also Nuland's suggestion (243) that we foster the hope in others that they will not die (and we should add, suffer) alone.

17. Mimi Reisel Gladstein, "The Indestructible Women: Ma Joad and Rose of Sharon," in *John Steinbeck's* The Grapes of Wrath, ed. Harold Bloom (New York: Chelsea House Publishers, 1988), 122.

18. See, for instance, Aristotle's *Nichomachean Ethics*, 3:6–9.

19. Poet Maya Angelou argues that "courage is the most important of all the virtues. Because without courage, you cannot practice any other virtue consistently" (West 190). While I will argue below that we should not give courage *absolute* priority, we should not underestimate its significance.

20. In the next chapter, I will argue that Ma not only fosters development of Rose's persistence and resourcefulness, but also proves to be a source of her hopefulness.

Chapter Three: Hopefulness

1. Will Wilson, Mr. Wilson's brother, similarly abandons the hope for a better life elsewhere because he succumbs to the paralyzing grip of anger at a car. Also, Judge Thompson warns Cedric to prepare himself for the trials he will likely face, especially so that he does not become an angry person. Anger sometimes paralyzes us; at other times, it mobilizes us, but the force of its energy tramples the patience and attentiveness needed to intelligently pursue goods.

2. Steinbeck significantly characterizes Tom as someone who uses his hands a lot.

3. Near the end of Steinbeck's book, Jim Casy shares with Tom the me-lioristic view that has inspired him to act. He explains, "This fella in jail, he says, 'Anyways, you do what you can. An'," he says, 'the on'y thing you got to look at is that ever' time they's a little step fo'ward, she may slip back a little, but she never slips clear back. You can prove that,' he says, 'an' that makes the whole thing right. An' that means they wasn't no waste even if it seemed like they was'" (Steinbeck 384).

4. A consequence of this involvement is that hopefulness has an intimacy which optimism (as a spectator's activity) lacks. As Gabriel Marcel argues, "the optimist, as such, always relies upon an experience which is not drawn from the most intimate and living part of himself, but, on the contrary, is *considered from a sufficient distance* to allow certain contradictions to become alternated or fused into a general harmony" (Marcel 34).

5. West reminds us that despair, like hopefulness, is participatory and so lacks the comforting distance that comes from being a spectator. Rather than simply observing despair, "you feel it in your soul" (57).

6. Victor E. Frankl, *Man's Search for Meaning* (New York: Washington Square Press, 1985), especially pp. 26–38. Hereafter referred to as Frankl.

7. A friend who attempted suicide explained to me that even though he had sought others' assistance and knew they cared, that was not enough to help him escape the growing grip of despair on his life. I say more about how we can re-spond to despair in ourselves and in others at the end of the chapter.

8. Marcel at one point defines hope itself as resisting despair. He argues that "there can strictly speaking be no hope except when the temptation to despair exists. Hope is the act by which this temptation is actively or victo-riously overcome" (Marcel 36). Marcel does not distinguish between the various dimensions of hope as I have, though he does offer more than one characterization of hope. I would qualify his statement by noting that resist-ing despair is one function of *hopefulness*, but not the only one. Its other, close-ly related role is energizing us and promoting growth. Marcel acknowledges this possibility when he describes hope as "essentially the availability of a soul which has entered intimately enough into the experience of communion to accomplish in the teeth of will and knowledge the transcendent act—the act establishing the vital regeneration of which this experience affords both the pledge and the first-fruits" (67). I will discuss Marcel's view of hope more fully in the next chapter.

9. Of course, efforts to establish or maintain connection are often im-peded by others. Sometimes hope must live in the midst of hostility, as Cedric learns from many of his fellow students at Ballou. Additionally, pris-

oners of concentration camps had little opportunity or motive to establish meaningful connections with others. Frankl notes that many who survived lost all scruples. Escaping despair in such circumstances increases the need for strong habits of hope. I will return to cases such as these at the end of the chapter.

10. The changes both undergo also affect their religious faith. I will discuss this in the next chapter.

Chapter Four: Hoping against Hope

1. *Critique of Practical Reason,* trans. Lewis White Beck (New York: Macmillan, 1956), 135.

2. *Religion within the Limits of Reason Alone,* trans. T. M. Greene and H. H. Hudson (New York: Harper & Row, 1960), 92.

3. For fuller explication of Kierkegaard's position, see Greg Beabout, "Kierkegaard on the Self and Despair: An Interpretation of the Opening Passage of *The Sickness unto Death,*" *Proceedings of the Catholic Philosophical Association* 62 (1988): 106–115.

4. *Fear and Trembling and Repetition,* trans. Howard V. and Edna H. Hong (Princeton: Princeton University Press, 1983), 17.

5. Godfrey argues (109) that absolute hope does not prevent all disappointments, but rather prevents us from being overcome by such.

6. Marcel's theory rightly captures the social and intersubjective nature of hoping. In its appeal to an absolute, though, it is problematic from a pragmatic perspective for reasons to be developed below.

7. Though such arguments can be found throughout their writings, James's most detailed discussion occurs in *Pragmatism* (P). Dewey treats this issue under the aegis of instrumentalism in *The Quest for Certainty* (LW 4) as well as *Experience and Nature* (LW 1).

8. Recall that habits implicate both individual and environment.

9. Godfrey similarly finds grounding absolute hope in an absolute Thou to be problematic. He argues that if the thou is "absolute and presumably without empirical character, then its reality cannot be distinguished from non-reality. Absolute transcendence of the thou-term is indistinguishable from no term at all" (Godfrey 211). He further argues that Marcel overcomes this problem by contending that absolute hope involves both an empirical thou and an absolute Thou. From a pragmatic perspective, though, the absolute provides no concrete addition that helps us choose or attain better objects of hope. It provides an empty guarantee.

10. Even Kant argues, as we noted above, that though our hope for happiness requires postulating God's existence, we must nevertheless act as though our own ability can secure such a hope.

11. Ernst Bloch develops similar themes in Marxist language. He denies the existence of God as a transcendent "throning-Lord-above"; instead, he argues for a future of human possibility that is partially conditioned but not fully determined by the present. Bloch argues that "[t]he highest good is itself the goal which is not yet formed, which in the tendency of the process is ultimately signified, which in the latency of the process is ultimately real-possible. . . . that which is the highest good . . . which is finally the realm of freedom, constitutes not only the purpose-ideal of human history but also the metaphysical latency problem of nature." *The Principle of Hope*, trans. Neville Plaice, Stephen Plaice, and Paul Knight, vol. 3. (Cambridge: MIT Press, 1995), 1324. Much like Dewey's notion of God as an ideal of the synthesis of the actual and ideal, the *ens perfectissimum* functions as a lure but not a determinate entity with antecedent existence (see section 54 [1312–1353]).

12. Suskind captures the spirit of the church when he writes that one of Bishop Long's sermons whips the congregation into a frenzy, "uncoupling hope from reason with the swinging ax of faith" (153).

13. Frank Darabont, the screenwriter and director of the film, explains the last scene as follows: "By ending with that final image, we've brought the viewer on a full journey that begins in tight claustrophobia defined by walls and concludes where the horizon is limitless; the movie has traveled fully from darkness to light, from coldness to warmth, from colorlessness to a place where only color exists, from physical and spiritual imprisonment to total freedom" (Darabont 158).

Conclusion: Celebrating Hope

1. Gavin De Becker, *The Gift of Fear: Survival Signals That Protect Us from Violence* (New York: Dell Publishing Co., 1998), 347.

2. Erich Fromm, *The Revolution of Hope: Toward a Humanized Technology* (New York: Harper and Row, 1968), 32.

3. Jonathan Kozol, *Savage Inequalities: Children in America's Schools* (New York: HarperPerennial, 1992).

4. David Bornstein, "A Force Now in the World, Citizens Flex Social Muscle," *New York Times*, July 10, 1999, Arts and Ideas section.

5. Robert Coles, *The Call of Service: A Witness to Idealism* (Boston: Houghton Mifflin, 1993), xxiii.

6. In *A Common Faith* Dewey argues that our churches need to dedicate themselves to social progress to remain vital in the world; they must "stimulate action for a divine kingdom on earth" (LW 9:55).

7. Recently, I watched college volunteers host younger children from a transitional housing program for homeless families. Encounters such as these give our typically privileged students both an education in the trials of those less fortunate and also an opportunity to share their own gifts. One volunteer showed a young boy some basics in diving. As the youngster gradually mastered the technique, he shouted with glee, "I can do it! I can do it!" By means of the sharing of abilities, hitherto not-yet-conceived possibilities became satisfying achievements.

Works Cited

Alexander, Thomas M. "John Dewey and the Moral Imagination: Beyond Putnam and Rorty toward a Postmodern Ethics." *Transactions of the Charles S. Peirce Society* 29 (1993): 367–400.

———. "Pragmatic Imagination." *Transactions of the Charles S. Peirce Society* 26 (1990): 325–348.

Aquinas, Thomas. *Summa Theologica.* Trans. Fathers of the English Dominican Province. Benziger Brothers, Inc., 1947. EWTN Online. Hypertext ed. by New Advent staff. Hypertext Version Copyright 1995, 1996. New Advent, Inc. June 25, 1997.

Aristotle. *Nichomachean Ethics.* Trans. with commentatires and glossary Hippocrates G. Apostle. Grinnell: Peripatetic Press, 1984.

Beabout, Greg. "Kierkegaard on the Self and Despair: An Interpretation of the Opening Passage of *The Sickness unto Death.*" *Proceedings of Catholic Philosophical Association* 62 (1988): 106–115.

Bloch, Ernest. *The Principle of Hope.* Trans. Neville Plaice, Stephen Plaice, and Paul Knight. 3 vols. Cambridge: MIT Press, 1995.

Buchler, Justus. *Metaphysics of Natural Complexes.* Ed. Kathleen Wallace, Armen Marsoobian, and Robert S. Corrington. 2d expanded ed. Albany: State University of New York Press, 1990.

Coles, Robert. *The Call of Service: A Witness to Idealism.* Boston: Houghton Mifflin, 1993.

———. *The Call of Stories: Teaching the Moral Imagination.* Boston: Houghton Mifflin, 1989.

———. *The Moral Education of Children.* Boston: Houghton Mifflin, 1991.

Conder, John J. "Steinbeck and Nature's Self: *The Grapes of Wrath.*" *The Grapes of Wrath: Text and Criticism.* Ed. Peter Lisca with Kevin Hearle, 625–642. New York: Penguin Books, 1997.

Darabont, Frank. *The Shawshank Redemption: The Shooting Script.* New York: Newmarket Press, 1996.

De Becker, Gavin. *The Gift of Fear: Survival Signals That Protect Us from Violence.* New York: Dell Publishing, 1998.

Dewey, John. *A Common Faith. John Dewey: The Later Works, 1933–1934.* Ed. Jo Ann Boydston, 1–58. Vol. 9. Carbondale: Southern Illinois University Press, 1989.

———. "Context and Thought." *John Dewey: The Later Works, 1931–1932.* Ed. Jo Ann Boydston, 3–21. Vol. 6. Carbondale: Southern Illinois University Press, 1985.

———. "Contributions to *A Cyclopedia of Education.*" *John Dewey: The Middle Works, 1910–1911.* Ed. Jo Ann Boydston, 357–467. Vol. 6. Carbondale: Southern Illinois University Press, 1978.

———. "Contributions to *A Cyclopedia of Education.*" *John Dewey: The Middle Works, 1912–1914.* Ed. Jo Ann Boydston, 207–365. Vol. 7. Carbondale: Southern Illinois University Press, 1979.

———. *Democracy and Education. John Dewey: The Middle Works, 1916.* Ed. Jo Ann Boydston. Vol. 9. Carbondale: Southern Illinois University Press, 1980.

———. "Educational Lectures before Brigham Young Academy." *John Dewey: The Later Works, 1895–1953.* Ed. Jo Ann Boydston, 211–347. Vol. 17. Carbondale: Southern Illinois University Press, 1990.

———. *Experience and Nature. John Dewey: The Later Works, 1925.* Ed. Jo Ann Boydston. Vol. 1. Carbondale: Southern Illinois University Press, 1981.

———. *Human Nature and Conduct. John Dewey: The Middle Works, 1922.* Ed. Jo Ann Boydston. Vol. 14. Carbondale: Southern Illinois University Press, 1983.

———. *The Quest for Certainty. John Dewey: The Later Works, 1929.* Ed. Jo Ann Boydston. Vol. 4. Carbondale: Southern Illinois University Press, 1984.

Eldridge, Michael. *Transforming Experience: Dewey's Cultural Instrumentalism.* Nashville: Vanderbilt University Press, 1998.

Frankl, Victor E. *Man's Search for Meaning.* New York: Washington Square Press, 1985.

Fromm, Erich. *The Revolution of Hope, Toward a Humanized Technology.* New York: Harper and Row, 1968.

Gladstein, Mimi Reisel. "The Indestructible Women: Ma Joad and Rose of Sharon." *John Steinbeck's* The Grapes of Wrath. Ed. Harold Bloom, 115–126. New York: Chelsea House Publishers, 1988.

Godfrey, Joseph J. *The Philosophy of Human Hope.* Dordrecht: Martinus Nijhoff Publishers, 1987.

Goleman, Daniel. *Emotional Intelligence.* New York: Bantam Books, 1995.

Herth, Kaye. "Fostering Hope in Terminally Ill People." *Journal of Advanced Nursing* 15 (1990): 1250–1259.

James, William. *Essays in Radical Empiricism.* Ed. Frederick H. Burkhardt, Fredson Bowers, Ignas K. Skrupskelis. Cambridge: Harvard University Press, 1976.

———. *Memories and Studies.* Ed. Henry James. New York: Longman's Green and Co., 1920.

———. *A Pluralistic Universe.* Ed. Frederick H. Burkhardt, Fredson Bowers, Ignas K. Skrupskelis. Cambridge: Harvard University Press, 1977.

———. *Pragmatism.* Ed. Frederick H. Burkhardt, Fredson Bowers, Ignas K. Skrupskelis. Cambridge: Harvard University Press, 1975.

———. *The Principles of Psychology.* 3 vols. Ed. Frederick H. Burkhardt, Fredson Bowers, Ignas K. Skrupskelis. Cambridge: Harvard University Press, 1981.

———. *Some Problems of Philosophy.* Ed. Frederick H. Burkhardt, Fredson Bowers, Ignas K. Skrupskelis. Cambridge: Harvard University Press, 1979.

———. *The Will to Believe and Other Essays in Popular Philosophy.* Ed. Frederick H. Burkhardt, Fredson Bowers, Ignas K. Skrupskelis. Cambridge: Harvard University Press, 1979.

Johnson, Mark. *The Moral Imagination: Implications of Cognitive Science for Ethics.* Chicago: University of Chicago Press, 1993.

Kant, Immanuel. *Critique of Practical Reason.* Trans. Lewis White Beck. Indianapolis: Bobbs-Merrill, 1956.

———. *Critique of Pure Reason.* Trans. Norman Kemp Smith. New York: St Martin's Press, 1965.

———. *Religion within the Limits of Reason Alone.* Trans. T. M. Greene and H. H. Hudson. New York: Harper & Row, 1960.

Kierkegaard, Søren. *A Sickness unto Death: A Christian Psychological Exposition for Upbuilding and Awakening.* Trans. Howard V. and Edna H. Hong. Princeton: Princeton University Press, 1980.

———. *Fear and Trembling and Repetition.* Trans. Howard V. and Edna H. Hong. Princeton: Princeton University Press, 1983.

King, Stephen. *Rita Hayworth and Shawshank Redemption.* In *Different Seasons.* New York: Signet, 1982.

Kozol, Jonathan. *Savage Inequalities: Children in America's Schools.* New York: Harper-Perennial, 1992.

MacIntyre, Alasdair. *After Virtue: A Study in Moral Theory.* 2d ed. Notre Dame: University of Notre Dame Press, 1984.

Manning, Martha. *Undercurrents: A Therapist's Reckoning with Her Own Depression.* San Francisco: HarperSanFrancisco, 1994.

Marcel, Gabriel. *Homo Viator: Introduction to a Metaphysic of Hope.* Trans. Emma Craufurd. Chicago: Henry Regnery Co., 1951.

Metzger, Bruce M., and Roland E. Murphy, eds. *The New Oxford Annotated Bible with the Apocryphal/Deuterocanonical Books.* New revised standard version. New York: Oxford University Press, 1994.

Nuland, Sherwin B. *How We Die.* New York: Alfred A. Knopf, 1994.

Nussbaum, Martha. *The Fragility of Goodness: Luck and Ethics in Greek Tragedy and Philosophy.* Cambridge: Cambridge University Press, 1986.

Peirce, C. S. *Reasoning and the Nature of Things.* Ed. Kenneth L. Ketner. Cambridge: Harvard University Press, 1992.

Rorty, Richard. *Contingency, Irony, and Solidarity.* Cambridge: Cambridge University Press, 1986.

Ross, Stephen David. *Perspective in Whitehead's Metaphysics.* Albany: State University of New York Press, 1983.

Seigfried, Charlene Haddock. *Chaos and Context.* Athens: Ohio University Press, 1978.

Shade, Patrick A. "The Contextualist Alternative to Rorty." Master's thesis, Colorado State University, 1990.

Sophocles. *Antigone.* In *Three Tragedies.* Trans. David Greene. 2d ed. Chicago: University of Chicago Press, 1991.

Steinbeck, John. *The Grapes of Wrath: Text and Criticism.* Ed. Peter Lisca with Kevin Hearle. New York: Penguin Books, 1997.

Suskind, Ron. *A Hope in the Unseen: An American Odyssey from the Inner City to the Ivy League.* New York: Broadway Books, 1998.

Thucydides. *On Justice, Power, and Human Nature: Selections from* The History of the Peloponnesian War. Trans. Paul Woodruff. Indianapolis: Hackett Publishing Co., 1993.

West, Cornel. *Restoring Hope: Conversations on the Future of Black America.* Ed. Kelvin Shawn Sealey. New York: Random House, 1999.

Index